Insights Toward Sanity:
The Art of Having Schizophrenia

or;

The Bird Cage for Spirit:
An Autobiography of Intense Philosophy

or;

Journey to the Centre of the Universe:
Coming to Terms with an Even More Radical Enlightenment

but;

(not necessarily in any comprehensible order)

Glossary:
INSANE = Interpretation Nurturing Significance Apparent Near Earth

To read this book, the author devised—since writing made painfully obvious—just one method: Slow down. Good luck.

The author was born on Nu'Chah'Nulth territory. The first structures of this writing began on Snuneymuxw territory. This book project was completed on un-ceded Coast Salish territory.

The author wishes to acknowledge his respect for the lessons and the expressions shared with him over the years by countless cultures, languages, and individuals, and the author wishes to directly state that historians, politicians, doctors, and industries do a disservice to humanity by not remembering very determinedly in the outset of their sense of their civilization's cultural projects that this Whole Earth bespeaks a serious conflict and must reconcile its idealistic goals with its buried memories.

Dedicated to all humans being who are stressed out.

If you need some support,
May you find someone such as an open minded MD
Yes a quack
Who listens to you and accepts you.
She will help. I know.

Thank you, Dr. Loewen, for being reasonable
And inspiring me to try to be reasonable.

Insights Toward Sanity:
The Art of Having Schizophrenia

Brenden MacDonald

POST EGOISM MEDIA

© 2012 Brenden MacDonald

All rights reserved. No part of this book may be reproduced in any form or by any means, electronic or mechanical, including photocopying, recording, or by any information storage or retrieval system, without written permission.

ISBN 978-0-9854802-2-6

Post Egoism Media
Eugene, Oregon, USA
www.postegoism.net

Table of Contents:

Part One: Teetering on the Edge of Poetry

An Epigraphic Conversation	13
A Telling Story— "The Poem that Never Ends (first part)" *by Michelle MacDonald*	19
Author's Introduction Beckoned by the Will to Talk	25
Assorted notes, phrases, poems, strewn through notebooks and folders <2003	33
2003< Very many really short poetic essays <2004	69

Part Two: The Birdcage of the Spirit

Chapter 1: Recognition of Chrysalis: The Early Stage of Life	99
Chapter 2: Acclimatization and Affect: Learning What Happens in the Real World	109
Chapter 3: Breakdown and Out: To Wander About, Wonder Through, and Escape from the Shambles of a Sick Society	123

Chapter 4:   137
Getting Weirder, Blasting Off

Chapter 5:   155
On the First Time I Disappeared Completely

Chapter 6:   175
On the First Time Assembling
What Had Shattered

Chapter 7:   195
Out of Hospital for a While…
Trailing Doubts, Between Sorts

Chapter 8:   207
In the World, In Myself

Chapter 9:   225
On Reheating Leftovers and the
Nutritional Deficits of Microwave Cooking

Chapter 10:   249
When Mind Opens Far…

Chapter 11:   261
Reflecting on Everything at High Velocity

Chapter 11.5:   269
Harder to Back a Train Down than Up

Part Three: Journey to the Center of the Universe

Essay 1: 287
Insights Toward Sanity

Essay 2: 301
Truth in Critical Theory and Simulacra in the World:
From Language-Games to the Defence of Meaning and
From Ordinary Language to Ideology

Essay 3: 315
To Inspire an Adequate Response…

Essay 4: 325
The Physical Future Awaits
Our Conscious Contributions

Essay 5: 337
Worlds Apart from the Same World

Essay 6: 345
Shifts of Focus: Encyclopedia in Dante's *Divine Comedy*
and in Niven and Pournelle's *Inferno*

Essay 7: 363
Imaginatively Fancying Nature from
Spinoza to Romanticism

Essay 8: 391
Spinoza, Deep Ecology, and Human Diversity—
Schizophrenics and Others Who Could Heal the Earth
If Society Realized Eco-Literacy

Essay 9: 415
Uh Oh: Do You Have a Brain Disease
You Didn't Know You Had?

Part Four: The Last Word

"The Gathered Part for the Book" 425
by Michelle MacDonald

Part One

Teetering on the Edge of Poetry

An Epigraphic Conversation

"It will be convenient to have a name for that part of reality which is not emotionally regarded as 'real' by the sane person. We shall call it the Outside.

The Outside consists of everything that appears inconceivable to the human mind. In fact everything is inconceivable to the human mind (if only because it exists) but not many people notice this."

—Celia Green, *The Human Evasion*
Chapter 5 : How to Write Sane Books

"Nothing in the world is more dangerous than sincere ignorance and conscientious stupidity."

—Martin Luther King, Jr.

"No longer will it be possible to read any treatise on phonology without deciphering within every phoneme the statement, 'Here lies a poet,' The linguistics professor doesn't know this, and that is another problem, allowing him blithely to put forward his models, never to invent any new notion of language, and to preserve the sterility of theory."

—Julia Kristeva, *The Ethics of Linguistics*

"Here is a fact I learned during my reading: We do not know how our visual system works. As you read these words, you do not really see the ink, the paper, your hands, and the surroundings, but an internal and three-dimensional image that reproduces them almost exactly and that is constructed by your brain. The photons reflected by this page strike the retinas of your eyes, which transform them into electrochemical information; the optic nerves relay this information to the visual cortex at the back of the head, where a cascade-like network of nerve cells separates the input into categories (form, color, movement, depth, etc.). How the brain goes about reuniting these sets of categorized information into a coherent image is still a mystery. This also means that the neurological basis of consciousness is unknown.

If we do not know how we see a real object in front of us, we understand even less how we perceive something that is not there."

—Jeremy Narby, *The Cosmic Serpent*

"Unconditioned sensations, the raw swirl of an unfiltered reality, exist as background noise... You cannot use butterfly language to communicate with caterpillars."

—Dr. Timothy Leary, *The Eightfold Model of Human Consciousness*

"...[T]here is a certain difference in attitude to people who would be called nuts, because there is a poem--an ancient poem of the Hindus—which says 'sometimes naked, sometimes mad, now's a scholar, now's a fool, thus they appear on Earth as free men.'

But you see, we in our attitude to this sort of behavior, which is essentially in its first inception harmless, these people are talking what we regard to be nonsense. And to be experienced in nonsense. We feel threatened by that, because we are not secure in ourselves. A very secure person can adapt himself with amazing speed to different kinds of communication.

In foreign countries, for example, where you don't speak the language of the people you are staying with, if you don't feel ashamed of this, you can set up an enormous degree of communication with other people through gesture and even something most surprising, people can communicate with each other by simply talking.

You can get a lot across to people by talking intelligent nonsense, by, as it were, imitating a foreign language; speaking like it sounds. You can communicate feelings, emotions, like and dislike of this, that and the other; very simply. But if you are rigid and are not willing to do this type of playing, then you feel threatened by anybody who communicates with you in a funny way.

And so this rigidity sets up a kind of vicious circle. The minute, in other words, someone makes an unusual communication to you about an unusual state of consciousness, and you back off, the individual wonders 'is there something wrong with me? I don't seem to be understood by anyone.'

Or he may wonder 'what's going on? Has everybody else suddenly gone crazy?' And then if he feels that he gets frightened, and to the degree that he gets more frightened, he gets more defensive, and eventually land up with being catatonic, which is a person who simply doesn't move. And so then what we do is we whiffle him off to an institution, where he is captured by the inquisitors."

—Alan Watts, "The Value of Psychotic Experience," a lecture

"A story is a little knot or complex of that species of connectedness which we call relevance. In the 1960s, students were fighting for "relevance," and I would assume that any A is relevant to any B if both A and B are parts or components of the same "story".

Again we face connectedness at more than one level: First, connection between A and B by virtue of their being components in the same story.

And then, connectedness between people in that all think in terms of stories. (For surely the computer was right. This is indeed how people think.)"
—Gregory Bateson, *Mind and Nature*, introduction

"Or the waterfall, or music heard so deeply
> That it is not heard at all, but you are the music
> While the music lasts.

These are only hints and guesses,
> Hints followed by guesses; and the rest
> Is prayer, observance, discipline, thought and action.
> The hint half guessed, the gift half understood, is
Incarnation.
> Here the impossible union
> Of spheres of existence is actual,
> Here the past and future
> Are conquered, and reconciled,
> Where action were otherwise movement
> Of that which is only moved
> And has in it no source of movement--
> Driven by daemonic, chthonic
> Powers."
—T.S. Eliot, "Dry Salvages" (part V)

A Telling Story:
The Poem that Never Ends *(first part)*
by Michelle MacDonald

Panic
Emergency   Who is he ?
                    Who am I ?
clues unheeded
determination
and how
a passport in hand
goodbye, hello

Phone phobia
set in

I left him (WHAT?)

okay

K.ask me is there

No one waits
and worries
quite like a mother

Another phone call
K.ask me has left him
but we know where his bag is,
mmm…..
the party is over

dial, dial, dial

Ginger has
the sweetest
friendliest voice
assures me
she knows

EVERYONE

(*County Deputy Cross
of Washoe County
doesn't care, he writes
his whole years quota of
speeding tickets today*)

She will look herself
don't worry
the weather has been lovely
only high 90's and
still warm enough at night
he will be fine without shelter
don't worry

I am WORRIED

I sent my first born
In to the desert with
Sea shells, stones and

intricate driftwood
to trade
for sustenance

K ask me knows someone
who's there

Alas, via satellite
K ask me has talked to him
he was
found, calculating numbers
situation, location in the sand
he wants left alone
to find his uncle at 195 degrees
and newcastle
no one knows

he recognized Xandra
so onward to St. Marys
hospital
set among
gambling maniacs
on vacation in the desert

Phone calls getting worse
a small voice says
mom, read me a poem

Xandra ,an angel. took
control
back to Black Rock City
only it's not, it has
been disbanded and
now falls

Dr. Green Peace
waits in Vancouver
while his new
communication device charges
then charges him self
to meet the ice queen on
channel 14,
25 minutes outside Gerlach

The phone Rings again

It is K-ask me, he is in the know
Did I know there is a raging dust
storm in their part of the desert?

Phone rings
it is HIM,
watching Star Trek
with his new friends,
he wants to stay

but, foolish me has
sent Dr. Greenpeace
back again, and
off they go to see
the Redwood Forest

phone rings
our son
has regressed to 3 years old,
remembers us all though
and says hi,
 he is on his way home

brief reprieve from
over the top worry
and
emergency calls
begin again
can't get worse?
It can

Ring, ring
We have your son,
It was close!
He came alone
did you know?

hang on son
hang on to life
emergencies
 explode in our hearts

dad is on his way

Author's Introduction:
Beckoned by the Will to Talk

I have learned enough about schizophrenia from having schizophrenia to write a whole book on the subject. In all likelihood, I will never stop learning more about it and will always write on about it in order to share my experiences and knowledge. I hope that I can articulate what it is like to be schizophrenic well enough to contribute to a deeper understanding of some of the processes involved in the condition. Indeed, with this book I hope to convey some of my basic conceptions and perceptions about how human minds work, because by contemplating and intently focusing on the general nature of the mind I have come to grips with more understanding of when my mind has not "worked" as well. I want to share the knowledge I've acquired over the course of schizophrenia, knowledge which helps me better understand my mental situation and which helps me better sustain psychological coherence and clarity of reason.

In this book I will devote the chapters to my personal, "lifelong" experience with schizophrenia, to my ever developing and personally unique understanding of the diverse facets of schizophrenia already well recognized by the psychiatric community, and to my hopes for reinterpreting and re-framing schizophrenia in new ways that I hope might help others as I have helped myself. All in all, I wish to add another perspective to the literature about this fascinating condition, and to give my story.

I hope this book will be able to convey an accurate sense of (at least my) schizophrenia to a person who has not read anything about it before. I intend to write as clearly as possible and will take measures to use accessible language to introduce the ideas to one who hasn't read any psychiatric theory. Mind you, I also know some big words and do think in complex ways. I will use this book to build up a whole account of what schizophrenia is, in terms of my own story and of other schizophrenics, in terms of today's doctors, and in terms of the general public who ought to know about schizophrenia.

A commonly accepted statistic for how many people in the world have schizophrenia is one in one hundred.[1] The traits involved are common enough that schizophrenia-like conditions can be found everywhere, so it is important that the non-schizophrenic alike with schizophrenic learn more. Sharing understanding always has inherent value, because knowledge allows for preparation and adaptation. I know that it would help in times of crises for the schizophrenic and his or her society to understand what is happening. If everyone happened to understand more about schizophrenia, in general and from an earlier age, then predisposed and activated individuals would have an easier, more knowledgeable time finding peace of mind.

In fact, it will even be an argument of this book that the features of schizophrenia do not inherently entail dysfunction given adequate understanding and integration by the individual and his or her social knit. I take a medication which holds my bizarre, audio-visual and emotional "visions" and false beliefs at bay and which helps me sleep, but I also know the potential yet remains for symptoms to return.

---

[1] See "A Report on Mental Illness" (2002), Government of Canada.

Hence, I have need for a long-term medical regimen. I can help myself be sane and minimize risky behaviour, even if the self-understood stress-triggers of my initial deterioration are still somewhat to fully present. The stress varies, and I attempt to be strong with varied success.

I take the antipsychotic med, and it helps in a few ways, but only through my active emotional reasoning will I voluntarily succeed, for instance, to maintain a set of intentional decisions, to keep using the medicine, to keep those audiovisuals away, and to not beckon them on recklessly. To feel strong in will and sparse of delusion, I've required personal contemplation and meditation and also needed to communicate and work thoughtfully with others willing to learn about my experience. I have needed to share with the ones I am close to, because I still have peculiar ways of being, feeling, and knowing, even when not off my rocker. I have a mental life that can get heavy and hard if I reject certain avenues of playful ways of being which bring me joy, learning, and grounding. Nowadays I aim for manageable eccentricity instead of insanity.

To say in a gist, I have planted my worldview upon a field of magical perceptions unfamiliar to most. I cannot help but take a whole lot in while I perceive anything. Much of my perception enters my attention with an insistence and urgency that bemoans that I do little else but in awe follow the magic of reality-awareness and action-response. In other words, any darn moment of every day might feel like the whole world hanging on a thread asking me to appreciate and frolic in the grandeur, or confusion, of blooming instances of sensation and thought. When fluttering from reality in "psychosis," I approach every situation with an ecstatic fervour. I focus on communicating and letting emotion overwhelm me. I fixate upon my wonder and curiosity about conscious being.

It may not appear to occur for this reason, but I get so swept away in the potential chance to communicate meaning and to feel human that I thoroughly lose the ability to relate via normal social methods. That's why psychosis can be defined as "a drastic disconnect from relevant, socially shared realities." I usually do this for the most part internally, but at times I may jump around, cart-wheeling and climbing trees and telling stories. The irresistible "magic" of human experience beckons me to deeply conceive learning, self-exploration, and sharing as the main priorities of self-consciousness. I cannot gate it. I obsess.

To have entered fully into such an experiential mode at some point in my development entailed ill-integration with the so-called "normal human world." I suffered when entering this unique mode because there is little peace it finds with the ordinary, contemporary Western social modes. I feel I may snap, freak out, and start yelling and wanting others to focus on self-consciousness. I want to start picking up every cigarette butt and other piece of garbage I can find and to show it to people until they don't throw them on the ground ever again.

I could not work at any normal job in such an extreme state, and I can say now in good recovery from my hard breaks that the stress is not gone of desiring to healthily integrate this extreme mode into the overall social picture. I want help in working through my modes to acquire peace and clarity of mind, not simple rehabilitation to have a normal job. I must focus on self-involvement and its ways, or I could perish within the potentially hyper-amplifying preconditions of another psychotic break from reality.

I straightforwardly announce that I believe the state of an ill schizophrenic to be quite distinct from the state of a healthy schizophrenic, and I do not believe for a second that a schizophrenic who has recovered from psychosis ought automatically to be defined to be entirely non-schizophrenic or aspire to be "normal" in character. I believe there are truly untold riches in the behaviour and psychology of a well-adapted schizophrenic. I believe the foundation of some cases of schizophrenia is a set of psychological features that are very intense in character, and dangerous to the self without proper knowledge and implementation.

I believe the ability to hallucinate audiovisuals and to work with incredible imagination would not automatically become pathological if the person who happens to set off the relevant mental functions finds the appropriate techniques of integrating the additional features of schizophrenia with the rest of ordinary human life. I believe schizophrenics need help to deepen and nourish their inherent psychological abilities, and I believe it is entirely socially constructed that the only viable life option for a schizophrenic is simply to "become normal again" and to resist all the other modes of experience.

The literature of every ancient civilization and religion gives account of the ability to hear voices, for instance, and some people called these voices the god within, the inner self, or merely conscience. I wager that in all times of human history, there has been the power of our body and brain to fill our mind with dreams either while asleep *or awake*, and I believe it very natural but poorly understood that the human mind can be filled with a huge amount of perception and meaning.

We don't need today to believe these voices, feelings, or visions are gods or their manifestations, but might try to fit them in ourselves in a healthy way nonetheless. Otherwise we may simply be medicated, near sedated, and in a rut with our "ill" faculties. I believe it very natural to have the ability to dream while awake and to see, hear, and feel in ways that others do not. That 1 in 100 statistic seems to be totally multicultural, except for prognostic fate!

I believe the source of illness comes from very poorly understanding or integrating in society that some people simply have more in their mind to experience than some others. I believe that as children of a certain cultural understanding, we aren't given a proper enough view of the mind's real and vast powers of perception in order to learn how, if the time comes, to facilitate self-clarity and sound reason when encountering an explosion of a bizarrely complex mental experience. Illness may result in times of stress from unfortunate adaptations to natural psychological states. For example, the sense of telepathically broadcasted independent intelligences (like God in the radio talking to Me) may be like a maladapted power to "make believe" weird and mysterious imaginary friends, similar but different than the ways some children do when they are young.

Along with visually seeing the sky and knowing how to tell a phone is ringing when it is in front of me, I live my life seeing and feeling with a great number of perceptual modes which include all that is normally perceived and which also carries a confusing, rich array of a whole lot of unique and constantly shifting perceptions and meanings. There is more going on in my head at any moment than there needs to be just to get to the other side of the moment. A gust of wind can convey a mood. I can't help but feel my life intensely, and I developed lots of problems with delusion around the onset of psychosis, the deep and acute break from reality. I didn't always have my present outlook on schizophrenia when I was ill. I didn't know where my perceptions were then coming from, and I became highly delusional.

I want to share my story with you and let you know how I fell into mental illness. I want to share the means of my recovery. I want to explain how I really feel about myself and the sources of delusion. I want to explain how I think the problems faced by some schizophrenics are problems given to everyone, and the problems have to do with the way of our mind and human, social existence. The patterns of our problems are in some very sure sense predictable outcomes of certain bio-psycho-social conditions.

I hope to convey the significance of the idea that a good number of schizophrenics might only find peace if their society heals and learns with them. In my own recovery, I am beckoned by a desire for expression. I want to share my knowledge of my path to health, which is a convoluted and colourful story. Pills can only do so much for us. I am a testimony to that, even though I take medication and appreciate it in some ways. Foremost in my journey, I have required much more: like support from my family, understanding from friends, effort to stay relaxed and being rational about my delusions. I want to share many insights toward sanity.

Assorted notes, phrases, poems, strewn through notebooks and folders<2003.

[[File random/significant]]
(Dating from early Spring 2001 until Spring 2003)

Written late in 2001

hiding
  in undr my shed
  out frum yr rain
talking
  a doing storm
  somniloquy
sticking
  within this symbola
  ths one u cast bfr
    me, u cast bfr
    me, i cast bfr
    it, an explanational
    anthem, my
    duty pitiful 2
    myself wretchid

round n round around here
its the silence i fear
  evrewun is so near
     (forever)
  the only sign our pain
  relucting frum its rain
  preferring to stay dry
  eyl nevr kno why
airy phantom by the nation's delude
resisting complee this deluge
  the way history repeats itself
    yr best bet is anything
i run the casino (case on u sheltr reign supreem)
  no u dont no-one does escape th rain completely

Written early in 2001

EVERYTHING IS RIGHT UNTIL IT'S WRONG

                   (it doesn't have to be nothing)
              ((straighten out your back))
   kept a certain pace
with sync-steppers all surrounding
we make a safe place
but a commander's fear to lose us,
     to be left under attack all alone
     or just left all alone
when we question out of face
and don't consent dismissal from this space
   brings hate and oblivion
cut from compassion
renders war motionless
holding both sides   let go
   let me   hear both
let me out of here
this mind,
our economy
virtual reality
and real virtues
1 n th same
the same 1
unknown
   what 2 do
paying for phreedumb makes sense

2001-2002—Assorted Insanities Noted To Self

i brand myself

—

nevr mind
what's real
wun's got
2 go

—

not both at once
weer multitasking machines
both at both

—

u cant proov th
pit is bottomless

—

separating and reconstituting assists rote abilities.
    how i was to rember what will.
        eym smart enuf to imagine absolute control.
does it stand to reason they cud

—

it smarts !
what does ?

—

I was necessarily confused by the world—it is
    a confusing place if that's how
        it is presented to our perception.

Time was also necessary to return mentally to
> natural belief and to separate (at first)
> the many pieces of societal education.
> It took me a long while—or at least a lot of
> thinking—to realize I was under my own control,
> or rather, under my own controls.

—

something like needing 2
release myself from bondage
slipping thru trapdoors   (flesym dellortnoc i)
but holding back, looking down

—

perhaps time and thot ar inseparable and permeant
as space is meaningless something immutable
> via thot in time.
Because/Therefore
Thru time we won't think th space away between us.
Thot and time indirectly proportions itself.
A little thot lasts nearly forever.
i cudint prove it fr u

—

You think too much for your own good.
No, I two-think much for more than my own good.
I used to think about going nowhere.

—

it can't be, because time
doesn't disappear, it passes
thru our minds

—

keep it, read it, throw it away, burn it, sell it,
       but don't give it back
I can't have it right now... Maybe turn the page.
—

Poetry precisely constructs abstract human
       thought and emotion
into tangible entities—which is exactly why this is not
       a poem.

Poetry 'abouts' inwardly indecipherable 'ing.'
—

ran back and forth
so much
while shopping mwallword that i broke
a sweat. They really should condition this air,
we are the crustomers, after all -and- importance.
i hope they make this easier.. on us..
—

from within the peak away from the hill underneath the
oceanic sky
—

Save Universe from God.
Love her like him.
—

eyelid implants
identity market
due process
the screaming soul of the cathode ray

and anode of my will
n2 T.empting V.oices
contact gaps
null transmission
brand via urinal
real world educaptives

everything u need to kno
to vertically disintegrate
–

fuck development
let what we envelop us.
i need economy. it needs me.
global economy b4 me.
i logopath.   eye premiss.
–

This is true despite a
discouraging silence on
the part of the concipients;
subjected, what promise.
–

now i giv up / / / gaim ovr
–

agenda of a social idiot:
skewl: neopragmatic insistence.
fewill: hypermarket metafarms.
werk: chex that yr paid off.
crushing Pandoraniscium: traffic marinades.
EntertainmeAnt: real life dramatization.
–

yes
ths is schism
ths is quantized
ths is cancerous
ths is grassblade
ths is not
ths is sumwrong
opposing, alryt?
b on ist
—

I believe in gods.
I don't believe a male named God created reality.
Rather, I conceive that
Optimal intelligence recreates reality's appearance.
Our existence is true and validates this.
Reality needs causelessness, in order to be true from and as a logical basis such as we purport any science.
Reality implies my completeness theorem:
All that is true follows from reality.
This is a self-evident axiom, given solely the meaning of its words.
When I am mistaken, my mind grows a new branch.

Note: There are a LOT more of these chaotically scattered writings and little things, but so many of them are so incoherent that they are little more than letters in some random order, or they are too personal in a way I do not want to share now. I won't be throwing any of my primary materials away soon, but there is a lot of stuff!

04/24/2001 – We are apart of them?

Sometimes I feel as if I'm sinking;
I stare into the light, numbly blinking.
I sit alone in my room, quietly thinking,
while spiralling away from else, my voice shrinking.

with the darkness of my breath as you
all fade away before my eyes, the mists
of far away still the air, steal my break.
In this state of subdued consciousness, a fog.

My surroundings, although through the fuzzy mist, seem
nearer to this death we used to see around us
when we could still see through our now closed eyes.
I thought I was running away.

Through the mist we go, to evade them.
I warn you if you wish to come with me,
you need to lose my trail and find your own,
or it's the else for you.

   Am I confused?
  We are particular? If, so.

added note from some time later:

subdued lacking previous articulation

(Grade 11 near end of school year):

04/25/2001 – Alone with Everybody

This grey world that's all around
can be so empty, bland, and selfishly unsound,
I gaze coldly at these which make me frown.
This emptiness surely cannot be what they were
        meant to have found,
These lack in feature, their souls turned to muddy brown.
Full of wasted hopes and might have beens all lost unbound.
Inescapable, my lonely fate,
        while they travel the spiral, down.
Imaginarily so, although; they wear confused crowns.

How easy it must be
to lose yourself from me.
still, you believe that you are free
but all of you are trapped.
unheard or unnoticed, as if it even mattered,
I drift away out to sea.

*(Grade 12 near hard time at school,
found in book below prior poem):*

01/15/2002

This lacks irony, lacks judgment; observation.
We can't be somewhere else. drifting...
away in the sea like there is somewhere to be
       in some other time, be.

I'm going there now, I can't do this.
I'm trying to stop so I can start,
then I will need like before to
try to stop, so I can finish this and go no there.
but/and there is/is not here.

We do/can't really exist/delusionally form.
       and/or happen anyway
beyond time. like before reality. if/and now, this is
       now/here,
like nothing. nothing/everything is/could not be truly real.
Real things begin from a previous state.
Not meanings; representative: random words.

04/24/2001 – Strewn about by all the wrong things

Thoughts from the sea blow all around my head,
they comfort me when all around are dead.
But without the breeze, by them my hatred's fed,
with all their joyous illusion that I try to forget.

In and of me, of all my insides, they wish it bled,
replaced with circuitry like all the freshly bred.
So many yelling at me
from one beautiful mouth on one beautiful head.
Although confusedly astray, they have been led
nevertheless down the path they did not choose.
But by what? What Demon, by this, could be amused?
Or maybe I just think I'm far away;
who knows, anymore, what is true.
For we are all in this, part of society's glue,

Gentle wind in my face,
    may I breathe away from here with you.
                  T
                      o
                        da
                            y...

(before I die apart...)

4/26/2001 – Scribble-Draw   (*Stream of consciousness*)

Little things are good, bad things are not good/
    try to correct the truth of that. Quit bugging
    the incubator, please pen work, I am in luck!

I can continue my descent into the limitless beyond
    or drunk rabbit loves cheese for flap shielding,
    thought box ridiculous,

trying to forget, leaving, inevitably returning,
    blurred reality on neon fire boosters.
    -smash mind, it's not much anyway!

Shrinking, circling, absently blinking,
    without a care for hair
looking for everything, hoping for something,
just feeling nothing rushing away... burying myself,
    losing my track,
following a nothing, help me run away, get away,
    kill myself

or you'll regret it if you even notice I'm gone.
so alone, so alone, so many faces, so alone.
why did I try to comply/ I'm so shy/ want to cry/
    wish I could die
not knowing why so hard I try. Please let me cry...

don't make me die, I'll unweave your infinite lie.

4/29/2001 – gone

gone   i try so very hard
just to forget all your lies
and illusions that make me
regret the time i spent
denying myself. absent
without leave, barely able to
breathe, taught what to believe
and how to perceive, I've slipped
away from myself.
     disappear into the dark, leave
everyone behind in rot
lose the war you never
fought surrender all you
hope you forgot
      ------------------> nothing

6/26/2001 – of my head

in circles spinning round
all out revolves unsound

outside's moved underground
inside remains unfound

sanity has unwound
insanity swirls around

unrelenting they hound
these terrible sounds

No date recorded, 2001 – Erase me, how.

have a cigarette, to start a bad day
smoke some marijuana, the voices fade away
drink some liquor, my mind forgets to play
chew a mushroom, reality goes astray
take a smiley face, I lose what they say
float away in a cloud, to obliviate today
no matter how I try, can't escape the decay
because I'm the one who goes away,
        it all remains right in my way

it surrounds and confounds me
loves to play the game of hate
why am I included just to want to be free
however bad it is to get I won't attribute
        anything to fate
otherwise I have no choice
then I saw, I'm not included—none of us are
we just happen… to disagree
I thought I saw you'd never change

then it was I thought I wouldn't
everyone is here right now
we've just forgotten or just started to
remember our reason.

This is about here, we can't get away
It is so clear, that this is our way
        We can only decide—The rest is up to us
started long ago, this is beginning
finally a reason to be grinning
interdependency we are winning
cessation of noise ringing
        Wow Now

No date recorded, 2001 – wake up to here

a robot arm pulled hair to through
my sidefaced burning arm wild release
of tricks up my sleeve, before we come home
we've got to say we've never been more
 ever enough... ever enough...
    white sounds a buffer through and through the in
    winding winds at hand of thought
    so tripping down a stair, relentlessly
stare into night, beautifully be

a child into night, mind pleasant
or ripely tracked mouse fangs attack!

mystery four brain---------one is trying to go
two forgets that I am-------------three seconds ahead of
four illogic reasoning, so true

so true   night sky   beautifully
                a universe will unite
for life is here of homes beneath

perceptive fields and forces.
quantum dawn.

No date recorded, 2001 – Questernity

Dried compact devices blooming with every care
A rain falls down spiral wind,
absorbent in this liquid sunshine

   falling on my ears   embracing every fear
   all infinitely near   conducive here

   to know the fading ghost   of replenishment
   to go bionic because   believe it or not, I care

Every morning I stumble
in or out of my dreams
to eventually waking up.
I will need to know to need will I
before I can implore the skies
swinging forth on starease.

   it won't/shouldn't be easy to come back
   it requires full-fledged interactions
   for this you would need no spare time
   and it can only take forever

   don't don't don't.... lie.   don't don't don't.... die.
You have nothing to gain, emptiness to lose, so drop
the lates the hows the whys and it can only take forever

lovely! We could fill in for boredom
if ever, we see this might end.

Summer 2001
(written morning immediately upon waking from a dream)

atreefloat   in a dreamy sex
with bluewhaleskysharks battling
flapaway to up to a tree gone from a house to tree

forest green hiding from my eye
re-member mind a mushroom tree

swinging by and through the energy
of starlight drifting underfoot
wild maneuver twisted airmouth
under footover   hiding

in the air up   to the sea fight
in a fright   through the nightlight
until floating   down from a
treeswinging through and of release from
wildflap balloonhands   un-swollen   spaceful

in a dream I pleasureburst into the spacebeneath
my feet under the seasky
watching over me-I-am

    over   in the bounc-
  sing air   singingly so wide
      so lovely   my over

Author's note: Many of my poems came in a spirit of personal exploration or philosophical defense. I believed writing got it out of me, got it on a page for me to see and to revise, feel, be aware of, and respond to what I was feeling with a record and interaction. Writing, whatever I was writing, always felt very disconnected, just flowing out of me, and when I would read it later, I would think: "How did I write that? Was I that angry? I don't feel exactly like that now, but maybe I used to... Why else did it come out of me that way when I wrote it??"

Hmmm... Read on.

2002 – You can make you

Join us in the creativity
live in beautiful fantasy
why won't you join your me!
you know (or don't); leave them be!
Someday too late, you'll see
that you've never truly been free
I ought to laugh, surely YOU would agree
but the unreasoned nonacceptance just makes me angry.

You seem perfectly content to lead a life of them.
I compel you to simply to be your one
but I don't mean to tell you how to be
I just see that you are lost and want to help you find
your way...

Lost hope crumbles into fragments
as you neglect to even see the pieces,
your personality splits and hides in far away segments.

2003—I Yearn to Flux the Wor(l)d w(Hole)

Meet me in the Lunaria. Bring your insanity.
Struggle for the family. Forgive the essence of Dystopia.
Live any way not harmful.   ask why...... imagine why...!

Why if I say to you today. Why not sureness in your place?
Just do it 'cos nothing can stop you, 'cos you're a peace of
real 'substance' for what is real, other than spirit.

Your soul it goes flash, the meaning of it flashing;
relevancy becoming clear, emponder careening near,
and there's the waterfall, follow the rainbow
only when in doubt just like its warriors.

The timeless flow of life forever, breathe please me
with it, please my survival; breathe with more of it;
live more, go stretch the limit of volition, bend
reality to willingness, to you; optipopulate the sky
with seeds, go all out and kiss the dancing sky
to life, the cosmos, coming to life.

The form of meaning goes !pow! flash
whoa and all the sadness and why, wow!
And all the beauty and why life comes
out of it completing its desire surging outcomes,
clinging judgments... wait let's just go—
nowhere; love growing wings or invisibility.

Love the essence of the need of the divinity
for your complete resolving happiness
because you're reality and it's right
that you ought to have FreedomLove
because nothing can stop you now.

2003—Untitled

Note: I remember leaving house at 4:30 in morning after up writing and thinking all night and power went out leaving me in dark. I went to dock close by and peered across the bay at town in relative darkness, emergency battery lighting on only. Then I wrote this at the dock.

When electricity hides..... we stop moving
as if our brains are unplugged because the power's out
but the weather doesn't go away... it doesn't ever need fixing.

Fretting flashlights for what? Our homes have darkened.
Artificial light to function, and see mobiles still circling
in dependency of what's provided,
        when we yet turn to face the sun;
here, quiet in comparison enters a chaos concrete jungle's
    face of stern logical convention.

2003—Untitled

we contend with pretend things
    and I intend that you attend to the deepest mysteries.
treeanimal symbiont breathing in reason to inspire air to
      unfold while containing life into a
      spiralling complexity.
given the organizamit, your willingness to breathe entails
you biological completeness; feed on the light of the sun,
remember the plight of 'rash fun. if you can save the world
no less, please just keep breathing and add to our
      catalytic ecstasy.
oh be the splendour sought, to be finished in
      continuous breath.
oh to cry and come aware with a joy untold of connecting
to the roots of liberation, but when you forget to breathe
you come to a standstill; you need the energy you
      system of catalysts.
you'll fall apart without your breath, so give to the forest
so we can live tomorrow.

2003—Untitled

And let the hollow rust consume the faded steelwork;
Aeon blue behind this face: nothing here anymore for us.
Crumbling above the towers,
      rats and mice come below from sewers,
hardly aware of ghosts that lurk,
      foraging in wasteland dust.

Rows of houses fringing lawns unnaturally
taken by life, grown over with weeds; shutters bang
in the wind over boarded-up windows, doors hanging
open unable to shut,
      of intrusion by dangling branches,
transcending green gods reaching both ways
        toward the city's heart.

2003—Untitled Set on a Single Sheet

Note: The following 4 poems were written on a single sheet of paper with a good chunk out of its corner. They obviously revolve in some way around some particular theme, if not just some single moment of several interlacing themes.

  A
Whittle the sparks
coming between reload,
I can hear the frogs!
Meetings arbitrary,
   u see? do u really?
      cos I can't
       anymore.
        it hurts
        to hurt
         u...

  B
Little box of evils, is it your choice?
Could you have any else? Pandora did a stupid;
no quandary! or repeat!

What I can only really wonder, u kno, is tho:
who the fuck built it? Why would someone do that?
Build a house for evil? Those knowing its right place.

Those on the inside.

   C
Missing the yellow brick walk path into the blinding
lite wait frogstomp, huh what's that??
Cataclysmic chaos. Apocalyptic aeons.
Yeah u kno another side of psychosobriety.
    Huh what's that??

   D
 Y if u half 2
  no prob
 now see here
 why don't u
  remember
  .my name.
   i don't!!
mean anything

2002—Another Page of Assorted Poems

      A
slipping thru the cracks, forget how to look back.
too tired to die, I'm on the right track,
      it's called the song zero.
help me pull the trigger,
      it'll feel better with him out of the way,
foggy window cracks, i'll wait for the sun.
      i'm sure it will be fun.
our day in the sun, i'm sure we could have fun.

      B - "Safety Bear"
Don't attract bears, store garbage and food securely.
Don't let it get away from you, it's not his.
Don't attract bears, run ahead as fast as you can.
It's your own mess, you did it to yourself.
Let it gone and spoiled rotten.
It's not my problem: it's all of yours and theirs..
You can't fix   it' s   working fine.
Just blink an eye, you've got tomorrow.
If lucky, you, you're on today!
      If lucky you,be bear aware.
Electric fence and scenic route,
      so pretty pretty, you are lost,
but worry not, it's still today: a pretty view and
      shocking fence will keep them on the other side.

      C
Wandering thoughts.
Devouring sands.
   move rock move   Move rock, move.

Tumbling waves
through crashing mind.
   Through and through.   thru n thru
Wash me away.
Slipping sand, true your fingers.
   Trip off my face into the moon.

      D
So dirty with a grin of play. When did I let it slip astray?
The door has slammed shut behind me;
     another opens up swiftly,
inviting me with candy.

2008—Re-Medicating The System
(note: old and revised lots)

the predicament we've found
of all language come unwound
is willing ground
unlike cement that's killing sound.

music is following me
straight into hell;
the cat dropped its tongue
so I strung round its neck
a flower for farewell
for we have an agreement
as long as I keep to my treatment:

I listen quietly
to hear philosophy
meant wildly.
you see,
minds with these brains can realize
the haul behind the mother train of thought:
eyes.

what's a thought, eh? ...sigh!
life is less complicated
yet so complex,
you'll experience the understanding
before it can be articulated
by our limited ideological syntaxes
blind to the differences
in following the dots
from following the rules

to figure out your taxes.

inkblots teach more about thought
than a reach for remotes
to transmit impossible tropes
that won't submit to the test
of the climb into the possible trance.

your words cannot save you but keep
conveying words in waves of meaning
that leap from idea to tongue,
portraying worlds.

give me what you have to say to that.
climb the rungs of the thought ladder
and join this dance.!.~

2009—The Birdcage for Spirit
(note: old and revised lots)

My mind breaks things apart
and sequences impossible order
to the meaningfully spontaneous.
I perceive a strange message conveying
while break-mind intervenes, inadvertently,
"breaking the spirit's focus from mind and body,"
one sense I have of schizophrenia.
Blinded by internal events too intense,
I easily wander lost seeking reasons outside
for my beautiful dreaming deep within.

A shared realm entertains transformation,
and I abide by the dynamic of biology,
mind, emotion, and soul.
Those reversed call for freedom,
response, articulation, and creativity.

If I ever forget my spirit, my freedom,
and reduce merely my dimensions to three,
break-mind squeezes my breath closed,
forces a halt.
I needed to accept a cosmic origin,
that I'm not just a meaningless chance.
If this world follows only physical mechanism,
and no soul-space has a you-essence,
where could real love live and who'd wait for true love?

To escape the clutches
of unstopping nihilist reduction
in this real struggle
for sane meaning
and in this yearning for my source,
my mind found a door to open
and I could let in my imaginings,
to find the embrace
of spontaneous expression.
And I could watch on this side of the door,
as this side of the world did turn
into a magic poem I could read.
The door to spirit slid open for me,
and I could disappear out there completely,
until then leaving it open,
letting the cool and warm airs of spirit fill my world,
airs of that open world that help fill physics with life,
with vitality, with my breath ongoing,
for the drawing and passing of air entices life
into our midst.
Pursue the lessons, oh, the joys, of symbiosis!

Schizophrenia for me has been a war against myself
and those devices planted in my brain, but hold on,
because I am not paranoid! I planted them myself;
they're devices for repression and devices for delusion.

One invents a device when a method of thinking is discovered, a method to organize meaning. Keeping in mind that I've never been able to well organize my room, my sentences, or organize my future, one could easily see the potential confusion for my mind released to wild nature. I feel at odds with my environment, extremely feel odd for sure. Do you

want to know my biggest delusion? I believed our society
was one grand illusion, for I couldn't believe in extreme im-
piety, the kind of society itself broken from reality, the kind
of society abhorrent to social, emotional, or racial inclusion,
a society that stomped Earth's biodiversity and stomped on
fellow global citizens in holy wars of greed and creed.
I became so deluded, because I wouldn't believe in true evil.
I made up a story that some god had weird plans, and now
forgetting that, I still won't agree to see evil thru to its end.

Please: if you dig this poem,
go to dance and sing some music,
and make love, communicate.
In my waiting out storms schizophrenic,
I longed to experience this world's sunlight again.
Feel the amazing release of your light,
deeply profound in every moment
because, really, you see, I've been meaning to explore and surrender to experiential discovery.

Gaia asks for tears, you phoenix,
so heal Earth with love on a never-ending quest.
Seek freedom in the sadness for the beauty that we are;
go emerge,
you can fly free from your cage....

2002-2004—Six More Random Notes,
Distributed at Random in a Journal

1. "many are waiting willingly to be eaten while they think not"

2. "i don't know if anyone was harmed in the making of this book."
(This was written near the inside cover "MADE IN CHINA" remark).

3. "is a narcolepsy of meaning real?"

4. "out raige the sceen"

5. "is meaning your consciousness?
or just its form, as matter from spirit?
if either were accurate, becometh the question irrelevant?"

6. "...nae man can tether time or tide..."

2003<
Very many really short poetic essays <2004

I had something of a common terrain of thought and concentration. I often asked the same questions, and sought to interpret many relationships. I wrote into a small hardcover notebook now and again, in spurts, maybe between 13 and 1.1 pages at a time. I always looked in the direction I had left off, and then carried on with my present concerns in the writing. I will be careful in array and selection to speciate the flow. I have made some edits for clarity and have rejected a few lines or pages for a few reasons, but these are primary sources of my confusions. Take these essays as schizophrenic investigations.

something like a preface

<Hello new book

What may I write in you? I think I'll write a book. It'll be about you and I; okay, book? That'll be ok.

As I'm drunk on a wine of my mind I'll float whimsical about my method of conduct. I'm simply easier to flow in an art-cling-beauty paradox of the smattering of poetic ramble ado so many a scientific thing of philosophy. Amidst the steams of light, I play-dance and sing a song I learned from gods who didn't quite know they were it and I wanted to be tagged.

I used to think and say in many forms that I simply was no different than any but just happened to be weird. This came to mind when I heard people preferring to be different but not just normal. I want to be apart from the human race.

I like the human stroll.

I'm just going to go walking. I'll see where I evolve. I want weirdness and to mutate. My race is hurting. I've had enough alternation, altercation, adulteration, so now I want something totally new, something serenely radical. I am becoming a novel

being with dominion over what? Only my free will. That's the only thing strengthened by slavery to systems. We need it to break free, but first and more profoundly we need free will in order to learn to structure, restructure, or to not structure our emotional responses in reflection of our desires with consideration of our benefit, our true benefit. (I posit this; I mean).

The problem solving ability works in this way for the goal **(of true benefit).>**

something like a chapter 1

<**The astral?** Consciousness without physical material sustaining its real existence is the reality of astral dimensionality. Imagination and desire, beckoned by will,

reign supreme as the causal principles and laws of the astral or conscious manifestations in the universe.

To say consciousness and a spirit exists beyond and independent of whatever physical vessel that currently informs it, is simply to acknowledge the uniqueness of the mind's reality, and this articulation does not imply that the spirit can exist without an essence of physique or that it may be able to exist and be mindful like we are without a brain attached to it informing it.

I think, rather, that *consciousness and its manifestations like the beauty of your lover have spiritual substance and reality*, just like physically manifest photons that possess the unexplainably odd characteristic of their own existence. Indeed, the only and most essential and irreducible quality of anything in reality is its existence. Therefore your will power and desires exist too, but why would they need to be physical?

I oppose the drive to *deny* **the spirit and freedom.>**

<The view I have adopted from the interpretations of others is that physical energy has no necessary reason for its causation into creation. We see this by interpreting the very creation of our universe of particles and waves from nothing, realizing that we have interpreted the spontaneous **creation of novel energy.>**

<This is defying improbability

The quantum mechanical model implies that the measure of our actions rely on the relation of the conscious with inanimate form. I believe the most plausible interpretation of quantum mechanics is that *The reality of an action is our intent toward and sense of its being acted out.*

This helps to circumvent the festering notion that events occur because of always blind causes, for the quantum mechanical model implies the requirement of the existence of an individual who may "collapse a wave-function."

[Note from 2012: "collapse of the wave function" is a phrase which represents a huge mystery in the physics of the last 85 years. You can look it up if you want more "accepted scientific" perspective.]

Essentially, the primordial vacuum pressure in the void of emptiness inside and surrounding matter's particulate forms is un uncollapsed wave-function. Indeed, a quantum reality entails that those particulate forms of photons and atoms, who like ghosts to the shaman we've held as so real and independent, must be properly conceived as "properties of consciousness."

Why? Simply because the potential for consciousness may be the only thing which can "collapse a wave-function," and the result of that is what a photon really is. [2012 note: "Copenhagen Interpretation"]

In other words, this esoteric formulation means that will is the glue that binds every form together through time. Sorry, that's even more esoteric.

I guess what I'm thinking is that there is a certain time between various instances of wave-function collapse, so one begins to imagine multiple universes arising out of the inherent flux of uncertainty in a quantum system. This is because we haven't sense of anything which provides substantial reason for saying that what we observed about an object in a specific moment needed to be that way because of an exact procession of states. [2012 note: "Many Minds Interpretation"]

What we observe is that there cannot be something certain happening where consciousness captures it, as was shown in the experiment where scientists prevented a "pot" of microwaved beryllium atoms from "boiling" by routinely measuring them. [2012 note: "Quantum Zeno Effect"] Did they decay at a slower rate because of **the potential for consciousness?>**

<Hmm... Life is often thought of as an improbable event in the cosmos because there's reason keeping matter from becoming complex, namely the tendency toward *entropy*.

I believe that soon spirit or consciousness could be directly and empirically confirmed as the root for the fundamental expression of life. This will come to fruition if my prediction is correct that it is too improbable for complex bonds to form and resist decay before a proper random collision can raise the products another notch ad infinitum, supposedly in reality manifest now, in Earth's living forms.

I like this prediction because it would mean that life is a matter of will because if there must not be a physical means for resolving the infinite possibilities, we have thus inductive proof of a ground for the necessity of there being an essential spiritual quality in the underlying reality.

The underlying reality is the continuum of freedom, the way and home of what could be. Imagine your body of animal metabolism and consider if you willingly ceased to support any conscious function and did this in a single instant.

Every muscle relaxes and the breathing halts, along with any thought in your head. Perceptions involving the senses remain but there is zero involvement, except for the sense of self, from the "soul" of your "consciousness."

Can you imagine this? Could you shut off? It's really scary when one does this in play, like when one intentionally stares blankly passed someone and shapes his or her face to express absence of any connection to the outer reality. But I mean something deeper, like simply giving up the use of the will and revoking your contribution to the third dimension.

So close your eyes sometime to perform this experiment: Imagine and toy with letting your head droop forward like whatever you're doing droops, as if these writings of mine you are currently reading, and the posture and position you hold, just fall out of your grasping hands, and the body of your desire's realization simply fall out or fall away for just a second.

What happened? Did you do it? Did you start breathing spontaneously or hold up your neck in case it bounced around to protect it, even if everything else stopped or got weird for a second? I also get tired yet focussed like I just came out of a **dream.>**

something like a chapter 2

<Something new beginning here;

      Sometimes there are moments when I lose track of my thoughts because there are too many

      On the possibility of losing Atlantis without a single trace of evidence to demonstrate technological sophistication before the last ten thousand years of modern civilization.

      Some perceive that the lack of civilizational remains of a ne plus ultra society of technology constitutes as proof that Atlantis could not have existed. But really, this is an unfounded inference based on our own paradigms of what makes a technological civilization what is is. Namely, I refer to the assumption that all technology suddenly abandoned or purged of human maintenance would simply not dissolve into nothing left we could see. But consider advances in biotechnology: Perhaps we will learn how to manipulate and create traits to make living technological artifacts that serve the same functions as our tools of inanimacy.

      One of the greatest flaws is slavery.>

<I'm talking to myself
 again. the words are
ringing in my head
my heart is fluttering
on and off my gut
is twisting making sound
 how you doing?   The
world free associates

a neck pain constricting
in around   my thoughts
what's on the inside
is it just me on the inside
 can there be an inside
 to the very deep you
 you're inside you're inside
i'm inside i'm inside
  i feel irreducible
  no one will reduce me
  neither could **even I>**

<I think of the difference between the metaphoric head and heart. I feel palpably engendered toward coming to terms with the nature of consciousness, that tangibly receptive outflow of the living things abounding in a sea of manifest reality called material energy, everything. I agree with Buddha that suffering is a truth. That compels me onward as well, in my inner foray of emitting articulation of the secrets of the physical universe, for I desire that truth be our guide, forever attaining to it.

Truth ameliorates suffering.>

  <Metaphors for heads
and   hearts, our thinking
and feeling ways.
    I loosed upon myself
the fathomless songs
   that you would faze.
    I woke up in a dream
of true awakenings so
   the thread of time frays

Breath came back to me
slowly, the more I held
my peace and calm,
terrified   of the maze.

I keep falling down
my head wanders away
from my heart who sleeps
and breath unites **the
travellers of the deeps
of the forests and the dreams>**

<i should just live this really
hairpin trigger for the choice to submit
but forgiveness is willing an amble could flit
to replace the cold march
and never take another hit
the beauty of expression needs me for my wit
the rest of the world is love
into which I yearn to fit

the living world is loving
  in emotional release
all the goodly voices
  enticing me with peace

   my heart of a saint
so I'd love to **take part>**

<The source of infinity is freedom of potential. Desire and intent must be deemed as independently free causal agencies. The observer has power to collapse their internal wavefunction into the nonrandom flow of precise and meaningful

articulation, emotionally, bodily, and symbolically, or so it could be easily interpreted to find the workable rationale of human experience and quantum mechanics.

It's that easy folks!>

<Even in Newtonian physics, gravity's always bringing things together, and life's what can lift itself and objects back up so they may fall again.

Yes I believe in the Radial Energy that Teilhard De Chardin wrote about, and in the Fourth Laws of motion and thermodynamics.

Life is the only relevant fact with which to consider **the cosmic ontogeny and ontology.>**

something like a chapter 3

<All writing prior in the book written during academic year 2003-4. here's summer

Sometimes we refer to our world as 3D, the physical dimension. In this situation, 'dimension' means efficient juncture for information transformation, the environment that contains the nature of objects and at the same time the collection that represents the unity of these natural objects into a whole.

This is a 'dimension,' and in 3D the natural objects are physical so the nature contained by 3D is what our language refers to as laws and mechanisms of physics.

By the Anthropic Principle, the conditions that prevail must arise in life. Creation of meaning happens anyhow. A lensing for symbiosis drives energy transfer ecstasy as **information expressions radiate.>**

    <furst
the release
of the children
overpouring
everexpanding
driven on
the first burst
here yet we are
not only revolving
a game evolving
i want your voice
a mystical note
sung engaging
trapped or caught (as in arms)
now we respond
have urgent breath
and necessary dance
cant help **so express**
a spiralling furst>

<Schizophrenia can consume.

    Are the majority of these writings the disordered delusions of me in sickness, or is this the imaginal adventure of a poetic and dreamy perception of the world? Personally I believe I linger in a spectrum. If I don't *believe absolutely* anything I write, the images remain poetic and indeed, even some of my philosophy must be considered purely poetic. But I believe values and activities and even meaning are expressed by minds. Creation is the question; we know evolution follows.

(I know I secretly assume we improve).>

<**touch and** be close and all that you want to be. I'm so frightened by myself at the same time I feel as to be becoming saner. My emotion yearns to flow yet my mind breaks the flow by judging cause with imagination.

I think about what is responsible for what in my life and external world of relationships, when the emotion is meaningfully expressed rather than caused. With this and the context of mind that includes social, scientific, and spiritual concepts and symbols, my imagination-judgments can be easily swayed to delusion-formation.

I do not intend to form delusions, but habits of traditional thought distract me from letting my experience be simply emotional without clinging to reasons for everything. Perhaps harmful emotional circumstances and lack of sense of will and viable options created conflict with the predominant mode of thought inherited in mimic communication during infancy thru adolescence.

I think awareness grows, (a not so hidden or missing premise), especially thru stimulus that **exceed thresholds for integration and challenge stability.>**

something like a chapter 4

<**Sometimes** I feel neglect.

    I feel that due attention is not observed at times. Even that undue attention is observed consciously, abounding from deep and drastic misunderstandings of the world, of our nature, and of the form of peace. I find myself striving in communication to shake the alienated sense of being utterly alone with coming to face a part of my being that operates as to alter my behaviours of and desires for experience.

    The clinical analysis leaves me with no aid other than a pill that chemically slows my brain, which certainly helps me function within prescribed social experience parameters, but I am still containing a powerful unresolved energy, evident if I forget my med for a day. I feel neglect. I don't like my basic perception of my experience reduced to terms of preoccupied spiritual ideation conducive to formation of delusion, even if I acknowledge that this happens. Again I state I feel misunderstanding abounds.

    I misunderstand too, and I feel this to be the actual source of my delusions, rather than their simply being caused by erratic, random firing of my nervous system; I don't have everything figured out, but this is what I feel. I think doctors presume too much to think that psychological factors play little role with the mechanisms of schizophrenia. I think it is implausible to find the entire reason for disabling symptoms in neurochemistry. I stress again, here I believe is misunderstanding. My medication assists me by suppressing perceptual expression but some of this expression feels good or feels like it could be good, if only I viably responded. To begin feeling good with who I am, I must interpret my natural condition of being in terms shifting from "individual in illness or insanity" to "individual in transformational potential or linguistic artistry," because then I can re-understand.

So I think the psychological mechanisms of schizophrenia and their disabling symptoms as actualized behaviour in our social context could better than illness or insanity be interpreted as having a basis in the natural, albeit extremely profound, capabilities of the human consciousness. My schizophrenic disability arises from the tension around an improperly integrated perceptual function. In my schizophrenia, the emergent perceptual function in question is the capability of the dreaming mind, expanding into the waking world. Where else but in dreams do we interact with objects and with people who come from inside us and where else but in dreams do we contend with the strangest, most bizarre, and most rapidly spontaneous meanings and feelings? Well? Psychedelic plant use and "self-immersion improv" come to mind, but closer to my life is the inner experience of being schizophrenic. In a few words, I dream of weird things when I am awake.

Imagine for a moment if you had a dream in the middle of dinner that someone poisoned your food, and suppose you did not know the difference between your dream and your world; imagine then your unwarranted behaviour and the untrue belief that the real food was poisoned. Many schizophrenics who are diagnosed and in self recovery share the experience of taming their symptoms thru recognizing their perception as "dreamlike" or as internally generated in some sense. In trying to causally link bizarre senses of objects or meanings to third-dimensional activity, I have found a source for delusion. Many schizophrenics share a range of adaptive approach, such as only listening to the kind voices or trusting serene emotions throughout streams of waking dream, or effortlessly maintaining a strong awareness and focus on the shared world.

It's as though some of us develop the experience of peaceful cooperation with our perceptual perturbation in exchange with expansion, and this in turn changes the nature and character of our whole experience of our being. It is personalized and idiosyncratic, in big way. Maybe we learn to accept and adapt to utilize what our brain creates, ideally. Hopefully we also retain the ability to enjoy an evening of good food with our family or friends without unwanted inner disturbance.

Do you ever find difficulty in choosing how to be? When confronted with internally generated versions of reality, I find myself freezing up and resisting action. My mind becomes active in "trying to figure out why," yet there are no external reasons for some of my feelings, no "external promptings that permit meaning." In a fundamental way, in a way, all meaning is internally generated and all the external world bears are the symbols for that meaning. To me, a part of "my schizophrenic problem" is that my mind and body naturally generate an immense and intense flow of meaning and emotion. In other words, symbols in the world seem alive to me and to be communicating in impossible ways, at least in my judgment of the rich and baffling feeling I receive sometimes when encountering language. Sometimes I just have no idea how to respond. I usually stare.

I don't know how to be, and whether to fully enter an emotional mode or remain social intellectual is not even a choice in our world where you must pay to eat food, drink water, communicate over distances, and have shelter. I don't have the option to float in linguistic and perceptual rapture while living in an apartment near a grocery store. Needing to work for a living requires a mode of being different than the mode of being where I live for free with every moment for free exploration and self-discovery of my powers of perception.

As far as I perceive my place in this world, I desire time and resources to embrace the full breadth of my humanity. For me being human must be far more than going to work to pay for life. In fact this keeps me from being human. I ask the question; is it logically impossible to provide for each other what we need to grow and to continue living culturally and technologically, without any stipulation of cost? Is it physically impossible?

Or is it only presently unreal? All I can think of now is the vast number of ecologists, artists, and activists who consider "mankind's conquest of economic progress" an impossible aim of a finite biosphere that seeks to sustain itself. Profit is impossible. Life just grows; who needs to invest in anything but compassionate activity? Wealth should be distributed. This poor schizophrenic would appreciate a **leeway for freedom.>**

<The world could be a better place if all were allowed to develop their natural interests instead of fitting to a world social system of business obligation. My natural interest is to explore my consciousness and experience emotion. I

enjoy being social and desire to teach and share philosophy. I desire a peaceful world where healthy needs are met. I don't want to ever charge a cover cost for my services of compassionate devotion. I just want to help the world, so I am confused by the insistence of others that I pay for living and to follow my interest.

Theoretically, instead of $3/kg, asparagus is actually free. It happens to be grown by light and nurturing of a farmer/gardener, to be transported by a distributor, and to be delivered by a grocer. In all this, humans moved and took action toward the world. Why do at any point we say "none until the money rolls"? Can't you imagine a world where all the humans wake up and enjoy their work and life for free? If the human race is so inclined that nobody is willing to get off their ass without pay because nobody is willing to share without pay, then ought we consider the path of our thoughts? I advise this strongly, for fundamentally and accurately, we decided to apply cost and we decided to accept money problems. Otherwise, life grows freely.

Life has a way of asserting and expressing itself by means of self-creation out of available energy. Life is the only relevant fact with which to consider the cosmic ontology and ontogeny, or the cosmic nature and origin. Life is to exist, and reality has no other plausible reason for being. This energy we call the world is like a dreamscape for consciousness, and we shape our results and the world to intended order and disorder.

Consider a moment the hidden purposes, knowledges, and histories required for this event, your reading this. There is a physical dimension for this process including the history of objects of pen and paper that are manufactured and utilized, including etymologies, or the history of symbols related to objects, of these words. Every part of this process is consciously generative when the pattern of physiological energy entails the purpose of communication.

This example of the external world of energy as a vessel for consciousness to bring forth form speaks to an ability of reality itself. We aren't beings caught in a reality; we're reality caught up in being itself. If this is a physical world, physical nature discerns itself willingly. Aren't we proof this is also a conscious world? **Matter lives and living matters.>**

<**Over the ages,** humanity has initiated a plethora of interpretational models of reality. I like shamanistic animism and sentient realism, for these modes accept and affirm a possibility of devotion and ecstasy in living experience, as though this is the natural intention of the basis for _____ (well.. anything). It seems to me that the world operates in a self-organized manner purposefully based for a perception of peaceful and emotive realization. It seems to me there is no other reason than to express and receive a future, in **the activity of work.>**

<**The world is for expression** and reception of life, for connective harmony between needs.

As I was just prior to starting this sentence, I was shutting the TV off during a commercial offering me "Life, Money, and Balance" for accepting the role of "one who is in debt."

The other night at work, my coworkers joked when I asked to see the put away sign-out sheet to allot my hours. One said "you can work for free tonight." Another chimed, "wouldn't that be better?" And I thought "yes, but everyone needs to for the system to work," but I sort of just froze up and went along with it.

Sometimes I feel uncomfortable around people because my basic views seem so distant and inexpressible in the normally accepted contexts. I've always had a suspicion, based on an observation of how people take what I say to respond, that there are things I think about that many people do not think about, and I also observe in myself a hesitance to think in ways that I deem as "normally accepted."

Before, I spoke of misunderstanding, and as natural a position as it may seem for a schizophrenic to misunderstand and to differ from normalcy, I have experienced many negative repercussions. I experience stress and maladaptation, when I aspire to act and feel the normal ways society expects people in our world to act and feel. 'Business as usual' and 'being normal' feel worse for me than allowing myself to feel and act ways that are judged to be weird.

Indeed, so has our ecosystem. It's normal to behave every day in a variably destructive environmental relationship. We know the number of fish in the sea are finite along with the trees in a forest, but economic progress and increased GDP like to stop the life to imagine profit. And indeed, an oil spill or an industrially driven war or genocide between beautiful individuals could raise the GDP by upping the barrel's cost, yet all this is imaginary! The concrete detail is the life being lost, squandered, and the abstract potential is to exuberate the condition of humanity.

The prospect of liberating my creative potential into the good work of devotion to the others of experience—wow and whoa—the amaze meant from it. I yearn to surrender to my truth—this lack of faith and lingering doubt yearn to submit unto emotion and meaning.

When will God overcome his greatest struggle to touch my face and yours? When will we listen to Mother Nature and the layers of infinities of beings which flow from **the womb of time?>**

<If beauty continues to exist in something, can we come to feed it perpetually to our hearts? Let me give me to you straight: I firmly know our nature includes not only physical food nourishment. Our hearts hunger for the word that means both emotion and meaning at once, in fact I know we need it like we need plants and animals. We need it from each other. We're a species, united in diverse potential.

I can't imagine a human world void of communication, and it strains me to see our world hesitant to fulfil our human desires to communicate. A means of living humanly cannot isolate itself to means of finding power to get food and stuff. For me we need expression and time to find love. Work, work, work...

I don't understand this beauty.

Except coming back to my senses has been exquisitely magical.
What I as a soul can remember or learn anew about the splendour and spaciousness of experience speaks to the presence of infinity, as though we may become beautiful forever.

Given peace and harmony in the ecosystem, I expect beauty to comprise the natural experience. Life forms can be appeased. Competition grows more irrelevant as consciousness evolves to make surviving easier, as has been the case with humanity, where competition (I am emphasizing here the self-assertion at expense of another) has proven omnicidally destructive, at this scale and manner, in our wars and social injustice as well as our suffering ecosystem.

I've had a long-feeling life of experience with suffering in it, in learning that normal people surrounding me were so misunderstood about human nature in peaceful relation to the world and others. How else could such destruction willingly occur? I refuse to accept any hypothesis that human events have a physically causal basis according to random chance alone. Enlightenment cannot be a matter of luck, or as luck in the matter, as it were in this case. The spirit is a necessary hypothesis because only freedom of sentience can give reasonable ground to an understanding of how consciousness expresses itself in our world as we observe, articulate, negotiate, and **emotionally involve ourselves with meaning.**>

<**Pragmatically,** when I foster belief in a mechanistic, marginalized existence of blind falling through space subject only to external forces, I wish only that something would happen and lose all notion of any way to make something happen. I affirm that my beliefs govern my behaviour, and acceptance of freedom in a physical divinity of conscious expression undergirds my hopes for world peace though understanding. Freedom also undergirds my hopes of maintaining sanity, to keep my **mind** from *splitting into*

fragments as in *schizo***phrenia**. I would have no desires or motivation for any part of life if yearning made no difference of sum to actions. I don't accept that this description can be put in terms or reconciled by a description of physical parts in automatic reaction. This is an "autopoietic" (self-making) response to cognitive dissonance, and I resolve it by accepting cognition, conscious and unconscious, as the means of living connected in sentient communication. Communication and expression events imbue physical potential energies into motion.

This would be an English, modern scientific rendition of some of the ideas of shamanistic animism and sentient realism as these have been perfected and multiplied by healers, shamans, sorcerers, druids, goddess-worshippers, and saints who understand the power of emotional devotion to experience. I'm using these ideas to contemplate Western scientific thinking, which I find to be ungrounded and misunderstood where the sense of free will is an unobserved problem or ineluctable mystery, rather than a revealing clue of spiritual nature being fundamental to **the observed events in life.>**

something like a chapter 5

<Someone once told me I was word-masturbating when I speak like I do or use a word, for example, like "fundamental." This person told me I used it simply to flash up my argument with words he thought I used superfluously without significant meaning. When I use fundamental as a word, I generally take the sense of "requiring at basis." To classify a thing as fundamental is to denote that thing's

properties as necessary in the "fundament" of what's being considered.

If I say spiritual nature is fundamental to observed events in life, I suggest that materialism lacks a sufficient explanatory or conceptual basis for living results such as the semantics of communication: the meaning, sense, and interpretation that occurs in perception. I think methods of materialism can only speak or ask questions about the transformation and embodiment of the formal characteristics of communication, such as sound waves traversing the air and neurochemistry waves traversing the brain and body. But these waves traverse between mouths and ears of communicators who have message-bearing modalities of existence.

(the formal characteristics thus include all symbols we use to convey the

[note from 2012: the last sentence was interjected at a later time in the bottom margin of a page. It trails off like that with an incomplete thought but with the space for a couple words.]

I think materialism is flawed to insist that it is not I who writes but that a chemical system of reactions generates the illusion of linguistic and sentient decision that consists in my sense of self. I believe the deepest part of us, beyond the physical, reveals the beauty that we are.

To the extent that materialism restricts the causal powers to mechanisms of a physical sort, it restricts sentience into a category of "the result of physical events and objects" and it even fits all events and objects into this category.

I think that makes life and culture misunderstood, their essence forgotten in **obscure ritual for the pay schedule.>**

<why do some consider explanation unreasonable, to be hostile toward emotion? Only where one is only forced to ask questions about parts can emotion lose its power as the reason for our actions and its will for explaining how **we carry action forth.>**

something like a conclusion

<Let me play...

What makes free will?

Free food means sustaining energies at no financial cost, which actually means sustaining energies given under no slavish symbolic stipulation. The sense of freedom gets confused. We are "free," by choice, to stipulate symbolic agreements to which we force adherence in others, i.e. "present symbol x-dollar bill or you don't get to eat, communicate, or learn" even if it's totally imaginary while inflation and debt just soar and dive. This "communicative agreement" relationship involving the sense of freedom may directly illuminate what would make "will free" as we propose by that phrase.

Free will may be those willing natures "free from" or existing without an adherence to some form of symbolically stipulated agreement. The agreements traditionally pondered are usually of three, the materialist, the transcendent, and the magical classes of agreement. The materialist agreement concerns the stipulation of energy as existent by physical mechanics and the transcendent agreement concerns the stipulation of energy as existent by divining intention. Thus in these two classes, will cannot be free from mechanism or divination.

Both these views, if accepting of will's position as free, see this only as a necessary result of things in mechanism or divination. Magic on the other hand directly asserts the existence of mystery and consciousness as the base from which any thing material or transcendent arises, so the will becomes determined to express and to make spells with itself.

The will is free from mechanism or divination as being seen as integral to every result, **seeing the will not as a mere result itself.>**

<the old new

I've been changing in a way that has brought both suffering and growth, and I perceive a transition toward more growth. The suffering is still here, still strong at times, but my recourse to calm is becoming, emphasis on becoming, a well-trodden path.

I've overcome a particular obstacle in my process of growth toward existence free from my own internal torment. The obstacle was an unabashed relativism that let me profoundly lose sight of who I really am.

I said to myself that intrinsically, the behaviour of energy, the universe, and 'the underlying' causes are arbitrary, that anything at all could be the case. I stopped listening to my body and my breath shallowed. My emotions were put on hold, and a fierce and chronic psychosomatic mechanism took their role in contextualizing my experience. I would hurt physically and think about how desperate I felt, with a physical sense of emptiness, of being a brittle shell, that only breathing fully can realize into strength filled with sensitivities.

And sometimes, when I do finally take a breath in earnest relaxation, tears of "I don't and can't articulate" feelings will form in my eyes, oxygenating my heart and filling the shell. Letting my breath roll in and out is one of the most beautifully engaged states of my being. Only love compares, and in a way that breathing is how I love myself. One way, at least, to rejoice in being.

Ask: what could this feeling turn into?>

finally,

<**Brenden** the little raven flutters,
 flies from the dark side of Luna,
into the light and view of Terra and Sol,
carrying magics of the night.
Little wings, flapping up,
in stirring a-fright,
at the chirp of a mysteriously compelling call.

He flitters and falters at times,
struggling through the great between,
seeking to convey the heavenly
gift of the magic called to emerge,
bringing Lunatic vision to the light of day's grasp.

-written in Phil 112>

[note from 2012: I note the poem was written in Phil 112, because otherwise understood the last section of these "short poetic essays" dated, according to a prior note, from the summer of 2004— that's after I would have been done my first year of university when I took my intro Ethics course. In this period of my life of free writing long-winded streams of consciousness, this poem was transported with some personal, but now speculative cause of significance, into this little note book, unlike the rest of writing in it, which originated in a linear fashion.

Cleaning out my binder sometime that summer, I decided it felt relevant to follow the quasi-poetic prose with this poem. I must have been in the middle of writing the prose when the poem would have been written in class. It fit here, after the fact.]

Part Two

The Bird Cage for Spirit:
An Autobiography of Intense Philosophy

Chapter 1
Recognition of Chrysalis:
The Early Stage of Life

In this opening chapter, I would like to share my first memories of life. I was born and grew up in a small town on Vancouver Island, close to the Pacific Ocean and thick forests. I was always close to Nature, and I had a nourishing family environment. I was allowed to be independent, and I was supported. My mom has told me I was always very unique, different, and odd... She used different terms at unique times, for it, whenever I was being odd. To be honest, my memories are always more vague than they seem to be for other people. My memories are conceptual and internal. I fear this book may be too conceptual, but for me to write anything else would be contrived. This is an autobiographical work, in part, but I am not good with chronology. There may be inconsistencies. It is more an "autopsychology" than a graphic picture of events in my life. It is highly focussed on what I thought about my thoughts.

To be all honest, from the very outset of my remembered life, as long as I have known I am Brenden, I have been acutely fascinated by being thoughtfully aware of what it is like to be me. Ever since I can remember, I have lived with curiosity about being alive. I have always remembered wondering what was going to happen next. Life was an amazing experiment for me as a child. I looked out to the world at others and behaved with a deep sense of awe and adventure and wonderment at the very fact that I was able to live it. I later learned in my philosophy education that my object of interest was "self-awareness" and that my most naturally found childhood play-tool was "freedom of imagination and choice." I've known ever since I can remember that I have been on a quest of learning more and more about the nature of my experience, before I even had words to describe it.

The joy and wonder I have, at the fact that we have choices to make and games to play, has never left me. My earliest memory is the memory of thinking about how beautiful, how truly demanding, and how inoperably free my next thought and motion would always be. Of course, I didn't have the abstract words to express it in this way, but there was something percolating in my mind from my earliest experience that was an abstract sense of self that was very compelling and often in my thoughts. I didn't know what to do at all, but I knew I had as many options as I could conceive and have access to. I knew from the initiation of my sense of identity that human life was a magic of perception and of learning how to behave. My schedule was open, and I pounced on every exchange with others and every moment alone as a source of learning, because that's all there was it seemed to me. Everything and everyone I came to had some contribution to my experience with which to integrate into my picture of reality. I didn't know the word 'reality,' but it seems to me I've thought about it forever. I barely even remember "childhood events of my life" compared to remembering thinking about "what it all meant."

Most of this experience has been non-verbal

throughout my life but has been explosively verbal in recent years, especially since reading a book or two or four score, I picked up on the fact that sages, mystics, scientists, artists, and philosophers had been enquiring and expounding directly for millennia on the subjects of my deepest interest. As I have been given language for it, my picture of reality that I've had since I was a child has become increasingly en-languaged and communicable. Regardless of sceptical arguments I have now heard in the philosophy of mind, and regardless of my initial need to learn language, I have always been inoperably convinced that all of reality is only *really* about conscious, living beings exploring and developing access to expression, experience, and energy. I've listened to the arguments as a philosophy major, but nothing sways me from the intuition that life and living (as I have imaged it, full of play) is the most important aspect to the nature of existence.

In the car on a family trip that took 3½ hours of driving, I was very hungry and cranky for food and cranky from the long ride. I remember not being able to see the ground from my low vantage in the seat while looking up through the window at trees, sky and buildings. I was complaining to my parents about my desire to eat immediately, and they were telling me to wait just a little bit longer. My dad finally got annoyed enough to burst my idealistic dreams with a logical point of truth: I could very easily sit and cry frenetically and "whine for food the whole way until we get there," or I could sit peacefully as I could because I "still won't get food until we get there, sorry...." And there it was: the birth of my concept of free will. I became quiet and rest assured that the choice was made up in the mind of my parents and that there was no use on my part in whining further.

I realized very consciously that I had learned completely the lesson of patience. It consisted in the willing choice to complain or be as calm or resolute as possible, no matter what your pangs of desire for a change in situation. They didn't buy me a drive-thru fast food burger, some junk food snack, to tide me over. I had been complaining every time I saw a convenience store or restaurant sign as I looked out the window. Then my dad spoke, and I remember quieting with the thought that emerged. I ate at my grandparents' house and was satisfied for the rest of the car ride with having realized that it just hurt me to complain when there were no good options. I just rested quietly and waited with the feeling in my belly, because I had some choice in how to react to a hunger.

I always strove after that to understand and contemplate my desires without responding to the situation by fighting or complaining. (I'm not always a perfect communicator, of course, and occasionally a mood overwhelms my sensibilities). As a result of this patience and desire not to fight with what the world offers to us, I eventually excelled academically at school, resisted bullies and defended the bullied, made great friends with people who seemed to not have many friends, and also could enjoy time by myself without being fed continual activity input. I was not a demanding child; instead, I was quiet and speculative, and up for experiencing everything I could see was available. My mom says my favourite spot in the house was always my crib, looking out a window. I was patient with situations while looking for ways to create the best from them.

I developed a sense of knowing myself to be in such a state that was totally different from the alternative of just living with a task fully at mind without self-reflecting constantly. Being self-conscious is almost a problem for me, while it is also enriches me. Quite honestly, I've been preoccupied as long as I can remember with seeing how the next moment will affect my consciousness and with finding something in this moment which I could bring to others. It has been easy for me my whole life to go amidst normal activity while quite deeply I am pondering how I fit in the moment, how I feel and how I will think next or relate with others. In childhood and early school life, I learned to think of myself as very unique, because I didn't feel that others felt or conceived their own experience as intensely as I did.

It occurred to me very early in my remembered life that I was a special thinker with unique methods of knowing and relating to my experiences. I cared greatly for the experience of experience, beyond the simple joys of playing with toys or games. When I had time to daydream I might wonder about what it meant to be alive and aware. Childhood dreaming during sleep was a psychedelic learning experience. I often have felt many of the people around me were just doing things without thinking as deeply about the meaning as I was. I felt my role in situations was ambiguous; I just went along with what everyone was doing while living a very rich inner life divided from the ability or venue to communicate it... yet.

If a philosopher of mind had ever spoke to me when I was a child, I would have been entranced and giddy with excitement. To have heard someone talking about free will and mental effort would have made an instant friend, but I don't remember that ever happening. When in grade nine or ten I found a philosophy book of nineteenth and twentieth century essays, I was amazed and intrigued by reading a bunch of old guys' views that made me think of things I had already felt I had enquired into in different ways by my own reasoning. It blew my mind to realize that many humans have thought over the ages about the intense and deep nature of consciousness. I suddenly felt like I was not alone in my long contemplation, and I realized there were even more perspectives and ideas than had occurred to me thus far.

I began to devour philosophy and ancient spiritual and religious texts, fitting my own experience of the mind into the ever-expanding picture provided by the life work of other minds. Until then, I felt very alone, albeit not depressively for the most part, in my kind of thinking, and my childhood was spent coolly contemplating for myself the nature of life and the world while participating socially, simply because it was easy and fun to, not because I felt embedded in it. I often questioned, inside at least, the 'necessity' of various behaviours others seemed to rely on.

I had so many dreams and deep contemplations and never knew what to do with them, because in feeling alone I didn't even realize at times that there were possible words and fellows in my way of thinking, somewhere out there, to communicate with. I felt huge wonder, curiosity, and desires about communication, expression, and experience. It just occurs to me now while writing that a reader might be wondering how this growth and curiosity of mine would get turned around into schizophrenia, a condition of great suffering and confusion. There is more to my story than my personal profound, beneficial experience with learning about and accessing the world.

I thus begin my book with a chapter about recognizing myself as having a deep conceptual and philosophical experience with this world. I'm weird, as many, many schizophrenics have been told behind and to their face, over the years, I'm sure. Of course, my experiences are particular to me, and generalizations are usually obscure, misleading, shallow, or valid only with degree. Thus, my experience of schizophrenia and my own consciousness is my own experience. Every case is different. This book is both autobiography, as well as forays into some generalizations. You will learn something, at the very least.

In the next chapter, I will begin to describe how I came to be schizophrenic, or in more specific words, what led me on the path to chronic and eventually full-blown storm-force psychosis filled with incredible hallucinations and delusions. I will begin to describe how I got lost in the mysteries of consciousness and suffering. I will tell you what I feel and think about my teenage life.

As a remark on the word 'chrysalis' (a 'cocoon' or 'pod-like' stage of insect metamorphosis) in the title of this chapter, I have come to believe that, especially for certain sensitive and aware children, the world's presence and meaning makes the mind into a kind of chrysalis for a type of adult individual. Children kind of live in a closed world of meaning where perpetual perceptual learning relationships with the world and a sort of profanely mystical unification with the world easily inspires one to imagine and reason. The metaphor of a chrysalis fits because babies are born, and *then* grow up to emerge slowly from their individualism into the profound relation of an incessant probing and forming of our psyche by nature, family, friends, and society. We enter the world once, but there remain other worlds beyond every start.

We all grow in a way similar to this, piecing together an idea of the self that we can't help but by nature consciously experience, an idea of purpose, function, and *career* as conscious self. We emerge from the chrysalises of development whenever we become able to understand and participate in larger and more complex domains of action and response.

In addition, we continue, hopefully even as adults, experimenting and following out the manners of life by testing, pushing, and pulling on anything with various degrees of wonder, openness, desire, and caution toward what happens. Every healthy child pursues such with the intention both of learning as well as inspiring glee in minds similar to ours. Of course, being still inside a chrysalis leaves an entity susceptible and vulnerable to several influences. I feel like I am always beginning to figure out what my nature is. Learning to play and playing to learn has figured in my sense of being a living explorer, once encumbered with great vision and no words, now starting to see and starting to talk!

Chapter 2
Acclimatization and Affect: Learning What Happens in the Real World

No one should find it hard to understand that our way on this planet is in danger. War can end. We can preserve our children's access to the bounty of Earth's life. Earth and its living systems could naturally flourish with the conditions that have underlain our complete evolution. The war against other people and the war against other markets have proven that humanity is in disgrace and immaturity. Nuclear wars of environmentally and socially devastating radiation pollution have been *tested and fought* successively even since Hiroshima and Nagasaki via depleted uranium bullets, bombs, and missiles that aren't seen by the world as the same impact as "A-bombs." Despite that, more radiation has infected whole populations and ecosystems in recent years than the A-bombs of world war two combined. These weapons are produced and sold like toys by people wishing to sway other economic forces in some direction.

Our economic-techno-aggressive cultures do not care sufficiently about food to worry about releasing pollution. We don't respect or know the ways we evolved enough that we can understand what ecosystems need. (Henry Ford: "History is bunk.") Many tribes of North American aboriginals lived for thousands of years, utilizing plants, animals, and stones in a ceaselessly spiritually conceived powerful awareness of how to live peacefully enough to have bounty easily. There was likely more than a hundred million of them living here, and they treated animals with enough respect that everyone who wanted a fur or skin cloak could respectably have one: the animal populations flourished to the point that Western culture would speak quite delusively and mythically of "untold, unspoiled, endless riches to be braved and conquered by destiny." However, things were endlessly productive here for humans by intelligence alone. Native populations were decimated, and in 1900, when the North American colonizer population was 70 to 75 million people, less than the original population, several animals were already becoming endangered or extinct, and the land was already under the road of eco-fracture.

The path of the modern man who thinks we ought to kill and sell first and hope for salvation through science later is just berserk. The cutthroat mentality of a daily race to the rat grinder is killing our ingenuity and prowess in the niche we co-evolved with. We do not have the right ideas in our mainstream endeavours. Culture is likely "psychotic" and void of adequate knowledge. Otherwise war might cease instantly. No one would keep fighting or polluting if they knew that was just a stupid form of cultural suicide. We should take hold of the bounty of living, conscious systems. If we were smart, we'd be willing to let our population decrease until we know how to live fairly with what space can be allotted for so many of us.

This is the perspective I have, today. My ideas are forceful and specific: my world is regularly crazy. Too many people know too little about how mind and plant nature work and have too many delusions about what is the right course of action. Sustaining an endlessly growing construction and real estate industry can be a massacre to the hopes of our children because that's where the jobs and money cannot be maintained forever due to always present ecological limits.

(Hmmm, post-"recession/depression" remark: I originally wrote that last sentence in 2007, it appears the official mainstream may recognize this now, somewhat, after the "housing bubble" popped). If we careen too far in a destructive path, we may lose all ability to wilfully change our lifestyles as famine and scarcity result from ecological abuses and changes. We do not need money. The more we exploit power and conceive the bounty of life as mere saleable commodity, the faster we change the Earth of riches we evolved inside to a "Holocene," the present geological era we are in, one of the greatest extinction events in the geological record. We may not simply be reducing human fare, but the overall productive capacities of the entire global ecosystem. I care about this enterprise of sane ecological stewardship more than any other global aim. I want sustained friendly forests, not rapidly growing deserts.

If you might conservatively wonder why this leftist rant about conservation is appearing in a book about schizophrenia, that is because you don't understand how the world went crazy before I went crazy. I have to tell you more about my childhood and life and these 'left' views to develop a proper account of the genesis of schizophrenia in my life, because my ecological and sociological views come from no ideology. The first chapter describes how I opened my eyes to living, how I first noticed the potential to learn from and actively participate in every moment. This early opening rendered me sensitive in a profound way to the identities of others and the world around me. On one side,

I was immaculately self-absorbed in my endlessly roving mind, and on the other, I watched endlessly to see how others were taking in the moment and situation as well as watching how the environment appeared and behaved.

Physics, biology, psychology, ethics, and art have never ceased to be lifelong disciplines of study, regardless of the fact I did not always have the language or had adapted my ability to articulate all that I am seeing and the ways that I am happening. My mom must have taught me very early (before any conscious memory for me) with her loving embraces what it meant to feel good, loved, and cherished in the effortless, natural, unstoppable manner of a mother. My parents always cared about and appreciated a green environment. We lived in a house surrounded by seemingly endless forest, and I picked up early that I liked picking up garbage and keeping our planet clean and biodegradable. I cared about people who fought and wanted to help settle fights and find ways to agree. I took it upon myself at a very early age to seek saving the world. "What did you want to be when you grow up?" was always a boring question that filled me with an urge of being everything I could as long as it mattered.

As my ideas of the world grew, I learned more and more about the existence of past and current wars and the immensity of the struggle to conserve the environment, which I just took for granted was universally hoped for and trusted when I was a school child partaking at Earth day. It occurred to me slowly in high school that kids thought of "garbage duty" as a punishment instead of a wonderful privilege of cleansing and moving outdoors, and teachers gave it as punishment. I remember kids had to do garbage duty if they did not have proper gym clothing or if they 'messed up' behaviourally. I started out one day to pick up garbage of my own will during lunch break after eating, and I was amazed and shocked and exhilarated and saddened all at the same time by the responses.

Some people said "right on!" and some people said "someone gets paid for that, so why do you do it?" But almost everyone thought to say something. The few wonderful souls who actually helped me one random day, I love you. Mother Earth is under the weather, right now, and I'd recommend to everyone that we should all pick it all up. Ethically and practically, we supposedly reason-capable humans must be the ones to either dump our junk and poison all over the living creatures or be as responsible as we can, and to be realistic we probably should be responsible, and have the opportunity by our intelligent nature to do so. But we have a tendency to make our choices poorly as a globe. All it takes is some basic intelligent, inspired negotiation. We can make a choice to let this Earth flow with the bounty we evolved in. Making money and throwing litter and pollution everywhere, burying the soil with concrete and pollution, we lose out on a truly phenomenal life of expressing the self-creation that we were made in. We are making the conditions of sickness.

I support these words fully, and later chapters or the essays in the latter section of this book will hopefully connect my experience to that of other schizophrenics and even people in general, who do not ubiquitously share my concerns or specific symptoms. But parallels and generalities will become evident later: for now I am building up my own story. In high school, I was mortally perturbed by what I felt was inaction, indifference, and apathy on the part of seemingly my whole society. Even if people cared about the environment, few seemed ready to learn and change everything we were doing right now. I was freaking out all the time inside and gaining a desire to change the world more readily and immediately.

I am ready for deep changes of lifestyle, ready to accept the tearing up of suburbs and the return to as much local farming as possible, ready to accept mass joblessness and the continued flow of transport, energy, and food, just so we can have the basics and not keep spoiling the globe with mass production and mechanical market growth. I'm ready first to join a ceaseless public conversation that never ends and personally feel we ought to raise an understanding of the necessarily fundamental general strike that is needed in order to take for the people some democratic control of food, utilities, production, development, and media. Certainly at least, the conversation is already starting among activists.

The latter half of high school was an increasingly horrifying experience, as I saw people becoming cynical and hardened into thinking they needed eventually to find jobs and careers and so many thought highly of money and senseless partying. I became ever increasingly aware and vocally active in conversations about life and experiences, and I increasingly saw that the global rape and pillage for wealth and profits was choking our planet and inciting wars of immense imperialism and terror. And I felt a blindness and violence in the paradigms of my society.

On one of the first few days of grade twelve in September 2001, I watched the trade center towers fall before catching the school bus. I really noticed the apathy and indifference and a hold out on or absence of emotions and reality on that morning of September Eleventh. I knew the third world war had begun, and so it has, based on the premise of stopping terror and upholding civilization (as every "good guy," no matter which perspective or side you look from, holds is the premise of their own defence and attack).

However, at "15 minute break," our mid-morning recess, I had realized my friends and teachers were not ready to stop everything and begin to brainstorm about the necessity to change the way we live. Others may be willing to wage destruction with despicable, Earth- and culture-harming ways of life, but we had to keep focus and not learn what life might really be about. We tried as hard as we could, as a social unit in our so thought to be far-removed separation from the goings on of the global situation, to focus consciously on doing our school lessons and in being the semblance of normal, not being swayed by the terrible events. I heard on the first morning of this present geopolitical era being violently ushered in a student about my age remark "I've already heard enough and don't want to talk about it anymore. It's fucking boring." A fear like nothing else overwhelmed me and spun me into chaos.

People didn't stand still during World War One and Two (well, I find out later that they did, but not all of them, and not in the long run), and I was shocked and mortified that everyone didn't realize the terrorist attacks could be an attack most exactly against the carelessness march towards "advanced civilization." Going on normal in a way that throws nations and majorities into poverty was the very nature of the rich business enterprise of the world trade center.

The continual criticism from the "conspiratorial" opposition to the "official story" has been to remark that regardless of the particulars, both the initial attack and response relate around money and that way of life that seeks to organize money. It was an attack on money and a defence of money, because money is the cultural status symbol of the situated normalcy which is globally destructive. It's not about biblical evil, terror, and democratic civilization. It's about not fracturing the normalcy. I saw all this in the first few moments of my waking period that morning. And when President Bush eventually mentioned foolishly that he was fighting a holy "crusade" against a "jihad" while telling Americans to feel safe shopping that Christmas, I mentally puked and felt ethically jacked.

I started to get very crazed and preoccupied with terror and about how people were living around me. I faced a set of internal and external events which I spun around in complex interpretations that devastated me that year. I deteriorated into a depressed, manic state. Previously in grade ten and eleven, I was in no way as preoccupied and mortified by the state of international politics. In those grades, I had been discovering philosophy of mind, as I mentioned in the previous chapter, and ancient spiritual texts like Sufi poetry, the Tibetan Book of the Dead, and the Indian Bhagavad-Gita.

I felt like the Buddhist conception of life as a natural state of suffering that we can enlighten was exactly what I was living through, and I was reading so many texts of different faiths and disciplines that my young mind absorbed like a sponge and got filled with wonder and curiosity at what the nature of spirit might be. I was a good student in science, English, and math, and thought the world was rational and intellectual, but I was intrigued at how art and the spiritual and religious systems bore relevance to my intrigue about my consciousness and contemplation that had begun as a child and for which I had no scope or possible bigger picture until those texts. I was more satisfied before my grade twelve year to simply explore myself rather than be so gravely preoccupied with the affairs and condition of others, but I was still sad and wasn't as adequately enabled to manage my growing concerns as I slowly became.

With the coming of September Eleventh and with the hyper-focus on global issues and activism that ensued for me, the world in my mind became doubly confusing and doubly rife with suffering. After all, I felt the world had just entered world war number three; really, the last two centuries have been as much about being "modern" as being about a long bloody history with brief pockets of cultural grief and remorse. I became overwhelmed with the perception that my species was killing itself slowly. I was tortured by the fact that everyone in my small, rural, economically troubled community was tortured by lack of means to money as though that would save them.

I saw my community tearing down trees to put up buildings and luxury homes in a mad rush to make a living instead of taming the trees to unleash the forest's riches of berries, mushrooms, herbs, and vegetables that could provide us with a means to locally live and trade with others indefinitely. Instead of sane, reasonable work as a collective community in a living environment, selling it to those with money seemed to be the only solution.

I knew the land could produce for us beyond our wildest dreams of wealth. We would have berries enough if we collectively aimed to grow them to sell to provide for every reasonable, modern convenience that came from the outside world. I saw people allowing the land's actual economic value to deteriorate and living for a way of life that can only end in deep suffering and voids of dwindling resources and more concrete, which is also a concrete, and not abstract, lack of community sustainability and self-sufficiency. The natural environment can allow us to prosper if we smarten up. Instead, I saw people with faded interests in anything.

I saw in my community suffering over bills and jobs and experienced all the endless partying. In my grade 12 year, I got depressed and stuck in a rut trying to figure a way to communicate to people what I was developing in terms of solutions to all problems: ecological sanity and devotion to the beauty of living experience. All the fun my peers wanted to have, I wanted to provide valid reasons for it and long term sustainability; I wanted to help out with what I saw as a failing society.

After September Eleventh occurred, it changed the way I looked at my peers and members of my community. So many actions seemed urgently required, but not many others seemed to notice. I began to enter a daze of preoccupation about others who, it seemed to me, had entered a daze of apathy. My final year of high school seemingly had set itself out for me. I was not going to stop thinking about these issues for a long, hard time. Watching those buildings crumble altered the course of my life forever; I crumbled into a heap of tattered dreams of childhood terrorized by the harsh realities of the adult world gone awry. I became so disillusioned about the fate of the Earth. I saw clearly that our course must alter immediately or our world would just sink deeper into its hell, which it arguably has.

Looking at the USA, I see, at the time I originally wrote this list, their invasion of Afghanistan and Iraq, their continued declining out of international agreements like the

Kyoto Accord, the Universal Declaration of Human Rights, and Economic and Cultural Rights, and the Nuclear Non-Proliferation Treaty, and their mad rush to run the global, destructive economy faster and harder have proven to me that their power structures are hugely corrupt, immoral, ignorant, and many other negative adjectives.

I still believe these things, but the formation in me of these concepts was emotionally and cognitively violent, urgent-felt, and strenuous. No ideology had me; I had my own ideas. My views arose from contemplation of the nature of life as boundlessly self-creative and evolving toward greater intelligence, which I saw power and profit seekers maligning in their solely self-supporting efforts. Some powerful people have entered a psychopathic trance which threatens to exterminate our species from the face of the Earth as we know it.

Immediately after grade 12 began with the happenings on September Eleventh, I would plunge headlong into a year of examining the relationships between ordinary living conditions in my first-world abode and the state of social and ecological war that was being ravaged upon the world. I looked at the rural community life I lived as intricately connected to the greater state of the world. I could smell the war-torn oil burning in the exhaust of cars as I rode my bike along the roads. I could see plastic bags and litter of all sorts up and down the main street.

I could feel how the lack of interest in my peers at discussing social issues was intricately tied to people in poverty-stricken places wanting to inflict "terror" on people in the first-world. I could see the disconnect between what the government and corporations intended and what the average person in the street thought about life. I knew the majority of people care mostly about providing a living for themselves, which can be difficult everywhere because of the behaviour of elites who steal resources and wealth for their own discretion.

So, by now in this work of writing, I have explained what I thought and felt prior to the more extreme symptoms and collapse. In the next chapter, I will explore my descent into what may more properly be called "schizophrenic symptoms." I have provided thus far a backdrop story, which most of us have. I could not easily tell the particulars of my collapse into psychosis without paying attention to the details that were relevant to my mind throughout the experience.

When I get deeper into exploring my personal story and discussing features of schizophrenia in general, I hope it will become clear that the schizophrenic's whole life story often provides an important element in understanding a beneficial course of action from the place of illness toward health. The delusions that eventually filled my head, to the real, genuine emotional concerns that can overwhelm me, it all has a place in the picture of my being, and a picture of my course to healthy living. I will write in the next chapter about how I grew over time toward heavier schizophrenic symptoms. It should give a glimpse of how certain mental functions can accidentally activate, how terrible misunderstanding can ensue, and how one can lose touch with relevant realities.

Chapter 3
Breakdown and Out:
To Wander About, Wonder Through, and
Escape from the Shambles of a Sick Society

I wanted out and wanted in. I was depressed about society, and I desired to flourish. I had activist sentiments, but more than that, I believed that my society was absolutely nuts. I was paranoid of everyone's thoughts, and my mind worked overtime every second of the day through my final year of high school. I would come home after school and meditate, write, and think about how I could effectively change the world and make a living situation of peace. I preoccupied myself with mediating solutions in the tangled thoughts of my civilization. In particular, I developed several habits of thinking that suited the position I found myself in, living through daily events with ferocity of intuition and interpretation and with a desperate need for changing it but feeling like response was not even possible nor acting without verbal response.

Because I so rarely felt an opportunity to express my sentiments, I developed a peculiar mode of thinking where I spent time alone wondering about possible social interchanges where I wanted to speak up. I imagined possible articulations of powerful statements that I wanted people to understand, and I imagined possible responses from whoever I was thinking about addressing whichever concerns. My concerns were those stated in the previous two chapters:

I yearned for a richer linguistic, spiritual freedom and exploration of emotional and bodily experience, and I felt we were flushing our planet and social opportunities down the drain with the various strains and degrees of ecocide and genocide. My response was the desire to communicate, but feeling little access in daily exchanges, I rattled off in my head, undertaking the imaginary composition of conversations to test out what I might say if I felt brave enough at the right moment. I never seemed to say it just quite right enough to effect a change of the magnitude I was seeking.

This practice developed to the point where it felt easy just to think and feel what I would say and where another statement would then enter my mind with the feel of an active, dialogic response. It felt literally like I was having conversations in my head, although I didn't at the time characterize the experienced conversation as hallucinatory. I knew it was imaginary, but it became forceful, because I still encountered and desired to escape stress triggers in daily exchanges and in a way felt like the imaginary conversations helped me learn regardless of my still not communicating outwardly very much. They helped me to turn inward and explore resolutions to conflicts, but I got more and more stressed out as the grade twelve year rolled on and my perception of conflict ever grew.

Don't get me wrong. Although I wandered through internal stimuli in high school, I also managed to be an executive member of my school's student union, a student volunteer with Crimestoppers, went on honour roll and received awards year after year, and managed to be awarded the Governor General's Bronze Medal for my achievement in grade 12. That medal is given to the student whose marks are at the very top of the class at the end of the year, with consideration of school and community service. I learned everything I could from those excellent teachers of my K-12 education and community. Like I said in Chapter 1, I love to learn anything.

    I did enjoy several aspects of school and was socially extroverted, I still joined friend get-togethers and went to parties, and I maintained participation in volunteer service... Though I did feel like some sort of a zombie in my final year of high school. I was soured on taking part in ordinary social discourse. I became known for ranting and radical opinions, and it is true that I have persistent criticisms about my society; however, in my grade 12 year the crisis of September Eleventh occurred and I wanted more of a global response. I saw that the attacks and response of a War on Terror needed to be addressed. Trade and imperialism for resources and power in the world ("World Trade Center") was choking out the spirit and health of every single human being on Earth. While I attended school and learned the lessons, I also deeply experienced the decay of our society, grown too affluent and careless and ignorant to maintain social and ecological peace.

    I finally left classes because I grew so sickened inside by extreme apathy about history and the situation of our world. I walked out of History 12 when the class was watching a film of an interview with a Jewish woman who was a girl in a concentration camp during World War Two. She was explaining difficultly how she watched her parents be killed in front of her eyes while soldiers laughed, and across the room I was interrupted by the noise of three boys I grew up with but now have not much connection to. They were laughing and mimicking the woman's accent, totally oblivious to the severity of their actions being exactly what the words "lest we forget" speak to. It was not their intention to hurt me so profoundly. "Boys will be boys" doesn't start to scratch the surface though when it comes to how a whole community relates and learns together about serious issues.

The apathy I sensed made it seem that there were *no* serious issues to the people around me. I was pre-occupied, and laughing at an accent without paying attention to the content of an interview is surely typical in any classroom. But I was shattered. I was shattered and spun much further into a deep angry depression connected to the values and activity of others in my society. I fled the school, wrote a note interpreted by my principal to be a suicide note, biked to and climbed a rocky hill in a logging area, and screamed a lot of tears at the surging Pacific Ocean.

When I had finished my outpour and felt calmer, I had a nap in the Spring sun, listening to the ocean and soothed by its salty breeze. I could not go back to classes for the rest of that final term. Laughter can hurt so incredibly hard in those most delicate contexts of perceived significance.

I went and aced my provincial exams earning the highest marks in my grade 12 class, but I felt like a visionary peacekeeper turned zombie forced to play a destructive role in our society's normal game of 'who can care less and face less truth?' Graduation ceremony terrified me on a subtle level, considering why I left school and how the only reason I went was to go along with things. My society terrified me irreparably at that point. I just machinated my body across gestures, smiling in place, getting my numerous scholarships for community and school citizenship and academic achievement.

While deep inside in a hidden place, I wanted to explode and scream at what I saw as the bloody murder of our freedom and horrendous past!! Our world really is falling apart. Wars are fought all over for our techno gadgets and cheap products. The ecosystem needs more care, and not a single additional condo. We need to turn around and face the truth that we've gone horribly wrong in our civilization and need to start talking.

We are neither ecologically sustainable nor peaceful. Violence and illness surround people in bubbles of "there's nothing you or I can do to change the world so I'm going to stake out what I must, and you better celebrate moments like graduation." I feel this world utters the "you're okay" mantra as a steadfast, significance-reducing symbol, to be merely repeated as often as it can, in order to keep the truth away that we need to change everything about the way we live, right now, because almost nothing is going just "okay."

It's *all* more significant than okay, what's happening to our complexly conscious species in an age of the crisis of a civilization with a barbaric history birthing into a global commons of high science and the open mediation and ongoing amplification of diversity in quality, form, access to, and the content of information.

We've gone too far, and I was totally willing to let it drive me crazy, my greatest fear was turning apathetic or immobilized and unable to instigate a joyful rebellion, which I did not then have. We need now to end all war and develop worldwide the knowledge of plants and earthly ways. Social symbols of progress like money and population and power are fruitless aims compared to ensuring Earth's ability to continue to nourish the blossoming of evolving intelligence.

I got so sick inside about what we were doing to the planet. I shut off so much and dreamed inside of ways to overcome our absurdities and idiocy. My intolerance of what went for normalcy subsumed and inflamed what before grade 12's intensity had been exploration of science, philosophy, and spirituality as a method of learning more about nature and the way minds can operate.

I began to develop a very sick and twisted view of psychological reality in a defensive manoeuvre to acquire some sense of spiritual security. I began to imagine after high school all sorts of ways this world could be an illusion, and I realized this was not a "sane" thought. Buddhism says directly that much of this world is an illusion to be pierced through by consciousness. Christianity says that some God controls the entire world and that what happens to people "was meant to be." I was desperate for honesty and understanding, and the old world traditions seemed to give not even a single sane solution to the serious problems, which long historical progression had invented.

In my state, I was never able to keep apart religious ideas, so all that I read fused into a picture of a weird world. In an attempt to escape what I feared was our reality, I began to imagine the world was not as real as I used to think. At the same time in late high school, I began to study schizophrenia and compare my experience to what I read about it, and I started to think reality was like a story book orchestrated as a weird illusion for me to work through to figure out answers to my questions. To reiterate, my mind was always roving very quickly. I spun around worldviews and interpretations, I kept thinking, and the agitation and stress slowly and eventually rose, like a tide with waves slowly reaching further up the beach...

Sometimes, like in History 12 class that day I fled the laughter, a big wave crashes up much farther, a storm is brewing fast on the horizon, and the highest point of the tide is hours and hours away. I kind of knew a storm was coming that year, and my response was to scramble intellectually and anxiously, trying to study the world and myself, and figure out a survival plan. As I became more confused and desperate for answers, I increasingly detached and acquired strange beliefs. With movies like the Matrix coming out and in discovering the poetry and philosophy of the mystics of ancient and contemporary traditions, I found solace thinking of different worlds and metaphysical possibilities. I came to an unsteady bliss thinking the world was an illusion I might pierce through somehow.

I used this response to my legitimate social angst as a psychological defence bolstered by a growing delusional hope that if I did something right in my mind, I might disappear and a god or whatever would whisk me away and give me freedom. Or that the world would be saved. A belief in heaven isn't normally called crazy, but I looked a great distance elsewhere from my immediate surroundings. A disconnect arose between myself and the reality, actual and consensual alike, of normal others. I came to think this world had to be a rehearsal for the life of a greater being to which I imagined I was leading my experience and realizations.

I just wanted to escape my experience somehow, to replace it with what I could imagine. I was never fully convinced of anything, forever sceptical of myself, since grade 10 knowing myself to have a lot of weird thoughts that needed sorting out and upon which I could not simply blindly rely. However, stress in my life accumulated after high school until I became quite psychotic and did become trapped in delusion and hallucination.

My first downfall into "acute psychosis" came about as a traumatic response to a sick relationship with another individual. I do not want to go over the whole situation and history I had with this individual, because it would go too long and would not be very relevant to my aims in this discussion. At any rate, lots of people go through traumatic experiences, and all such experiences vary vastly. Their only relevance to my story is that any trauma either psychological or physical figures greatly in the possibility of anyone becoming sick in body or mind.

I believe in poetic existence. In other words, I believe mental life has a profound poetic quality. I have found ways to integrate my schizophrenically strange capacities of thinking into creative endeavours and art experiences. If you understand my writing, enough, up to this point, you may detect I am coherent and reasonable. I am convinced of the power of the human brain to manifest peculiar perceptual and emotional experiences. I have come to revere the mind and its potentials.

I think this world of ours boundlessly and beautifully lives in a free sentient vibrancy overcome by no other force than the choices made by the living. Notwithstanding that most people who live care neither to explain to their sensibility nor refute such a view, I experience "freedom of will" as a fundamental mechanism of nature, instead of pondering it as a philosophical curiosity to blindly accept or scientifically/theologically assert or deny. It might be standard that any views of this sort are "logically" inadequate, and one would only ever need to explain or defend such claims to those who demand philosophical justification. Everyone else basically accepts they are in control of their lives in some manner. (I do, however, provide some philosophical justifications for my views in the essays after the autobiographical section).

The last three paragraphs were kind of random, but there are reasons I feel this is all relevant in sharing my understanding of schizophrenia and how (at least) my mind works. The more our conscious and emotional lives are actually consequential to our health and disposition toward illness, as Gabor Maté discusses from a medical perspective in *When the Body Says No—The Hidden Cost of Stress*, the more I am led to doubt non-psychological interpretations and therapies which believe *only* in "brain disease" and "anti-psychotic pharmacology." I do not disregard the contribution my meds have made to my recovery, but 10 years after starting on them and starting my recovery, I can't explain *just how great* I feel this past year, slowly weaning myself down in dose, with a doctor's support and cooperation, of course. As those long term side effects ease back slowly, I feel less disabled, less sleepy, more stable, and more emotionally alive!

The more our theories obfuscate the potential role of an individual's intentional behaviour and habitual modes of conscious experience, the more we obfuscate our capacity for change. I don't mean to assign a blame or ethical responsibility regarding the sad state of affairs for the too heavily medicated mentally ill. As "physiological disease" is increasingly treated holistically and the role of stress is increasingly understood, I hope that the medical community realizes that "psychological disease" also would benefit from a more holistic understanding that regards the individual as a nexus on influences, traits, and possibility. I am asserting the ability to form more proactive responses, rather than point blame at the historically recent tradition of pharmacology. Medication has a place; it's just that the real problems have deeper solutions.

Someone curious about the prognosis (or outcome) for individuals with schizophrenia should understand something simple which might not sound so simple until one lives it: I find hope only when I hold onto a scrap of a sense of genuine spiritual freedom to choose healthy realities from a field of open psychological possibilities, because even as I am indeed a creature of biology, I have a capacity to think and feel in the directions I sense are open to me. Mental health has no more deeply profound ingredient as provided by real, personal freedom *and the time* to understand and pursue methods of stability and cohesiveness that provide a sense of meaning in our lives. Basically, we all need to hold steadfast and to fortify our minds with a habitual core resilience, or else we risk losing self-direction and healthy response to our stressors. We want to avoid getting subsumed into delusion, preoccupation, and hallucination!

An example of such choice-making and its importance to maintaining sanity, I direct myself with my own will every day to take my psychiatric medications as prescribed by my doctor. Without those meds, or if I go off them suddenly, and if I don't monitor my stress management, I could easily fall apart and lose my ability to string coherent sentences together or to maintain the composure to relate with others on sensible terms. Recall some of the incoherent poetry in the previous part of the book. I choose to stick to my meds and choose to stay away from other drugs.

Of actually greater significance, in my own perception, I choose not to entertain delusional thinking. I make lots of choices about my mental experience in order to keep myself grounded and healthy. I have a gesture pneumonic which helps me remember my intention and helps me be strong in the face of delusional thinking. I think I talk about the gesture more than actually do it in practice: I hold my two index fingers in a cross of protection around my head, intending to ward off the evil from entering my brain. Choosing not to entertain those thoughts, or *thought patterns*, of the past which led me to delusion was an important part of stabilizing my mind and diminishing the delusional tendencies. My hope became rejuvenated, my desperate preoccupations with apathy and the disorder of our society subsided, and my opinions and knowledge of my interests evolved. The core of this paragraph will be discussed at greater length as the book proceeds.

For now, I just want to highlight that I did successfully overcome my depressive and obsessive preoccupation with social issues. I was able to get out of the position I had slowly entered. But before describing how I got better, I want to first elaborate upon the getting worse, which occupied the last few years of high school and summer after. I suppose my chronological order is all over the place, but I hope that so far I've provided some early context and situations, which I see to be relevant, as well as provided what have been more eventual reflections on my past.

I've talked more, so far, about reasons for stress than the symptoms that arose. My schizophrenia developed slowly, and there were many warning signs, flare ups, and progression in my condition and symptoms. I became weirder and weirder, mostly on the inside, as I descended into more and more chaotic states of consciousness. I accumulated strange patterns of thinking and perception that would eventually erupt into a full blown severe psychosis at the end of the summer after I finished high school.

Maybe a moderate emotional psychosis was spurred within History 12 class that day. It stands as relevant that schizophrenia is considered by doctors to be a "chronic psychosis" and a condition that can easily and progressively deteriorate without intervention. At any rate, there was more going on in the changes in me than simply angst before I became acutely ill. For instance, the conversations I alluded to were quite the thing, and they started quite early, became worse, and other symptoms slowly emerged.

Chapter 4
Getting Weirder, Blasting Off

The "shambles of sick society" from which I escaped were the intense framework of self-doubt and false rationalization that my piecing together of history and contemporary life built into the structure of my mind. My mind was the thing left in shambles from my stressors. My behavioural responses and dispositions as developed through high school were the formation (or dilapidation) of the shambles. The way I reacted during September Eleventh was highly precipitated by my already growing set of non-urgent preoccupations and curiosities. I started talking about these directions last chapter, but I'll go into greater detail here about the earlier years of high school.

In high school I bore a general kind of spontaneous and loose thought patterning arising from always being very independent with my ideas and attention. I was always reading as a kid. When I started getting curious about various literature that seemed better than most I had been exposed to, my ideas grew into more concrete expressions rather than the abstract, intuitive free flowing childhood self-conscious self-awareness that I had. But I didn't think quite like a normal grade nine kid of my age, mainly due to my increasingly "adult" and "academic" reading material. A public library book, Philip Kerr's *A Philosophical Investigation* exposed me to a murder mystery with large words I had never heard and heady, historical-philosophical concepts, which I sort of intuited while reading, but was putting together on spot into Kerr's words. That's when I went and looked for a Philosophy book, and I found *Philosophy: The Basic Issues* in my parents' bookshelf, which marked the first flash foray and exposure to the ancient traditions of setting controversial ideas to paper.

Like I said last chapter, I learned to fabricate whole, many-peopled conversations within the space of my head. The perceptual quality of these conversations eventually startled me. I was not merely going over possible kinds of responses in hypothetical conversations; I became able to mentally talk and receive fully articulated responses that naturally arose in my mind. At times it "sounded" like thoughts and at other times it seemed to have a real sound, or at least it felt so different from my own thinking that it could be called to a degree hallucinatory. In the second half of high school, I was not as delusional as I would become during the months following high school, but I was close to hearing voices.

It was a tactic to test out concepts and explore by myself what I wanted to say, since I did want to say a lot. Sometimes I was waxing philosophical internally in order to set out ideas in a way a personally understood. Sometimes I was debating with friends or explaining to them the way I feel about the world. It occurred to me eventually that I almost literally heard the speech of my friends and argumentative quarrels when I imagined their responses. It still "sounded like thought" but it also eerily had a tinge of them; it sounded like them but without "sounding" fully audible. I thought in isolation about what exactly I might say if I were to open up and express issues important to me. I would go for a walk out back behind my house into the forest, find a spot, and pace back and forth while imagining and muttering under my breath both my words and the words of others. The experience gave me an eerily realistic sense of meaning that was exchanged and developed through the imagined dialogue.

This progressed until I could not shut off the perception of imagine-hearing others make statements, even when with them at school. I began to make up responses and follow-through statements in the direct midst of actual conversation. It happened when I would walk by a group that was talking, and the "sound" of these extra statements began to feel a lot like my own thoughts but attached to other personalities than my own. I had been reading ancient to new-age spirituality as well, and at the weirdest times, I imagined with some disbelief that I might actually share thoughts with others.

The characters seemed consistent. The thoughts kept appearing in my mind without any impetus or desire of mine to think about them. Yet I also didn't resist when I thought I could learn from it as I initially intended by testing out hypothetical conversations. Something that felt meaningful then would eventually cause me to reflect in university Philosophy classes when I learned more about Plato's writing of dialogues between Socrates and counter-sayers to best mimic the actual exploration of an argument. I always wanted a dialogue to occur between parties to which a subject is relevant or significant, not just to "have my own opinion."

In grade 9 and 10 I spent a lot of personal time reading and thinking, and by grade 11 I started to write in a journal and write poetry as well. To be honest, at the time I started writing for personal reasons, I was already in an internal situation of feeling strange with some growing confusion and suffering of the existential sort. One day in the fall of grade 11, I skipped class and sat outside by the end of the hallway doors, on a bench on top of some rocks, under a few trees. I decided to take my pen and paper out and to write a couple sentences. I did already recognize my perspective about the suffering of ecosystems and about warfare at that point in time, but September Eleventh had not yet precipitated the intensity of that trend in me. I wrote the following three sentences sitting on that bench:

"What can one write when there's nothing left to say? if i could write what I felt, I would not be here today. should I just give up, and accept the boring grey, and have a formless block to show, for my mind's clay?" I had no idea what I was going to write, but these are the first words I had, up to that point, ever written in any context outside a school directive like an assignment. It was first time, but not the last that I consciously did not capitalize the word "I" or the beginning of a sentence. It was a few lines of poetry rather than a journalling, but the words expressed a conflict. I became tense, I felt quiet, inarticulate, and sub-expressed. I took out my pen and paper and the words flashed out the end of the pen. They rushed out of me, then I sat crossing things out, editing. That's what I ended up with. It didn't occur to me until later that I felt kind of like a squished, amorphous bug in high school.

The way I welcomed the internal dialogue surely figured prominently in the rest of my collapse toward acute psychosis, for I became geared on a track with a confused direction, full or words that finally burst skipping class one day. Eventually in the angst-crescendo of grade 12, the conversations became intensely disordered and aggressive, but earlier they were always about my ideas and more relaxed interests. My mind became a playing ground for multiple voices, illusory words flowing through my mind while imagining circumstances for deep discussions.

Between grade 10 and 11, the words took over my private life, filling at times even moments when I interacted with real people. Starting to write in Grade 11 made it slightly easier to participate socially as the writing time compartmentalized my preoccupations, but I think it would have been much better if I could have shared more of what I was experiencing with the social knit that was perturbing me. That was the hardest, when I could not divert my attention from the mental chorus of my splitting thoughts. I would carry on by attempting to act appropriately with people when they have started talking with me about something. I did okay most times, but surely began to be regarded as having some odd behaviours and views.

It happened like this, because I got to brooding in the conversations when I was alone in thought, even in the classroom, just doing my work or whatever when we were left to our own devices for a while. The bell would ring for ending a class, some snippet of insult or something I overheard from a peer would revolve around my head as I vocally but internally confronted it, and I would wander through the halls toward next class in a semi-daze entranced by what I was think/voicing about the previous hour.

Now, this phenomenon did not exactly occur constantly through my waking hours. There were rest moments, when I focused on writing which I did a lot of, for school at first, personally later, or when I focused on interacting with friends and family. I had not become totally psychotic, even as the inner dialogues did represent a deterioration of thought stability and coherence. And, I should definitely talk about how the dialogues were not the only deterioration of my thinking.

Words (beyond the conversations) began to take on greater significance in my mind before and especially after I started writing for personal reasons. I saw the beginning of my stumble into intense word salad, which I will try to examine in detail. Before I started writing poetry, words were already becoming significant and I was reading lots of poetry and mystical writing. I liked words and learning what they meant, and I started to identify with the power of language to express thought. At the later high school phase of my schizophrenia onset, I delighted in words as I wrote poetry and philosophy with deep metaphor and emotional intensity. One could definitely describe my poetry of those years as very dark and pained, and I'd say my philosophy was chaotic and mystical as well as poetic in its own right.

My poetry and other personal writing increasingly left the bounds of conventional spelling and grammar. I felt like I needed new language that I did not have yet, in order to understand my thoughts and experiences. I began to shape my school writing, too, in ways that my answers to many assignments started to represent my increasingly irregular and idiosyncratic interpretation of history, current events, arts, and languages. During high school, my math and sciences remained strong, rigid, and proper, through all else my head took from other classes.

I loved how words sculpted meaning when they conjoined to frame and express concepts, and with my private concepts, with my private philosophical thinking, I could rejoice in wonder at how profound ideas could be.

I'd say the raw creative potential I experienced in those years hinted at becoming the high functioning side of a loose (open-minded) and spontaneous schizophrenia. I knew I had "issues" and I did try to remain an individual who wasn't in particular risk and managing stress, but still would be different in how I think. It's safe to say most people know that some "mentally special" people of whatever sort are often very artistically minded. I certainly was and was also very linguistically geared.

One time, in the late Spring of grade 11, I skipped my afternoon English class because I was particularly distraught for some reason and didn't want to interact with my English teacher who I always felt some competition from, and I didn't feel like being outwardly vocal that day as I usually was in that class, spinning off my fancy interpretations. Instead, as it was beautifully cloudy blended with sunlight, I went to the very middle of the school field with was surrounded by a 400 m track, and I sat in the grass with pen and paper, a fitting "skipped English" activity.

It was quite an hour (I went to my second afternoon class). I wrote a bit (I don't remember what), but the interesting part was a group of other students who were walking around near the school. I don't know if it was a class or other skippers. Probably a class, because they were on school grounds and it was a lot of them. Maybe they were doing garbage duty as some punishment. "Why aren't you in claaassss, Brenden!!?" I suddenly heard and looked up, at a few students but one in particular yelling at me in some overt concern that I was getting away with something. "What are you doing in the middle of the field?" "Do you love your books? Why do you think you can skip class, nerd!?"

143

I do not remember more of what was said, but I do recall it continuing for some time as I tried to sit quietly and meditate because I was too distraught to write. I sat for about half an hour with my eyes closed, and the yelling stopped probably 15 minutes or less into the meditation. All in all, I was in quite an activated state of mind and body, feeling both ostracized and driven to remain indifferent and in my desired activity. I felt kind of electric after finishing my inner quiet and decided to open my eyes and look around at the sky.

After my eyes had been closed for so long, I expected the sky to be very bright to look at. Instead, the blue and silver-white bands that I saw were previously in life, an unseen colour to my eyes. It seemed my brain was in a heightened and lucid state. I felt calmer than when I stopped trying to write because of the yelling, and even the sun was not too bright. I didn't stare too long because of reasoning, but the blue was different, and I found I could stare directly into the big light ball for several moments without any feeling that it was too bright. The light was cool and refreshing.

Metaphor was very important to me from an early point, and my preoccupations with society provided a rich array of material for my metaphors. Sitting on a field instead of sitting in English class, and having a social experience of being ostracized like the young guys in the Outsiders that we read that year in English class, and then blocking it out, zenning out, and having a literary moment observing my inner mood and the cool sun in my eye—This all seemed very "metaphorical" to me of something deeper and broader in scope that I was going through during high school. In my English class poetry assignments and even more so in my personal poetry, certain common phrases and certain objects of our society spoke to me in various ways. Electrical systems, highways, plumbing, building structures, television, and much more all took on meaning in metaphorical poems.

My affection toward artistic language developed more into "word salad" with time, a common trait among many schizophrenics. It went that way with my poetry to a severe degree, especially when I became more distraught and lonely in my yearning to communicate. The tripping into word salad became more prominent when I began to think of metaphorical meanings out of context from poetry. Imposing the metaphorical meanings onto real objects started to come naturally. My ability grew quickly to associate and dissociate words and meanings across multiple contexts and situations. I now recognize the feats I pulled off with meaningfulness as sometimes stretching too far the limits of linguistic imagination into where it had no usable domain. It wasn't poetic at that point. It was deep in confusion.

I began to watch the world around me as if it expressed poetry directly, as if there were a natural grammar and meaningful expression taking place in the way everything was set up: how it was "literally/literarily" set up, to give a telling example of the random word associations I would toy with. An analogy for this phenomenon of my thought patterns is taking a bird as an omen or sign for something, but in my case there were omens a million fold across every object that graced my attention. The wind rising, cloud movement shadowing or revealing sunlight, the fall of rain, and innumerable aspects of nature began to affect my mood.

The mystical poetry, art, and spiritual philosophy that I was reading also fostered this "literal world as poetry" feeling. I do not discount the many spiritual traditions of several cultures that the world and forces of nature are spiritually alive and can be communicated with. However, I also strongly count the many possibilities for an individual with a lot of stress on their plate to not quite get it. I strongly count the possibility of being confused and arbitrary, of being just incorrect in the sense of what something means or if it even needs to mean anything.

Strong relationships developed between my experience of nature and abstract thinking about what was going on meaningfully and socially. I took in the natural world metaphorically as well as literally. I thought that everything meant something and that nothing was out of place in the grand scheme of things. I now recognize myself as having psychologically distorted reality to a deep extent. If my thoughts were so inclined, I would listen to my perceptions as though what I saw was in conversation with me and only me. My imagination ran in hyper-drive and interpretations ran wild. In a "classical" sense, I was intermittently fleeting into moments of mystical dissolution with the universe. However, I had no refined, established cultural framework for my experience, and I had anxious despair and compulsive preoccupation. Slowly, the worms of delusion laid into my brain.

In this phase, words took on huge significance beyond their normal meanings. Whatever somebody said echoed around my mind; the words went through poetic filters straining out strange meanings to which only I seemed privy. I mentioned that during grade 9 and beyond, I was reading texts of spirituality and philosophy and melding many diverse spiritual concepts into a confused and contorted whole. I was picking and choosing beliefs that seemed to help out my perspective on things. I picked and chose, basically, what would relieve some anxiety, in some way.

I did not believe in a Christian God, but I definitely entertained notions of how the world was less naturalistic and more illusory and magical, like many of the world spiritual systems hold in their principles. I entertained notions of angels, elves, aliens, and secret brotherhoods of mysterious humans. I was becoming aware of many of our species' stories and myths, and taking them very seriously compared to how much importance my Canadian culture usually places in them. I began to live like every word that people uttered and every interaction they had was based in the act of a myth creating itself. My strange collection of beliefs was the basis of the filters for my perception of everything. Through them, I took aspects of everything and took from it all anything I could imaginatively interpret that felt coherent amidst my ever-fluxing field of reality concepts.

Shortly after high school, direct communication with external stimuli replaced the inner conversations I used to have with imaginary debate quarries. Through the last year and a half of high school, in a way I felt liberated that I could enjoy the world like a storybook or imaginary friend. Less and less would I have inner dialogue with real people I knew like developed after grade 9 and through until grade 11.

I didn't have other people's words floating around my head at that point anymore. Instead I experienced loftier and loftier thoughts and sensations of connection between external events and personal experience. The spiritual texts just rubbed it in. I did feel like the Buddha's remembered idea that "all beings are completely enlightened in their natural state" definitely applied to me, even inside my despair. After all, the first Noble Truth that "life is suffering" should logically still be true even after one has realized an enlightened state.

In this phase, I also felt liberation from my preoccupations, because I felt the world was less substantially real than before. I felt precariously balanced between invigoration by my experience and being overwhelmed. Predominately around this time of late grade 10, summer, and early grade 11, I was reading extensively about schizophrenia and deciding I could see it in myself. I love the internet. But at the same time, my spiritual beliefs and strange perceptual experiences pushed me along in a direction. I was delusional but just hadn't realized it yet. My thought was becoming very disordered, a typical sign of schizophrenia, but I thought that was a necessity given the depth and complexity of my ideas, given my age and then present knowledge. I was enjoying my strange experiences and altered states of cognitive ability, even though I knew explicitly that I was going, or already was, quite insane from many perspectives including my own.

I was in prime condition for a collapse in a big way, but intense (even traumatic) events were to occur at the end of the summer after grade 12 that would derail what stability I had. Until then I was able to coast in a daze of weird inner experience while I interacted with friends and family. In hindsight, family members and friends have told me I was beginning to act weird at that time, but I never talked about my strangest experiences so they stayed hidden for a long time. For a long time my mind spiralled into deeper and darker chaos before I received any informed support.

I enjoyed some of my experiences, but there was a darker tinge to it all, as I was getting more confused and more poised for psychosis all the time. It's a weird nether region for a teenager, beginning to believe firmly that the world is ephemeral and governed by wacky rules. I entered a solipsistic point of view readily as my surface perceptions of reality grew weirder and distanced me from the reality of others. Solipsism can refer to the view that only one mind, your own, exists. I took a weird version of solipsism augmented by new-age principles of "meant-to-be" and "we-all-create-our-own-reality" spiritual ideas and combined many other traditional spiritual concepts.

I imaged these concepts into a single picture that showed any particular mind or soul is eternal and that the reality we're in is more conditional on our own being and states than the collection of everything working together. I felt I was making sense of reality in a beautiful way that was consistent, albeit disparately crisscrossing, with several world belief systems. One of my reasons for constructing weird beliefs was the conviction that all the spiritual systems had some truth to be discovered and put together.

Consequently, a radical form of reality relativism held sway in my beliefs at this point, and my solipsism held true to that: I wanted to believe somehow that every soul might find peace if any individual, namely me, could take on the right state of being. Quantum mechanics held a powerful influence on my belief system, particularly the interpretation that parallel universes branched out for every initiating event of possibilities. Assuming that each person's life could potentially meet many different spiritual outcomes, I conceived of a larger reality than by most traditional religions which hold that the world works in one way only. I wanted to leave no one out but I half felt them to be illusory or believed I could spiritually escape from their world, as they from mine. I insisted others were real, but since in my mind our futures could separate, my mind felt as fragmented as the world I imagined.

I never found a way to reconcile how everyone's reality could be different while we were together, but I worked hard to do so. I found relativism to be the central mystery to my philosophical confusion. However, I had been a thoroughly interested science student in high school and had been somewhat a mechanist if not fully a materialist (believing in mechanisms of reality if not quite materialist ones). For my age and education, I had a pretty good knowledge of chemistry, physics, and biology, and I loved learning about the way the physical and living world worked.

It was a gradual progression, inspired by stress of many sorts, toward fixating on how a mechanist reality could provide for my spiritual convictions. All along the last few years of high school, I had been reading about spirituality and philosophy but also about speculative physics and biology. However, the curiosity in relativism had not ushered me into delusional thinking until just after high school. Before that point, I was a free thinker, but increasingly my thoughts were binding themselves within tight knots behind strong bars.

So strange were my aberrant perceptions that led me to take my additional curiosity in world spirituality way too far. I think the stress of the final year of high school that I talked about in detail before led me by fear and obsession to emotionally abandon the world. The final point in that history class when I walked out and did not return until exams and graduation changed me deeply. I began to want out of society so bad that I abandoned my scientific mindset of high school for an urgent, emotional mindset, while the scientist/mystic in me continued full steam ahead. My metaphysical confusions subsumed my attention.

The summer after high school was a strange period from the stress of before, because I was dealing with some twisted emotional experiences, taking street drugs including ecstasy, mushrooms, and crack, and delving deeper into word salad and aberrant perception. The drugs were powerfully devastating to my state of mind, driving up the intensity of my thought and perception patterns, and I was doing them with the people with whom I had troubled emotional relations, which didn't help things. I was losing grip on reality while changing my state of consciousness with substances as often as every couple days. I would binge with friends on coke and crack for a night or weekend, then go home for a week and not seek to take it home with me to use it all the time. I would get just wrecked on it at the time of use. It particularly amplified my weird perceptions, and at the time I wanted to experiment more and more with my consciousness, so I precariously travelled through intense high after high.

The mushrooms heavily amplified my participation in word salad behaviour, causing me to aggrandize the meaning of my psilocybin-influenced thoughts, which were always very interesting to me. I would become perplexed for hours contemplating the nature of the world and my being in it while having minor visual hallucinations which I let tell stories with my imagination. I did mushrooms and had these experiences throughout high school, but the trips steadily became more delusional with time. As many mushroom users will report, there can be long lasting changes in the patterns of the mind after coming down.

Doing mushrooms off and on for as long as I did definitely feels like it changed the way I think about the world, in some ways, and at the time when other stresses and thought patterns in my life were compounding together, the mushrooms may have played a strong role in my developing more extreme schizophrenic thought patterns. That fungus changed the way I responded to language and emotion, accelerating imaginative thinking as a way to interact with elements of my mind's behaviour. None of my friends who usually did the mushrooms with me ever had serious psychological problems quite like mine. The friends I did cocaine, crack, and ecstasy with did, however, have more serious problems. Really hard drugs are only consumed when there *is* a precondition of serious problems, I am fairly sure from my experience.

I don't know how much I want to talk about the emotional relationships, because the details are so personal and people who know me might read this book. Also, many of the specifying details and particulars about these relationships are not very much relevant to what I have to say about my becoming sick. These relationships did stress me out and introduce me to drugs and damaging emotional situations, and that's what's most relevant to this book's undertaking: stress, emotional warp, and hard drugs are never good, especially for someone already experiencing confusion and disorder. The stress of life after high school compounded the earlier stresses of high school and put me just on the verge.

All in all, the drugs and messed up relationships really set me up for the disaster that was to strike upon September following first summer after graduation. They catalyzed my strange perception and behaviour to the point where I was ready to fall apart and spiral into the heavy delusional and hallucinatory experience of full-blown psychosis. So I come to the end of this chapter and will start to talk about my first psychotic episode, about how it occurred and its aftermath, in the next chapter. I have set the stage for what followed; everything just gets more interesting from here on out.

Chapter 5
On the First Time I Disappeared Completely

Disclaimer: Upon reading the manuscript for this book, my mom let me know that my retelling of this story skews the timeline. Rather than try to edit it, I leave it as my memory experienced it. So, take this as you will: an experience. In "The Last Word" at the end of this book, you will hear a mother's perspective.

All I can imagine is one room.

I have the forest I want to explore beyond the top pane of a mostly opaque glass. Now and again I am aware of a hall with desks around the corner out the window of the locked door.

I have the vague impression of the nurses coming down the hallway as I peer at them from the window in the locked door. The door was kept locked unless I was given a pill to take. I only remember the pills; I don't remember eating or sleeping.

I don't remember clearly, but I believe everything was coloured grey-white except the yellow pill and the green forest. I was there a whole week, and I remember taking a med only once or twice.

Even if I had thought, "this seems like a hospital," I did not really take notice to why I was there and was not curious. They said (as I later heard) that I often talked and looked around as though interacting with hallucinations while alone in the room.

Apparently, I cooperated with treatment, but I had no idea where I was. So began my first psychiatric stay in a hospital in Coos Bay, Oregon State, USA.

But how did I get there? I had taken a trip with somebody to the Burning Man event in the Black Rock Desert of Nevada. The event is a weeklong city in the desert, for sharing arts, games, and community. I should not have gone with the person I went with. That person was bad news for me; one of the ones responsible for the drugs and twisted emotional states I mentioned in the last chapter. Once getting to the event, I was scared enough about what this person had in mind that I decided to leave their company. I had spontaneously run into my uncle, who had also travelled to the event that year, so I had a safe place to go. However, my mental state was not nearly as safe as it could have been. I don't think my uncle suspected anything was weird about my state until the end of the week when things had gone bad and when I needed someone's help.

Through the week, however, I enjoyed the reckless, precarious freedom of having escaped a bad situation. I wandered without very much direction every day and also through most of each night, interacting with all sorts of people. I did not sleep much, wired as I was. I had a little bit of food at my tent, but mostly ate when food was offered to me by strangers who were eating. So many "burners" take on a character persona and play act in games spontaneously while they are there that I had fun with my theatrical interest from drama classes in high school. The beginning of the week was full of playfulness for me.

The week also contained a high amount of weirdness. It felt like some people were playing with language with me, but I now think it was mostly me doing the playing. I would talk to someone about something philosophical and had a lot of fun partaking in weird conversations. Other weirdness included my growing aberrant perceptual processes concerning text, image, and environment. As the week went on, I became more and more entranced by the art displays people set up and by the messages that were everywhere, like on people's vehicles and the graffiti in the portable toilets.

At one point, I even looked at a little warning tag for an electrical device and thought it had a message I could interpret. I don't remember what, though. What made things a lot weirder for me was when I ate magic mushrooms and took a tab of acid in the same night. After that, my experience spiralled beyond my control. I did not come down when I should have. The psilocybin and LSD wore out, but my elevated state did not. I had quite the high and, frankly, had gone fully psychotic by then!

That drug experience was one of the weirdest times in my life. At night time when I did them, I wandered around stunned at my perceptions. At one point, I had extreme time and space distortion. It seemed that distances stretched out longer before me and that I perceived myself in slow motion. I felt my muscles as though they were moving regularly, but the timing seemed way slower, like I was taking a long time to step. But I didn't feel like I was holding my legs up longer or anything. It seemed I just had a different perception.

One of the most invigorating parts of the acid and mushroom trip was when a group was setting off coordinated fireworks in the middle of the night. The part of my schizophrenic experience was highly activated during the fireworks of taking in things from the environment and matching them to my internal state like signs or symbols. I felt like I was dancing with them, guiding them with my mind, similar to how I've read about spiritual practices of dancing with fire or thunder and lightning. It seemed like the fireworks were an extension of my desires for activity. It felt like it was me exploding into the sky. I was lucky enough to watch it from beginning to end, and I just jumped around alone in the dark watching it above and in front of me, feeling an intense synchronicity with it. Sensing synchronicity between external events and inner states would prove to play a large role in the subsequent developments of my psychosis.

One of the following days, perhaps the next, I walked around the desert in the heat and must have acted weird in front of someone, because the Black City Rangers (the onsite security and police) came to take me to the medical tent. They got me when I was drawing circles and math in the sand with my finger. They believed I had dehydration delirium in the heat of the day, and that I was acting weird for that reason. Little did they know I was entering a highly psychotic mode that would last for a long time. They asked me questions which I don't know how well I answered. They tried to give me an intravenous solution to hydrate me, and I watched them try two places in the veins of one inner elbow and once in the other unsuccessfully. My blood pressure or something was too high and I watched the solution try to get in but not make it, pulsating with my strong heart beat.

After I had calmed down a bit, they took me to a sanctuary tent to rest the remainder of the day and night.

I remember all sorts of people came to see me and make sure I was okay. I had an air mattress, and stuffed animals for pillows. I remember relaxing and talking with people about the weirdest things. I remember everyone seemed really understanding, but I don't know how much sense I was making. As the night progressed, I realized it was the climax of the event, the night they burn a huge effigy of a man (hence the name) with a flame made by a lens with the light of the sun at the beginning and sustained alight through the week. I could tell by the noise of people I could hear from the sanctuary tent. That year, there were about twenty-five thousand people at the event. In celebration, that many people generate a lot of noise.

I had another strange encounter with synchronicity at that moment when I knew the effigy was burning. They had loud fireworks going off at the same time which compounded the noise of the crowd. I basked in the incredible noise performing what I would call bed yoga, where I stretch around every angle while laying down, tensing and relaxing all my muscle groups in a random, intuitively-ordained sequence. It feels wonderful to me. My thoughts still swirled from the intoxication a couple nights before and I was having quite the mystical experience listening to and feeling all the noise and energy of those tens of thousands of people.

I don't remember what felt so right about the moment and my inner state, but I felt I touched divinity that night. I behaved in contrast to my previous pattern through high school which expressed more mechanistic and scientific thinking about ideas. It was then that I started to think I could really believe that there was an organizing principle spirit or entity like a capital G God that would have the powers needed to produce the strangest of experiences of synchronicity that I was having. It didn't occur to me then that I had recently taken hallucinogenic drugs and was entering a psychotic disconnect from the reality of everybody else, letting my perceptual aberrations and conceptual fluctuation get ahead of my rationality and composure.

At some point I passed out or fell asleep from that night's dizzying experience, and I did not wake until it was light out the following morning. My state of agitation and confusion from the previous day or two had calmed quite a deal. I felt rational and clear-headed again, but inspired with thought of the prior couple day's experiences. I also had memory of the idea I had stumbled to before sleeping that a spiritual entity was probably the thing responsible for my experiences.

I left the sanctuary tent (I woke up alone, and no one seemed to be around), and used a portable potty that was very close by. When I came outside again, I was to have one of the most memorable experiences of my entire lifetime. When I left the potty, I walked around the corner and met a man, who appeared to me smiling and greeted me, shook my hand, and invited me to sit down beside him as there were a few chairs. I was no longer feeling the influence of drug induced trance like the last couple days, fully awake, aware, and clear-headed, but I hallucinated an entire person.

In full calmness and sobriety albeit a wicked and fresh attitude from the last night, I sat down outside the sanctuary tent for a conversation with an audio-visual projection. It did not seem he was waiting for me particularly, but that he was just there and waiting for whoever might be interested to chat. The whole time, no one else would walk by to interrupt our conversation or to tell me I was talking to myself, but I soon realized that I was not talking to a regular human being. Shortly afterwards I judged the interaction as an experience of being visited by a spirit entity, my award for having taken on a diligent belief in a higher power the previous night. He looked natural enough at first glance, but I started to think this man was beyond ordinary when he introduced himself.

Calmly articulated, he told me "I Am He Who Has Seen Each Path," and he gave me an intricate, earthy looking necklace that looked like hemp fibre with various wooden, shell, and glass beads. The necklace had a slightly rounded centre wooden bead with black words burn etched on each side. The bead was sort of a rectangular prism with two sentences alternating on the four sides, so each sentence was repeated once. It said, in all lowercase, "you are god/thou art god/you are god/thou art god." After I had taken it in my hands and examined it, he clasped the necklace around my neck and smiled.

Thinking back on that moment, the vividness this hallucinatory experience had astounds me. The audio, visual, and tactile senses were all activated in what now seems a perfectly compelling replication of an actual experience of interacting with someone. All the perceptual details were wholly convincing. The scope of the concepts we discussed clued to me that it was not quite a normal conversation with a normal human being, although at that time I believed him to be totally real, just not of this plane one might say. I'm astounded at how genuinely real and complex a hallucination can seem to the one experiencing it. The sense of external realism can be entirely seamless, down to shadows, handshakes, and independent personality. I think nothing could have convinced me then that I was having a merely illusory dialogue with a being entirely made up from my own imagination and dreaming brain. It felt so real and like part of the world.

After the introduction and giving of the necklace, we proceeded to have a wild and interesting conversation. We talked about a great number of things: The potential evolution of gills behind our ears in humans by accidentally choking water down the nose; The limits of language in expressing profound truths because the truths are about complexly existing things which betray simple articulation into words; and, The mystery belonging to events of internal and external synchronicity.

On the topic of synchronicity, he pointed to a vehicle with finger-drawings in the coat of dust upon it. A rainbow and sun were drawn, as well as "BM # 2". We laughed about how my name was Brenden MacDonald and how I had sort of been reborn since the last night into a new kind of attitude and conception while the person drawing on the vehicle was thinking "Burning Man number two."

He said it was legitimate to take things in the outer world as signs for your own meanings. Though, it was safe only as long as one recognized that every ambiguous event also has an independent history and future, regardless of the moment's metaphor, free association, and significance. Some of these details are fond in my memory, still, because regardless of the fact I was hallucinating, I also still see the real validity of the ideas we discussed. I was totally psychotic, yes, although it really feels like my subconscious had a notion that would be good for me to hear somehow.

This also feels like the natural outcome and intensification of those imaginary dialogues I had mastered in high school. I was already quite comfortable with talking in my head and "hearing" a meaningful, articulate response. This time, it had now become so real that it was more profound and literally apparent than typical dreams in sleep get for me. And this time, the subconscious dialogue was relaxed and deliberate, rather than as aggravated like the angst ridden dialogues of high school had been. It was guided mostly by my interlocutor developing ideas and my reflecting on them rather than by my turmoil in trying to express my convictions to my school chums.

I remember walking away with him from the sanctuary tent into the rest of the festival grounds, but I don't remember when we stopped interacting and when he left. Forgetting is not because of the time lapse between the experience and the writing of it. I found myself wondering about it as soon as I noticed I was walking alone. Just a little while later when I was walking around, I had my second hallucination, but this time other people were around. I saw a jovial, loud man with long and wavy brown hair at a little stand where they were selling or handing out lemonade.

I approached, interested, and when in proper earshot, I heard the man say loudly and as if telling an inside joke that he was Jesus Christ. I thought it very ridiculous, but I played along, in front of the other people at the stand, who were looking oddly at what was happening, it looked like to me. In actual fact, they were watching me talk in a fairly incoherent manner and watching me claim to be Jesus Christ. In the middle of hallucinatory experience, I could barely recognize any reaction in the people who saw me acting weirdly. I thought they were being weird and ignoring the man I saw, but he was not even really there. I was fully engrossed in the hallucination, and totally unable to pay attention to the actually real people and their statements.

After me and my hallucination walked away from the lemonade stand, we had a weird talk about mystical experience and possible forms of existing in different dimensions, but I don't remember much about it. What I do remember is him giving me two pieces of intricately embroidered cloth folded together. I unfolded them and looked at them. It seemed they would have told a story if I looked carefully at it. I folded them back up and put them in my pocket, and he told me that they were something like tickets for me and another to travel across a river such as the Acheron, Stygian, or Styx, a river of the dead or of some point of transcendence.

I was very perplexed by all that this vision had said, but only suspected he wasn't real when I went to look for the pieces of cloth and did not find them in my pocket. I knew they could not have fallen out of the pocket I had put them in, so I clued in that this "Jesus"-guy was different like "he who has seen each path." However, it was not until much later that I would altogether deny the two figures existed or that they only existed as mental figments.

Just like the first hallucination, I only gradually realized at some point that I was no longer with my second hallucination. They just faded from perception and I carried on with whatever else I was doing, which at this point was wandering the emptying desert after the festival had come to its conclusion. I had no more full-blown hallucinations of people that I remember. I remember that often during my walking, I would hallucinate a large crowd making noise in my head. It felt like a commentary on my actions and felt like the echo of the real noise of all the people I had heard.

The noise would come sporadically and suddenly when I read something or moved a certain way. I could not predict it, like most of the experience.

I was supposed to have left the desert to get back to Canada with my uncle's help, but the chaos I was in had prevented me from meeting up with him when I should have, so he had left without me and I had forgotten all about our plans. Upon getting in contact with my uncle, my parents began about then to worry about me and to attempt to track me down. Their first approach in finding me was getting a hold of my uncle's friends who were still at the event and a hold of Burning Man officials. The officials had heard of a boy of my description (because I had been acting weirdly), but they could not find me. I think I found my uncle's friends first, and they took me in.

In quite the state, I got taken by them to a hospital in Reno, about an hour or so drive from the desert. It was a very weird trip. I was very docile and accepting of where they wanted to take me, and the landscape and features of civilization were very weird. I thought I saw a nuclear power plant, with its distinct, steam-billowing cooling towers, but I may be mistaken. It would be the only one I've seen, if it was.

The light seemed surreal. It had been days since I did the hallucinogens, and I had been calmer since then. But now, it seemed like I became more and more disconnected from others, as the psychosis set deeper in. Everything about the trip fascinated me. My uncle's friends were talking with me and I was so interested. I showed them art of mine that I had brought with me to the event to show to people. I didn't realize they were taking me to a hospital until I got there. I was having fun travelling around.

The first visit to a hospital in my state of psychosis was far too brief. Apparently, I was in a trance state and my heart was beating 10 times a minute. I felt tranquil even though disoriented and not knowing what was going on around me. They stabbed a needle full of adrenaline directly into my heart and were monitoring me until it slipped out of my mouth that I had done mushrooms and acid. They took my state to be fully accountable to the drugs, and swiftly kicked me out of the hospital, luckily with the people who brought me there and not out with the police. Fairly calm as I left, we had food in the lobby/cafeteria before leaving. Then we returned to the desert.

I was supposed (by my parent's planning) to wait with my uncle's friends until the person I came with to Burning Man returned to take me back to Canada (the person had left after I departed company), so they had a tent set up for me and told me to rest. I wasn't aware of the plans at all, or their desire that I stay in the tent until they return. I might have slept for a while, and then I ventured out of the tent.

No one was around, but the wind blew hard. Sand was flying around, even. The desert had become mostly empty by this point, and I saw where the vehicles were leaving the desert to get to the highway, so I walked that way. I stuck out my thumb and got a ride to the highway, and began to walk toward Gerlach, Nevada the town closest to the Black Rock Desert. Another vehicle, coming from the festival and heading toward Gerlach picked me up and dropped me off in town.

By then, the wind in the desert had picked up into a full blown sand storm, so it was good that I had left when I did and did not walk around deeper into where the storm would have been. A magnificent sight, the sand flew up and down and around so much so that the middle of the desert blurred from the ground to low sky. I have seen hardly anything ever so spectacular and unique, the ground lifted up so high into the sky. I watched for quite a while and then decided to walk around a bit more to explore the town.

I proceeded to pick up garbage that I saw everywhere on the ground. I guess I looked like a non-local hippy, because this one man threatened to beat me up; he told me to get lost and that he didn't like my kind of people. I dropped the garbage I was carrying and went in the opposite direction, claiming to be innocent and claiming that I liked the area and was trying to help it out by cleaning up.

He was hearing none of it. It was a rather disgusting experience. A few minutes later when I was walking by a house with a school bus parked in front of it, I met a lady who was going to her house. I was a bit shook up from the prior experience, and she asked if I was okay. I told her what I had been doing and what had happened; she felt sympathetic.

She was a more reasonable individual than the angry man. She asked if I was hungry and gave me part of a watermelon and some chocolate. We parted ways and I walked to a building that had something to do with elderly people where I asked if I could use the washroom to wash my hands and if there was a garbage receptacle for my watermelon rind and chocolate wrapper. The lady there was very nice and allowed me to wash my hands and throw away my stuff.

No one seemed to notice very much that frankly, I was walking around disoriented without much direction at all. I finally walked up to a building with symbols on it that I recognized from the Burning Man event. It was the Black

Rock City Ranger Station in Gerlach, sort of the home base for ranger activities, but I really had no meaningful awareness of my whereabouts. I walked in, totally unaware that at the moment I walked in, several people knew who I was, who had been in contact with my mother, who were busy searching for me at the time.

I don't really remember what it was I wanted when I walked in, but shortly, I was comfortable sitting on a couch watching Star Trek: The Wrath of Khan and eating pizza. I don't know how they felt about my demeanour, whether they knew I was basically very psychotic, but they seemed calm around me. I remember a few of them staring at me with weird looks on their faces. I must have looked a mess, dusty and frazzled.

At one point soon, I talked to my mother on the telephone. I don't know whether they called her or whether she called them just after I got there. The conversation I had with her is vague to my memory except I remember explaining to her how I would get home on my own. At my own pace I would go west to California, then follow the coast north.

I didn't have a clue of what I was going to do that very night, let alone of how I would get to the coast or even of a good direction toward the coast from where I found myself. My mom told me to wait there because someone was coming to pick me up, in fact the person who took me to Burning Man in the first place, the person I wanted nothing to do with at that point. However I did not explain myself well enough at that point or at all, really, or things might have turned out differently and not so mentally explosive for me.

I left under supervision of someone without my best interests at heart. I want to carry on this story while not being vague about why I was at risk with this individual. It is hard though to share this in a book I want lots of people to read. But here goes. This individual had a sick and intense obsession over me that had been only culminating over the summer, and had gone full blown by the time we were at Burning Man. I had been growing more and more scared of the person as time went on, but I was also deteriorating on my own, with all what else I had to chew on my cognitive plate. I agreed to go to Burning Man only because I loved the idea of the festival, not because I wanted to spend a week together. It was so good that I had found my uncle, for the week, but bad at the point where I re-met the person.

I don't really know how to carry on with the story without exposing too much detail that I don't really want to share and that makes the story about something other than schizophrenia, which is after all my overall topic here. We stayed the night in Gerlach in a motel and my memory fails me on exactly what happened, but I think I may have been raped. I'm not sure, but I know the individual wanted to be sexual, may have drugged me, or who knows what.

I did not remember much of anything about the previous night on the following morning, but we headed off toward the Californian redwood cedar forests which was the original plan of weeks ago. By this point, my psychosis was getting fairly radical, but I wasn't totally off the wall with extreme behaviour. I remember looking at the person's sunglasses while driving and thinking the person was the devil. For most of the day long drive up through California to the Oregon coast, we chit-chatted and got along fairly well I guess, because the interaction was more like when we became friends, instead of about the obsession which was being vocalized more and more regularly.

When we got to the town where we would stay the night, things took a sour turn again between us. First, we got drunk, which was a very bad thing to do at that moment, because the emotions started to flare. Eventually I was left alone and awake as the other slept, after we had argued about the obsession again. In a state of alertness without tire, I stayed up brooding over the seeming hopelessness of getting the idea through to this person once and for all.

I started watching television, in the most extreme way. It seemed instantly natural to assume that the subject being discussed or narrated in the imagery and dialogue was solely me. The first sentence made me think about my own situation, and every one after that had the same feel. The evil huge imperial robot ship was attacking the planet, and the Powerpuff girls were saving the day.

Whatever broad similarities my mind may have drawn at first, the experience became more intense and focused as a perceived dialogue between myself and the television. This common schizophrenic symptom of delusional self-reference is stereotypically expressed in the example of "hearing God in the radio." This symptom in full force can feel like absolutely every signal into your senses is consciously intended as a communication to you. I totally accepted the synchronicity I had read about in both ancient and new age spiritual writings as a plausible source of veridical communication, believing that all of reality became an actual partner with whom I could enter a dialogue.

I watched for a few hours, becoming more and more excited, until I became very agitated and decided to wake up who I was with. I started yelling, and confusion was the response, but shortly the obsession became the topmost topic, and it was "why won't you love me?" bull shit, and very loud. Under so much stress, my own psychological state was flaring and I decided in a spontaneous fashion to draw the line in a very radical way.

I took a bottle of sleeping pills that weren't mine and I downed the whole bottle saying something to the effect of "this is my proof that I don't want anything to do with your obsession. My will is my own." In retrospect, I know I in some way believed that the effect of the pills would not be the end of my conscious experience, like I would live on or reincarnate into another form. The desire to swallow a bottle of tranquilizers and knowledge that the act may be suicide was not brought on by a desire to end my life.

It was a very, very linguistically oriented act, with the express purpose of communicating something to this person. Elaborating on that to say the least, something I wanted to convey was the force of my emotional separation and incongruence with what was coming at me from the other direction. At that moment I uttered an absolute refusal, all sense of healthy response broken apart.

My memory has a hole in it, but the next thing I remember was being told by the person to stick my finger in my throat and puke up the pills into the toilet; by the moment of recognition I was beside the toilet. An ambulance was called and shortly I was whisked away to the nearest hospital. I don't even remember being taken outside of the hotel to the ambulance. Everything was starting to blur totally out of my conscious perception.

The next time I was conscious of my surroundings, I was in that white hospital room with a three-quarters opaque window that displayed out the top a forest I desperately wanted to explore. I was barely cognizant of what had been happening to me. I had no detailed knowledge of my whereabouts except that the forest had a familiarity, as I happened to be in Oregon, where exist many of the same plant species as the place I grew up.

Apparently I was agreeable to taking the medication they wanted to give me, even though most of the day they observed me talking and gesturing as if to actual people in the room or interacting with objects invisible to them. For all that time I have no conscious memory of experiencing anything. The first moment of recognition of my self that I remember was looking at the clear top pane of the window and desiring to see what was outside my line of sight. I took the chair in the room to the window and stood to look through, out into the world.

The recognition that I was in a very white room with a door did not occur to me as strange at this point, and I didn't quite have any clue of reminiscence as to where and what I had experienced the week before at Burning Man or during the nearly week-long hallucinatory trance in the hospital room. I basically didn't have any memories for a time prior the moment I wanted to look out the window, except maybe taking pills they were giving me when the door opened.

However, I may only have been aware of that *after* the recognition of the forest as a real attainable goal focused me into the reality of being in a hospital room that I could potentially get out of. I don't know when I even understood with literal awareness that I indeed was a patient in a hospital. I might have had dropouts of memory between the window experience and finally leaving the hospital, but the crucial moment of knowing I would be okay and the point from which I wouldn't again have memory dropouts for the near future was when I saw—arriving to accompany me back to Canada—my father enter the room.

As reported back to me, my reaction was one of letting exhaustion overwhelm. It was like I knew it was safe to sleep. I remember complete relaxation and emotional peacefulness (not just peaceful behaviour, which I had given the whole time). I think at that point, one of the nurses or doctors indicated somehow to my father that I had returned.

At least that's what my father indicated to me. I remember suddenly being at ease with the situation, without the anxiety of my desire to see the forest outside or know what lay beyond the turn in the hallway I peered at through the door. But now my father was there and I knew home was not too far away.

I have so much compassion for that 17 year old I was, 10 years ago, who had no conception he was turning 18 in just a few weeks, or had just botched starting at UBC in Vancouver where he'd been accepted earlier in the summer. Really, my struggle was closer to beginning than over at this point, but that calls for many chapters yet.

Chapter 6
On the First Time Assembling
What Had Shattered

I don't remember being led out of the hospital in Coos Bay, but I vaguely remember getting into the back of an ambulance with my dad, and once in the ambulance it was recommended I just lay down and rest. They said I could use a rest with what I'd been through, and I didn't argue. Knowing I was headed for my home of Vancouver Island, I think during the long ambulance ride I began to realize where I had been the previous week.

I apprehended the last clip of time in fragments of images, social interaction, and shredded imaginings. It felt so effortless to simply lie back in the ambulance and not to resist or question what was happening. I just did not and could not at that time understand the entire sequence and consequence of the last couple weeks. In that ambulance I very much was, but also felt, more like a passenger than an agent in what was coming next.

At that moment very little context had entered yet into my consciousness. I knew I was in an ambulance with my dad, but other than that, I hadn't realized that they knew I was emerging from wreckage in the aftermath of psychotic break. Everything about my knowledge of the situation was simple and at one immediate level of interaction. I had no contextual knowledge of the world beyond the ambulance and my secured safety knowing home was coming. There was no analysis on my part to interpret a clear idea of what had happened to me, even though, as I've said, I had read about schizophrenia and had decided that I had it but did not yet show psychotic symptoms; I did not clue in that this was what a post-break is. I just rode in that ambulance in oblivion, not noticing or projecting anything about the destination.

Most of the time, I just relaxed lying down, but every now and then we stopped at rest areas so we could relieve ourselves. What I remember of them strongly shows what I mean by lacking contextual knowledge: My core personality and desires shone through my mentally disconnected behaviour. As these stops were my first post-hospital voyage into a normal social arena, they jogged me more to my sense of surrounding, but this sense still possessed limit in a peculiar fashion. The most prominent feature of the landscape, as related to my social preoccupations, was the huge number of cigarette butts littering it. It was my sole desire on the rest area stops to pick up the cigarette butts and other garbage that people had splayed about disregarding the provided trash cans and ashtrays.

Obviously, this is a gross, unsanitary job unless you have gloves and a garbage bag, so the ambulance staff wanted to stop me from doing it, but not without commending me for my attitude. They were heart struck at my incoherently articulated defence of my behaviour, about my desires and intentions to help out ecologically. They were heart struck because my world had crumbled inward, shattered, into a fractured but kind, caring personality of primary impulses and motivations, without secure, knowing connection to the world outside.

What shone through in that moment were my deep set convictions about what people can do by themselves to help the world be a better place for all life, and that heartened my navigators so taken by the gravity of my inner state. It was amazing that with such devastated emotional affect and incoherent thought I managed to express a clear desire that signified (especially to me in retrospect) that I was still me at my shaken core. I was still me, but I was living in uncohered pieces. I felt shattered in the sense that only pieces of my personality, values, and desires came through either my psyche or behaviour. I could hardly feel any sense of a whole reflective picture of what had been happening in my world.

As I have stated, even in my incoherence I knew that having my dad with me meant things were going well, that I was headed home. First, though, I was headed to Comox General Hospital's Psychiatric Ward. It was probably an eleven hour or more ambulance ride from Oregon up through Washington into British Columbia, across on the ferry to Vancouver Island, and up island a ways. Sleeping or not thinking much for the majority of time yet not even capable of boredom, the time passed without attention. Stepping out of the ambulance and walking into the hospital having had a substantial day's rest and the innocent assurance of heading home with my dad, I must have come across as quite relaxed and at ease. The past few months had not accumulated in my awareness, blinded to the emotional stress in my life and to the delusions that had been forming around my preoccupations.

I would be calm for the next bit, but soon chaos would distress me as in surged memory and in flew delusion. I was able, in retrospect, to reconstruct the timeline of events up to this point, but without my mother's memories I wouldn't have as clear a timeline about the first while spent in hospitals. I got to Comox General on September 10th, 2002, a full year shy a day since the fateful events that first sent me on my way toward compulsive interest and delusion about my world.

I would be there for a short while in Comox before going home, and it's a blurry time. I remember being emotional, childlike, and not yet concerned with the previous months and years of deterioration, of my descent into a madness. Top preoccupations included the sound of ambulances leaving and coming to the hospital. I was worried immensely for the safety of people who might be in them. I also liked mustard when it was a condiment in the meals. By the end of the second week, I had realized where I had been three and four weeks prior, and I was mostly settled in the eyes of the doctors.

By then I had not yet received a psychiatric diagnosis, and it seemed my mind had settled. They knew the LSD and mushrooms had played a role, but no one had looked into my recent mental history yet. Having realized where I had been after getting relaxed and comfortable with where I was at the moment, with my long term memory becoming accessible again, I remembered some of my weird experiences at Burning Man and afterward and I remembered the intense spiritual interpretation of events I had developed before going completely incoherent for over a week.

I didn't tell anyone, of course, remembering that in a psychiatric hospital, such admissions of thoughts would be grounds for continued admission of body. I also thought I would be okay, mind you, as I was calmed down. Nothing was too out of whack yet in terms of the experiences I had already had and which would follow, so I believed I could handle figuring things out on my own. I still felt sceptical, as always has been the case concerning the nature of my bizarre experiences. I had realized some of the figures I interacted with in the desert were only there to my eyes, but I did not know where they came from, whether from just my brain or from some non-physical domain.

I cannot, after my experiences, join the ranks of atheistic materialists and outright deny the possibility of consciousness beyond biology. However, I also knew even then from the range of beliefs I have variously held that it's very true, even if some part of my experience was genuinely spiritual as I have felt, that I have surely still been prone to delusional and disorderly ideas. I think the heavy medication made me sleepy and slow to think, so I didn't seem too messed up, but what was the pill to do for my strange ideas? So I hid my ideas, for more medication would make me more sleepy. I wanted to actually change my mind.

So, they released me and I went home with my prescription. I must have appeared either sane or dazed and sane to be released, so I must have hidden my growing sense of desire to further my self-exploration that had been taking place over the summer and intensified at Burning Man. I was eager to go home, and being clever enough to realize the dynamic of being a psych ward patient, I got through their checkups on my state of being in the short order of two weeks. I had no idea I would be back in as soon as a week's time. Little did I know that my confusion period was still just beginning to really fortify in my psyche.

I got home finally for the first time after leaving for Burning Man, and it felt nice to have a forest in my back yard again to explore and be with plants and earth. Too bad my delusions rushed too quickly back to the forefront. I had a TV again; damn! Seeing the news again, and at my fingertips again having my weird books to read and also the journals I started in high school, I quickly got back into the groove of word salad. Now though, I had the memory of interacting with "He who has seen each path" and of our conversation about reading the appearance of the environment and its stimuli in order to spontaneously relate meaningfully with the world. That's bad news with a TV, a hyperactive imagination, emotional recoil from an abusive situation, and plenty of time to percolate without psychotherapeutic intervention of any sort.

 That first experience in the motel room at five in the morning, while listening to the TV tell me a story about my self, was a meagre beginning compared to where eventually the self-referencing reading of spontaneous stimuli would lead. After a brief reminder of the TV-viewing anomalies in Oregon after I turned one on at home, I was quickly amazed at how profound it felt to have a TV blaring randomly in seemingly precise coordination with my inner stream of consciousness. I realized at Burning Man, without TVs, I had been "reading" the artistic features prevalent there while exploring the event in an air of being in a storybook. Once in front of regular social stimuli, I had entered a whole other realm of information that was highly dangerous considering this state of being.

 It occurred to me in full force that I had a few weeks before encountered a shift in my perception that I had no precedent for, except for growing ideas about the world being a solipsistic illusion (the Buddhist Maya). Now that I had remembered attempting suicide with those tranquilizers, it seemed one potential interpretation that I had died and been put into a learning lab or that my time in the standard illusion I already started to think I was in had ended. Maybe I was in the bardo afterlife I had read about in the Tibetan Book of the Dead. But maybe some spirit was just using the world and I was alive. These all gave me some reasons, not logical or coherent in total between them, to accept that now the whole world was being a messenger system from beyond to little old me.

So after a few days, I decided to stay up two nights in a row watching TV after discontinuing my medication. I felt it was getting in the way of my experience by making me sleepy and emotionally flat, all after a couple weeks of starting it. Luckily, I had a first appointment with a psychiatrist the following day after I had been up two nights. I decided to bring my journals of word salad, and after stopping the med and giving myself a sleep deprivation re-psychosis, I was a tad excited, to say the least. The doctor told me five weeks later that after a brief look in my journals, noting when I said I had started them, and her brief listen to my highly energetic speech and idea flow, she knew my case was full-blown schizophrenia and not just a toxic psychosis brought on by the hallucinogens I had taken.

She told my parents to take me back to Comox right away, and I was there shortly after night's fall, one week from my first release date. It wasn't just because I stopped my meds that I got sick again right away, but a combination of that along with not having been convinced in any way that the majority of my experience was really delusional and not mystical or spiritual at all. I didn't have a conceptual or practical framework for every day. I just had a pill that didn't change the content of my mind except to slow me down, put me to sleep, and give me a headache if I thought too quickly. I left the hospital without having worked through any delusions at all, so I was definitively a sure candidate for medication stoppage and relapse. The following four week stay in two wards on Vancouver Island after my initial two week stay in Comox would be a rougher time emotionally than when I was first too dazed and un-remembering to put together much of any agenda, unlike now that I had my memories and delusions at ready grasp.

I went into Comox General psychiatric ward a wreck with a strong agenda. I was resistant to taking my medication, and I thought everything that was happening was part of a plot. I think the first night, I was put in an isolation room that was totally concrete and metal on the inside. I was very disorderly and crazed. At one point, I ran around the rectangular room banging my skull against the wall. I wanted out. It was terrifying, looking back on it. I became totally disconnected from everything except acting on bare impulse, and not in any understanding of the way that would help me get better.

The experience was like I was driven and randomized by emotional stimuli, acting on any thought however momentary. I wanted to let them know I wanted out of the room, so I ran around the room banging my head. Totally random, but it was going on. I was in that state, the middle of going totally crazy or falling down and becoming quiet in extreme exhaustion. In the fiery moments, I was very much in danger of what might happen next were I not to slow down and think of the risks involved in my behaviour.

Like I was possessed, I just went with any spontaneous gesture of emotion. I had no clue of who I was; it was like I was what Western culture calls "animal," except I had my human language and sense of demand. I blew up in that isolation chamber; somehow I needed to be restricted but it was horrible to be only in my own disordered momentum, unrestricted into my problematic, altered state. I don't know how long I tried to get them to let me out, but eventually I woke up and was much calmer after that long explosion had subsided with sleep.

Something had changed. When they let me out of the room there were several people around me and they talked over with me what was going on. I was kind of dazed. They told me I had schizophrenia, which wasn't news to me by that point, having researched it by myself a long time prior. I would need to accept the medicine they had to give me and I would need to be gentle, not wild. At that point I had no argument. I vaguely remembered the run around the room the night before, and shuddered. I was told I would be in the hospital for a while to make sure I was better this time before leaving. I knew that whatever had happened to me, though I was not letting go of the delusions yet, meant for certain that I was out of whack and not clear on how to operate.

I would be in Comox General psych ward for three weeks. My love for mustard increased exponentially. I wanted it with every meal. I found a use for it somewhere. I did all but eat it by itself. I enjoyed the meals and didn't fuss too much about anything. I got it into my head that being in a psych ward was the best place for me and I began to think that every aspect of the care routine was a good thing for me. After the initial wavering on the medication that accelerated my journey back to this place, I did not resist it in the same way as I felt I wanted to in the time between first release and first seeing my doctor.

(I would more or less, give or take a few experimental moments in the long run, remain steadfast to the medication from there on out. The times I would not take it most often were forgetting and just a few times because I wanted to go without for a night or two but would carry on the next day. Nowadays I take it every day and hardly ever forget. I would never have a "bad trip" when I experimented like that, and it would never make me loopier or more disorderly or more delusional. It was often because the meds would make we fall asleep when I was still getting used to them and I wanted to stay up and read, think, write, and play with creative mental states. However, after this point I knew the meds helped me keep a stable sleep schedule and did suppress the sheer pace of my brain (even if they did little or nothing to my capacity for delusion).

Speaking of delusion, in those three weeks at Comox, I watched a little bit of TV to weird effect but also watched "A Beautiful Mind" about John Nash the schizophrenic mathematician and that actually helped put things into a more proper perspective. I realized through the dramatization of the experience more about the tenacity of inner perception to insist on being true and materially objective and about the power of the mind to help the belief structure seem true, by making and running on untested, unchecked assumptions. I knew a great deal of my experience was delusional and incorrect, but I didn't know what. That's probably why I accepted the treatment regimen and being institutionalized.

I still couldn't help but think it was about me, but this time I remembered "He who has seen each path." He had talked about reading the random signals as pertinent patterns of significance, while not snagging the 'container for the meaning' away from its own independent causal history. There was no mention during that hallucinated conversation in the desert that I would soon be feeling like most stimuli were orchestrated just for me, but *my* path had been foreseen in a way.

It had turned out that this event in my schizophrenic perception gave me the conceptual guide to dealing with a rising experience. I would have just healthy enough a modicum of doubt, in the compelling idea that my own mind was adequately powerful by itself to strip stimuli of every sort from its random context—from spontaneous conversations, and light patterns, to inner bodily sensations—interpreting a meaningful and unified narrative stream. I would still think for a long time, though, off and on, it was possible that I was a lonely solipsist, in a world of just my own being, in conversation with some overseeing mind which was simulating everything I thought was my world. I wouldn't let go of multifarious conclusions, and my imagination ran in overclock.

Now, I should say, it wasn't every moment of waking experience that I felt this forcibly bent out of shape. I could have lucid moments where scepticism was thick, and I could also get in the groove of having normal conversations without thinking every sentence was a double sent message from outer space. It was surely compelling at times, however, to think so, because the meaning I interpreted often felt so incredibly consistent and continuous.

Sometimes I felt something like a sixth sense in my strange interpretations, feeling like communication was happening with a real, external conscious entity. I truly wanted to believe that I was not dead and that people had their own minds, and often felt that most strongly, but an odd sentence in a commercial or from a group walking by me on the street could throw me for a loop into taking my communicative stance toward random stimuli.

Sometimes I would not have any tinge at all of extra meaning, and if I tried to turn on a TV, I would get a headache and not be able to force the experience. In those times, I might feel low, bored, sluggish, and like I would rather be having messed up thoughts. In the next 3 years, the experience would ebb, flow, and ebb again, but could surge intermittently and strongly. It would go from occupying half or more than half of my time awake, down to a tiny fraction of my being awake every day, down to eventually going days without the strangeness before I would be knocked square on my bottom in a bad moment and left dazed again for days.

As I will talk about in the next chapter, I strained for a long time to abate my experiences toward psychological manageability and security. I wasn't then able to monitor my stress factors and knowingly observe my symptoms receding or peaking slowly, because delusion drove me on rather than a model for healthy living. The stimuli interpretation happened a lot, at first, when I was thinking to myself personally about various things. A random external signal would interrupt during a pause in my thought thought stream.

It would seem seem in a figurative and relevant way to instantly respond, seemingly with direct intention, to my inner processes. The experience developed into something even stranger at the most intense phases: it was not just random signals or phrases that would set it off. I would eventually learn to speak back and forth with an actually real person, while for me the conversation was occurring on a completely different level. I learned to say the right words on cue as would fit the Earthly conversation a real group of people thought I was having with them, but on another level I felt I was interacting with otherworldly consciousness.

These traits would take time to set in though, and around the time of my first hospitalization, I would spend my time tentatively nourishing and intentionally expanding the strange behaviour. It was natural, as I felt I was learning and gaining from it. In Comox General, I got a taste for how my attention span would take on an increasingly normalized disparity.

My thoughts would become vividly split between two kinds of awareness, and I was on the path of developing intellectual methods to withstand, in striking parallel, two separate but simultaneously primary experiences. At the start, I could only go between, and back and forth, in either one state of mind or the other.

Temperamentally crossing the schism from side to side, I could not yet see that I was becoming desperately confused about the nature of reality. Distrusting or ignorant of the inward spontaneity and force of imagination in my cognitive behaviour, my compulsive delusions reigned supreme.

When I felt ready to leave the hospital in two weeks, time after my doctor had just sent me right back in, I was told I was not ready yet—I had to finish "settling." My behaviour was still a bit erratic, but I was calming down. I was in the mood by then to stay on my medication, because I realized it was helping to keep me more calm and more in synch with those around me. I was somewhat giving my consent to reside in an ordinary, shared reality. Being emotionally driven by the bizarre perception appealed less and less to me, compared to the prospect of calmly and intentionally learning from it. Temperamentally, I realized I wanted to continue to have real conversations with my family, instead of perceiving a broken, world-permeating mind intervening in all my affairs. At this point (though unbeknownst to my caretakers) I still fully intended to keep communicating with and learning from that entity. In numerous ways I kept flirting within my beliefs, feeling that both an ordinary and relatively mystical experience was possible to interchange in sequence or parallel. The conceptual content of my delusions and the compulsive desires to entertain them were the easiest thing to hide after the emotional warp on me subsided as the medication made me more passive and subdued.

    I cannot insist this point more in thinking about the course of my recovery: Neither before nor after medication did anything change for delusions already etching into deep habits of responding to various triggers, or for delusions freshly chosen and concentrated upon after hospitalizing. With the particular compulsion that I should keep my delusions secret for the most part, I was basically on my own to face them. I had a lot of conflicting notions about my social and metaphysical existence, and the med seemingly didn't touch the perpetual rearrangements of my mental order.

    I lost all bearing inside the self-reconfiguring maze of a bizarre reality stock full of commanding perceptions and perplexing concepts. Schizophrenia is a lot more than a "brain disease," pure and simple, when the mind can consciously fuel and stoke the embers of delusion that might gradually become hardwired and imprinted as an automatic habit—as I would suggest is the hidden truth in these theories of psychiatry. That is, eventually what the mind does by its steadily applied and conscious efforts becomes slowly quicker to fire off in the brain's customary networks of behaviour.

The more I would voluntarily choose delusions, the more I'd have weird feelings, thoughts, and even some hallucinations, although the med did seem to suppress perceptual intensity. Except for the queer sense of communications with spiritual entities, my hallucinations had never been forceful or à prominent part of my experience. In the most extreme moments of my initial hospitalization in Coos Bay, as the medical reports indicate and not my memories, hallucinatory experience overwhelmed me for days on end. Without having started medication, my hallucinations possibly could have worsened for some time. I am on board with attempting to create safe and effective medicines for schizophrenia, but I definitely know from experience that chemical methods hold the smaller part of treatment. Social and cognitive treatment is quite likely to be necessary, especially if delusions and other intellectual commitments have settled in for the long stay, as I experienced.

As my time in the hospital was affirming, delusional tendency was the greatest obstacle to my "settling" and becoming more like the old me. I wasn't as sane yet as I would have personally liked to be, and the nurses' insistence that I needed to keep calming down was a revelation. I would need to keep adapting my methods to integrate my wild language experiments with managing life in the shared social world. I decided to endeavour toward fitting in with my old experience of the world while consciously developing my abilities to create or transmit wild meanings and to have interesting learning interactions between spontaneous stimuli and my cognitive responses.

I would flip flop in and out of delusion, trusting my doctors sometimes that I was coming out of sickness and back to reality, nevertheless succumbing sometimes to the idea that I was coming into clarity and deeper contact with previously hidden realities. To this day, I think I've had a bit (or a lot) of both sickness and spiritual growth, while today I have come to terms with the fact I was mostly grossly muddled in a dark moment of my life and was mostly just getting sicker, for some time. It felt back then as though I was constantly pushing forward, but I seriously needed to check my head and pursue a healthier tendency. The power of the mind to represent beautiful and strange meaning is what speaks to me nowadays, regardless of which directions the information seemed then to be travelling.

I've had a deeply reflexive focus on my mental experience since before the age of six. By the time my birthday had passed unbeknownst to me and I was 18 in Comox General psych ward, I had attained an entirely new and awkwardly even more self-conscious focus. I would be set at that time for several years into directing and enticing my cognitive machinery into various schizophrenic activities. The questions and overt concerns of doctors would not impede the notion that I could get through the delusions by myself if I spent time and effort directing my attention to the truth.

I thought if I answered "yes, I am experiencing delusions" that a heavier dose of my drug would only increase my headaches (figurative and literal both) and stick me deeper in my rut. I therefore hid the delusions very privately from anyone else. I even hardly wrote them down, although I would in the next year, beginning in the hospital, write lots of poetry and philosophical prose. In the madness that came to be, that was one thread of continuity between my early childhood years and my late teens: I had a long lasting and profound focus on my inner being, and the content of my experience which has been most profound has typically been quite hidden from the views of others. Through my early years, into my first hospital stay, and up until my early 20s with a second major hospital stay in the works, my life felt mostly like my own private adventure.

Hidden in the background were seeds of the intention to maintain the rest of my life in some kind of ordinary form and to sort through my intense and chronic psychotic symptoms. In this state, I became more calm and resigned to my personal journey by the end of my second visit to Comox. I was moved closer to home, to Port Alberni, and was there only a short while.

I finally got to go home after being ambulated between two countries and three hospital wards across a roughly five week period. There were those delirious nights in the middle of that span, of course, that I spent unmedicated and sleep deprived in front of a TV preceding my first aware visit with my first psychiatrist—who had observed me at Comox initially and now quickly ascertained, between my lasting confusion and the evidence of scattered, tattered written notes I presented, that she had a full blown case of schizophrenia before her.

In the next chapter, I will go deeper into some details of my strange cognitive behaviour as well as go into my experience of the "negative symptoms" of schizophrenia, as they are called. The "positive symptoms" are what I have written about so far: the hallucinations, delusions, and disordered thinking, for example. I didn't totally get away from these positive symptoms, as you will read, too.

Negative symptoms include subtler and less overt problems that schizophrenics are likely to develop, both preceding the onset and after the immediate repercussions of more acute psychosis, which often exemplifies more positive symptoms. A schizophrenic in "psychotic remission but expressing negative symptoms" might, for example, appear depressed, socially anxious, withdrawn, obsessive-compulsive, and more, in various depth, while also having subdued positive symptoms at some times.

One thing is that schizophrenia, in general, may be well defined as a "chronic psychosis." It involves a disconnect from healthy cognitive, emotional states that is not only episodic, but rather persists in many identifiable ways (i.e. the lasting negative and positive symptoms). Schizophrenia influences the entire domain of a human existence, not merely with incorrect beliefs or random voices in the head. Its disruption involves the whole mind and body, and prolonged healing in schizophrenia entails sensitivity and a range of responses.

Chapter 7
Out of Hospital for a While...
Trailing Doubts, Between Sorts

There were cracks most of the way through the post-psychotic tatter assembled as myself. I didn't know then that slowly the tremble of the pieces would exceed the pace I could glue and would eventually rip apart four years later. Specifically, I mean that I was a mass of subtle delusion and thick mental tendencies, hiding what I knew to be "crazy" from my doctor and others because I felt like I had control over my behaviour. I had some doubts in what I thought I was experiencing, but it still had a strong hold on my psyche, now that I look back. Going through another hospitalization in 2006 turned down most of the noise, but how I went there again is an interesting story, full of trance, turmoil, and tremor.

What "fun." I cancelled a starting semester at UBC for fall 2002 (as it occurred to me much later, having been totally unprepared, with no place lined up to stay in Vancouver and no class registration done)! I had to take some time to myself to get better, and better I was in a way compared to how I was doing prior to the first hospitalizations, in high school and that summer when my preoccupations were becoming pathologically intense and my mood fell to despair. The "better I was" included headaches when I had disordered thinking and preoccupation, a huge amount of sleepiness, deepening social withdrawal, and a generally flat mood, a blend of medication side effects and negative symptoms. So, to be charitable, no longer was I able to think as treacherously fast and as chaotically or have as much trouble getting to sleep on the semi-regular. However, my community interaction highly declined, my mood darkened, and my delusions concerning the stressful world largely became stronger instead of weaker, through my first "recovery" from psychosis.

That is why schizophrenia is considered a "chronic" form of psychosis. It all typically lasts for a considerable amount of time, affecting the individual in variably severe ways perhaps through his or her whole life. It has given me the belief that schizophrenics need more help than a pill in most cases, which I have also kept taking quite consistently since my first bout in 2002.

I didn't always want to, wanting another "fun" at times, a bit more of my quickness in thought and bubbling in emotional affect. I'm not really sure the medication does much other than mellow me out with sleepiness, slow my brain, and make creative thought more painful, which affectively dampens some kinds and extents of positive symptoms; but this doesn't offer methods of managing the stress and triggers which underlie what are my voluntary responses to my intellectual and emotional experiences—the stress and my responses to the nature of my own experience where I most identify "cause" in my condition and the possibility of managing it.

There is all this theoretical talk of "brain disease" and "genetic factors." Can I please not dispute the rational claims of reasonable scientists and yet suggest a philosophical notion of being in crisis? Of course genetics play a role in brain development, but those genes and brain have a correlate: I am a person with an experience. Nearly universal with the flaring of symptoms in mental illness is some sort of "stress" affecting the person, and it seems at least partially known that people sometimes behave with "conscious effort" in effect.

The management of stress and cognitive behaviour, over a lifetime, reasonably plays a role both in the activation and emphasis of genetic processes and in the unhealthy chemical habits of the living, thinking, feeling brain. If my experience stands for anything, self-management has played the biggest role in my becoming healthier to my own standard, not just deemed "less crazy" by the system reeling in subtle symptoms and feeling slowed down too much by a medicated daze all the time.

In my case, it was the apparently magical sequence of events and hallucinations during the peak of my onset that stuck with me and so affected me into arguably wider degrees of delusion. I became entrenched in a few strong ideas and regularly achievable mental states. I wrote earlier that I went into the hospital for the first time after a suicide attempt. One of the incorrect ideas that formed in my interpretation of my experience was that I might be dead but had only died in the material world to be reborn in a spiritual world that was all too similar to the world I came from. It seemed to help explain the strangest of feelings and perceptions I began to have during and after psychotic onset.

In the final poem I included at the outset of the book is a line, "the world became a magic poem I could read." I also mention that "my greatest delusion" was that "I believed our society was one grand illusion." I said that right before I swallowed those pills and the day before my quick re-hospitalization, when I was watching TV with a strong apprehension of direct and spontaneous communication betweem some intelligent agent and my inner thoughts. Little could I have guessed then in which direction or to what extent would grow my experience of non-ordinary intelligence and my altered sense of reality.

When I temporarily decided to go off my medication, it was because I felt it was blocking a proper understanding and blocking the working through of my experience. That, and I also felt exhilarated by the bizarre perceptions and thoughts. It felt weird to perhaps be in a spiritual afterlife or perhaps under spiritual invasion into the world and my psyche. Whatever I felt was happening (and it changed all the time), I had not when going off my meds so suddenly yet suspected that the majority of my strange experiences were internally generated dreams (or nightmares, given the mood).

Speaking of mood, any pressure residing those first couple years to go off my meds probably had to do with the negative symptoms I mentioned at the end of last chapter. Lack of emotional affect, when not experiencing intense states of meaning transformation, led to convincing reasons to enjoy and desire the stranger psychological events. When I wasn't in a dizzy high, which was continually variable, I often felt subdued and exhausted and felt that it was due to the medication that I felt restrained emotionally.

In the year and a half prior to my first hospitalizations, non-medicated, my mind would more freely move to where I wanted it to without the headache which has very persistently accompanied open, deep thought since I started on medication. As I became more disturbed in my thinking over the years, I got used to being able to keep delving into higher states of feeling, but after the hospital, my feelings felt estranged from me. They felt less vivid.

The personalized, direct, vivid feel of communication with alien entities through TV, music, and text enveloped me instead and then eventually trespassed into overheard conversations held by strangers but spoken from beyond, then to actual conversations I was having face to face with people's higher selves, it could have all seemed. I had paranoid delusions that people were part of a huge conspiracy talking in code about me or to me, or that spiritual power unleashed the potential to communicate via the signals of the world's ordinary events with higher order conscious entities. I began to rationalize how parallel streams of existence could take place, like being half-dead, with the physical world's normal, fairly predictable mechanisms being employed in extraordinary communication from beyond. The wind and rain could convey intense moods of astonishing synchronicity with my internal (e-)motions and thought.

I would faintly, or strongly, perceive in certain moments how every single double meaning I perceived in otherwise ordinary circumstances could have been contrived in a poetic context and confabulated on the spot. However, in an instantaneous and spontaneous fashion, the meanings just arose in my head indefensibly at most times. I didn't need to try, and it hardly "worked" if I did "try" to make it happen. When it would not happen, I would be a subdued normal me with my ordinary world, kind of despairing about how empty my connections to others were. When it would happen, I could think fast in my personal train of thought while a lot of sensory and conceptual stimuli would randomly affirm, deny, or in some way the world seemed to respond like I was actually interacting with an independently thinking mind.

Do you know the strong and sometimes amazing feeling of being addressed, having your eyes looked into, or being physically stimulated by another human being? I do not mean by an automated recording. I mean the feeling of actually knowing that the person beside you talking to you is actually a real, conscious being and conscious of communicating across the connection with you. This seems to me to be strongly a bodily apprehension, as much as it is some intellectually simple thoughtful recognition that "*you are with someone.*"

I don't mean a simple sense like the one that recognizes your personal objects in your bedroom or bathroom. One can hardly relate to a toothbrush like the connective and attentive attribution of personhood can create relation of one conscious to another conscious. In my out-of-hospital between sorts, I sometimes could not escape this feeling of directly apprehending a conscious entity in deep contact with me. Even when walking by a radio that was on or walking by some strangers talking, I felt immediately and personally addressed.

Because I could not stop the seeming exchange of meaning when I wanted to and could not make it happen by choice when I wanted to, but since I also felt it so often and it felt so genuine a connection to conscious intelligence, I thought I had compelling reasons to assume the world or I had transformed or become reborn. It didn't help that a lot of "new age" (and old age!) religious thought affirmed my delusions, considering demonic possession, ethical judgment from above, and all manner of religious fluff that intentionally dismisses and self-assuredly denies the claims of science. But for a while, the strangeness of my experiences began to make too much sense to me as genuine conversation with God or some such hyper-conscious entity.

Now, I don't want arbitrarily to join the side of close-minded intellectual scepticism to all deemed to be paranormal, supernatural, or spiritual, but I admit I had almost no scepticism for a while. I do know it is too difficult a task for me to try to weasel now how part of my experience might have been the result of some genuine spiritual agency and how part was simply an unreal nightmare/dream. There is hardly any way to sort or test it now, but I have totally discarded the idea that this world and human society, with its ways and manners, is a grand illusion or hallucination.

In another vein, because I could not stop the "exchange" when it happened, parallel processing or multitasking between ordinary meaning and 'hypermeaning' became second nature. I could do both, but it was indeed much more heart-warming to think of my family and friends as real human entities in themselves like me. That provided a compelling reason to affirm and find the truth out about the independence of minds and matter in the universe. I developed a sceptical impulse toward the entities from beyond, and I contemplated my parallel processing, poetic inclinations, and the times when the experience wasn't going on by its own and I was trying to force it to proceed. I eventually, gradually realized it was highly possible that the majority of my weird sensations were simply internal streams running parallel to the actual, independent reality. I realized I could have a fast enough mind for it, actually.

What finally broke my grip on the thought that my world and friends and family were puppets for a spirit master was the recognition of disgust for not being able to hold a normal conversation. Especially when I started again to believe with certainty that I hadn't died and that Earth indeed had humans just as real as me living on it, I could no longer believe that some entity was puppeteer for everything under the sun. So when I still could not stop the apparent communications, I became somewhat depressed. It probably took me a year to get back on track with knowing myself to be fully alive and never dead, but the exchanges of meaning unfortunately persisted and took a lot longer to fade out.

The conversations that felt out of this world, regardless of my attributing any or no reality to them, did usually seem to be a constructive learning game. I felt that I was actually learning about myself and about the world in various ways. That's probably why it lasted longer than my belief in it had wavered. I could still perceive the warm reception of a mind that understood everything about me, even if I knew at the same time my friends, family, and the various other media of communication were entirely self-inspired by their own free will, and were naturally contained with precedent within the order of our world. I felt like I could learn by a metaphor game that I thought my brain could play, safely. However, it was a long transition with a strong tendency for flip flopping on my various delusional alternatives.

I could sometimes augment but not totally direct my experience at will, so patterned responses like delusion formation were still present, throughout my trailing doubts. I was subject to irregular and incorrect beliefs that continually shape-shifted and revolved with one another, because I did not have a clue really of what could be the source of some of the meanings I felt were being contorted out of the TVs and my environs or social surround. Sometimes, the meaning felt with such an intense degree generated outside myself and self-involved that I could not shake the feeling of being talked with.

Sometimes I went from this stimulus to that stimulus while real sounds, words, and visuals around me were the most perfectly coherent and thoughtful points of dialogue with my own inner thinking to myself. My brain moved at light speed taking in stimuli from random sources in the manner of conversing with foreign entities. The delusions would not abate until the experience did, which took years. All through it I was sceptical, as I have mentioned, half the time believing my communications were simply a result of my hyperactive and poetic cognition.

So the last few pages have been a very general description of my symptom experiences in the time after my first hospital stay. I was diagnosed safe to walk out the hospital doors, but I had kept it from my first psychiatrist that I thought a spirit was informing me through her words to me that my meds would help me stay on the level enough to play and remain indefinitely half way between my nether and normal life. I only ever half thought it you see. I did tell her I still felt the triggers to delusions that were full force in my psychotic break and not yet doubted and discounted, but I was trying to be clever and figure it all out without letting people know the secret interaction. That might get me more medicated, which at the time following the first round with psych wards, I did not want. So the next few pages will be a tale of the social experiences I had in the years preceding, you guessed it, my second psychotic break and hospitalization in the summer of 2006.

It was four years steady enough to hold it together, and the story getting to the second falling through illuminates how schizophrenia's turns and toils have uniquely played out for me. I mentioned university plans. That was still on my agenda, but I decided I would take a year off to cool off and get more stable before starting my post-secondary education. So at the beginning of October 2002, I was feeling pretty slick, having got my memory back and realized I had emerged into the clear of the sick relationship with that individual, had enjoyed Burning Man, and had a slew of new psychological abilities unleashed in the wake of my psychosis. I felt liberated, but the oncoming years of folding halfway between delusional tendency and coherent mental order would off and on trouble me. My symptoms became a persistent compulsion in the background.

The internal schizophrenic condition can be like the deepest, darkest maze of confused ideas and feelings, involuntary or self-amplified and subtle or intense hallucinations, and energetic hardship, in no particular order. Feeling halfway between visionary and utterly lost can be normal, as the course of the mind and body oscillate.

Chapter 8
In the World, In Myself

There were cracks most of way through the tattered and shining octopus skin of my inner organism. I lived those months after hospitalization as an infernally driven, internally focused observer-intellect-artist, earning my conscious living at play every day on a panoramic work site. It was the plane of my most personally intense schizophrenic behaviour: getting lost in the altered state I will hereby describe as Interpretation Nurturing Significance Apparently Near Earth. The INSANE void, my body floating in an allegorical poem performed by TVs, books, and gods in the radio: mystical significance near, beneath, and inside what I knew to be the literal structure of reality.

I cannot emphasize enough, even with my flowery language, the compulsive pressures to accept incredible make believe stories in different regards about this symptom. The experiences of feeling, perception, and thought were so strange that I felt the need to theorize in order to explain what I felt couldn't have originated in my own brain. I came to resist less forcefully the incomprehensible, evidence dismissing manner in which delusional processes interacted with hallucinatory processes. Less resistance obviously helped both survive. A hallucination, mind you, is not merely sounds, sights, and textures, and a delusion is not merely a belief. They are not the same thing, but they are often confused in people's way of speaking about it, in my experience.

They are those, and also in my experience they can be similar in content but more different in how they feel to play out. Thoughts on whole can jump into the head in a certain phrasing, not quite fully audible or very similar at all to more stable thought patterns, which generally feel much more volitional than automatic and intrusive. "Delusional" content hence can start forming in what is more like a "hallucination" of thoughts and feelings that aren't logically connected but which impress on a faltering mind in convincing ways like perceptions do, without being consciously thought through like a problem. After delusions are 'formed,' often simultaneously with hallucinations which "happened," they may take on a force in virtue of the choosing mind's power to hold on to its beliefs with unquestioning faith.

In addition, there are probably other 'sensory' and 'conceptual' manners than the ways normally construed in the language of both our sciences and popular vernacular, so influenced as they are by dualistic concepts, monotheistic tendency, materialism, and secularism For instance, are thoughts perceived or do they arise by act of the intellect? Is what our senses tell us distinct from ideas?—Do we have ideas, consist of ideas, or contain ideas?

Or does the thought that "we have a mind" just sound redundantly true, while actually false, and our body may be the only idea we are? While this all may sound like philosophy speak, it is, and it is true that people who spend a long time thinking about these nuances usually have thoughts which sound confusing to most people who don't.. But these nuances make for complex experiential events which involve the manifestation of hallucination and the construction of delusion, simultaneously, with plenty of interactive process and development.

For instance, I don't think the feeling or sense of talking to someone face to face is entirely identical to the idea of talking to someone directly. When a schizophrenic converses with voices in the head or feels the radio might be talking to them personally, that sense of *being addressed* may present as incredibly prominent. Talking to aliens, one's higher self, or to God, seems to be halfway between schizophrenic hallucination-delusion and ordinary new (and old) age spiritual and religious experience. In any case, having an experience of being 'with' some other mind is common across cultures and not only reserved to when other human beings or even animals are immediately in attention—or to insanity.

I could constantly feel like I was in the throes of being addressed by the environment through physical sense signals and in thought and emotion signals. Sometimes I assumed no difference between the nature of external signals and the status of my own subjective, conceptual-emotional responses. A voice from the radio or a word internally freely associated could do for me as both meaningful streams of consciousness or as communication. In the months post-hospital, I bounced from watching TV, hanging with friends or family, to surfing the internet, to listening to music, to simply letting "my own" thoughts surface in bouts of meditative absorption; all the while I felt and thought I was in a learning game or living encyclopaedia which could transmit from some unidentified source intense content whose comprehension involves a great sense of revelation. I lived through and orbited around meaning.

Before the fall of 2003, when I started school at what was Malaspina University-College and has become Vancouver Island University, I toyed lots with cutting off meds for a day or two here and there. I also entered a relationship with my first girlfriend and worked a couple jobs. I also did a lot of bad drugs. I stopped taking psychedelic hallucinogens because I felt they too powerfully compromised what stability I barely had. But other drugs, from marijuana, alcohol, a bit of ecstasy and quite a bit of crack-cocaine were a grotesque way to regulate my state. I would go up higher on a party night as the feeling of being in a story about me accelerated. I would lose almost all ability to have a lengthy conversation, and I would do more drugs and get messed up even more. I would lose focus of reality in many dimensions, but then would wake up Monday and go away from the party for a week or two in a subduing daze of non-accelerated consciousness.

Maybe because I was under the influence of so many drugs when the feelings were more intense, and because I would have way less 'world poetry' outside the drug abuse environments, I came to think more readily that the phenomena of feeling addressed in every signal and word whether meant for me in any way indicated a personal cognitive ability being heightened by the drugs. It seemed normal to me to have a hyperactive mind, but I still thought also that there was a mystery in how the endless chatting that goes on at parties always could seem to be about me, to whatever degree accelerated neuro-chemically by doing drugs or skipping meds, both in my case examples of drug abuse.

As much of the time was a blur of disassociated sensation, chemical behaviour, and internal narrative, my memories of the time after hospitalization and before school started are quite discombobulated. I have several memories, but can't put them in a linear sequence. I just rode along, basically. The particular delusions that I went thru I have partially discussed and surely they are interesting to read for someone interested to read about schizophrenia, but my most significant conscious reason for elaborating on them in this text is that I believe the recovery of a schizophrenic from his or her shambled and often acute psychotic breakdown requires great attention to abating the delusional wake of the psychosis. Delusions and some (especially vague and conceptual) hallucinations did not go away as the overt visual and auditory hallucination dissipated. In light of what cannot go away on its own, the active behaviour associated with such reticent and especially subtle processes can yet not dissipate.

Early intervention plays a role in the prognosis of schizophrenia. If a first psychotic break can be deterred, for instance, then a great number of symptoms may not arise in the first place meaning the amount of work needed might diminish in setting the course to secure sanity. I slowly deteriorated in the last years of high school, setting into place several types of behaviour and cognition which would wreak havoc when I began to be delusional and compelled to find resolutions for the problematic tension building inside me.

I could have been caught earlier, before my psychotic break, but it is no fault of anyone. Definitely an increased general awareness in the society about what schizophrenia is and how a person can take hold of it may have been very beneficial for my general outcome; anyway, some people are very good at holding up appearances against the pressure.

I know from discussions with people that for a long time I seemed to be okay enough and just a bit off—though getting weirder—and all was fine until the pressure finally surmounted.

Holding up appearances against pressure needs more discussion. I can reflect on memories of drug partying with Idea Nurturing Significance Apparent Near Earth. Sometimes my mind reeled on world-denying solipsism and a martyr complex. I had no clue what to think of the intruding sense that everything referred to me. (Psychologists call them delusions of 'grandeur' and 'self-reference,' but as I have implied and somewhat directly eluded, there is an aspect to this kind of "delusion" that is straightforwardly more hallucinatory and sensual than idiomatic of belief, idea, interpretation, and verbally articulated 'theory'). Nonetheless, it did not get in the way.

I was, and other schizophrenics might be, able to deal with a *huge* systemic array of bizarre and aberrant perceptual and cognitive functioning, all the while holding up a conversation with a real person in three-dimensional real space. I wasn't as healthy as I appeared. I could interact along the lines of delusional self-reference very well while uttering sensible, coherent, and appropriate responses to a conversation while the responses of both conversant and of me still eerily waxed metaphors of supreme divinity in my mind. It wasn't ALL the time, but most of the time I was thinking about it and hence looking for metaphor actively when it didn't just streamline in. Some schizophrenics have paranoid conspiracies about things like the CIA and religion that might be very resilient to meds.

Whatever the believed context for schizophrenics' delusions of self-reference, in some way they are, I would say, uncontrollably hallucinating the sense of being addressed or implicated in whatever situations. They follow that sense by taking an active role in the cognitive process perhaps best described as a stance of prosecution. Sides of argument and evidence are considered and out of that a narrative account of the symptoms of experience are derived that otherwise do not picture legitimately into the shared and actually inhabited reality. Severe schizophrenics, in diligent response to their initial motions, simultaneously act as witness, defence, jury, and judge in face of the confusing, cognitive injustice they commit and are victim to in the existential predicament of a twisting mind.

Reality falls apart for the afflicted while she or he scrambles to make a case that can win over the conflicted testimony from all sides both internal and external, especially when a sense of huge conspiracy and journey reigns. Such was my fate in a perturbed condition; I was left adrift in a torrential storm of contradicting and powerful currents. I felt alone and didn't reveal the severity of my condition to my doctor or to anyone else, so I effectively left me alone to combat the waves of my symptoms without either ambulance or personal floatation device.

In time I would develop devices of reason which I would first organize then confront my diverse experiences with, which (to summarize) range across: 1) delusional preoccupation with issues related to society to which my response basically stemmed from a *deep* Deep Ecology perspective (look up Arne Naess); 2) playing in various language activities including the makeshift imaginary conversation games I wrote about and the writing of journals and poems ranging from autobiography to philosophy; 3) imagining talking with gods, to put it most succinctly, or sharing INSANE consciousness with ancient and alien intelligence that seems to inhabit the chains of causality, to put it elaborately; but also 4) a host of those which belong to the negative symptoms of schizophrenia. The negative confronted the active processes running on. There was left a wake of delusions and involuntary mental processes of the relatively severe psychosis, but a lull affected me and energy went down.

The negative symptoms, such as perturbations in emotion (there can be untoward lack or excitation of affect), avolition or the lack of motivation which affects social and personal behaviour, and speech disturbance, all found me here and there. When particularly dulled and unmotivated, my speech could slow down and I would tend to be quiet and be unresponsive. That was rare, as I usually have a busy mouth, but sometimes I just find it hard to come up with what to say. I take in the meaning of what's been said to me, but can't find a way to easily output my response. Especially this happens when discussing emotional and interpersonal issues in a serious, personal conversation. I do have deep emotions, but in some way they don't come either to the light of language unless I slow way down in my speech or to bright, energetic feeling unless I'm closer to a psychotic state.

An intellectual recognition of the negative disability I faced, along with the intellectual recognition I had since grade 12 that I probably had also the positive symptoms of schizophrenia, put pretty well in check the notion that my experience was verily otherworldly. I had strong doubts while my post-psychotic perspective on metaphysics and spirituality was constructed over several long months specifically in order to rationalize my strange thoughts, feelings, and sense of communication and meaning.

My ingenuity alone in making up potential rationalizations was in time a help in raising doubts, because I could entertain such a large number of simultaneous explanations, such as being a ghost in an afterlife, being contacted by God, breaking thru illusory physical causality to communicate with spirits, or finally I might simply be hyper-cognitive in the sense that my bizarre and complex experience stemmed totally from within me while the world was still the same old world. This last option was not tantalizing in terms of the cognitive dissonance of feeling so strongly like some*one* addressed me directly, but it was a much stronger contender than several of my so-called plausible justifications.

It is important that I had doubts; I think sane insights saved me. Perhaps the medication only went so far, because I didn't report the delusions to my doctor, family, or peers and hence no one increased my medication dose, but perhaps the mind's power of choice and effort maligns to arbitrate, regardless of dosage, in part by force of what the intellectual reason 'passes' with an 'A+.' Dosage is at least in many ways unrelated to decision making about thoughts. I suppose very generally it is a sure necessity, in dealing with a wide range of conditions of mental illness, that the intellect, effort, and choices have a role to play in assisting the afflicted.

Mental resilience and high functioning prior to my psychosis helped me defend against the stressful predicament I also found myself contributing to, post-break, by will. Before going to university I came to recognize that I could not very well go on in my daily affairs under so many delusions and near delusions as I had. I took an independent effort from any official treatment plan to work to rationalize my interpretations in terms of being ill. I knew I was ill, but I still had an open mind to much more than I do now. My worldview was, albeit confused in deep ways, sophisticated enough to keep me primed for 'extraordinary' communication signals. In addition, I could still at that time easily lose phase with the semantics of a word stream, effectively doubling the apparent meaning of things as I've described like a spirit was in control of things.

I can render (or articulate) my semantic phasing in terms of performing a role in or reading an allegorical play. I might for a minute or two, attention suspended, play apart from the worldly content and context of the experience while at excessive rates my brain somehow 'got' a profound stream of ideas, insights, metaphors. At a moment of question, had it come, I would have been able to wax philosophically about any phrase and run off in a huge number of imaginative directions with it.

At first in post-psychosis, after it had indeed developed to its full unintended thrust, it was uncontrollable. I would be in a storybook fantasy classic epic sci-fi with me in the world at centre focus. Later, in gradual time scales and in morphing dimensions of quality, the inability to keep away from moment to moment allegorizing with its sense of divine intervention shifted deeply. Eventually I would sometimes have trouble avoiding a watered down sense of intervening external minds in my phasing of the meaning. Other times I would simply have the phased meanings apparent to me, without a driving sense of intervening agent.

The doubt I spoke of previously definitely contributed to the watering down, but the practice had ingrained devices of interacting with language and environmental stimuli (as though it were language), disposing me to be quick with my mind, which had always been quick. The extreme initial experiences quickly blew "ordinary" totally out of the water. It was like being a savant of literary and psychological analysis. The meanings flashed by in such quick succession but I would at least feel like struck by insight. Citing and only slightly editing a line in a poem I wrote in this era, "dancing the form of meaning flashed the form of meaning flashing…"

By *form* of meaning, I think I mean the overarching purpose for some exchange of meaning as well as the semantic structure and content of a particular meaning. I don't mean the medium for the meaning, the external signals, words, and bodily and mental sensations, which all realized the meaning in multiple ways in an arbitrary way. Basically any signal I could be conscious of might pass before an incredibly powerful linguistic lens while simultaneously being decoded for its real world significance.

At first, I interpreted or felt the flood of meaning as not possibly a personal manifestation, but rather a beamed message. I doubted much of my experience but only strengthened the ease of the habit's occurrence until I would learn to exert doubt upon the phased signals instead of enjoying the facilitating of the conscious stream with effort. Whatever doubt I had at first was only another thought out of hundreds flashing in my head.

So far in the course I'm depicting, these descriptions may exaggerate the predicament of the first year after hospitalization. There was a lot happening inside me that I could not control well, but I also kept it together very well. I thought I might have been in an afterlife or in the INSANE world (my world of "interpretation-nurturing significance apparently near Earth," to remind the reader) of minds and forces of causation beyond what is physically determined and willed by independent agents. All the while, relentlessly nevertheless, I also 'got' ordinary reality. One foot danced on clouds while the other was stuck in mud.

I became adept, to repeat what I've said before, in parallel processing such that I could totally comply with the ordinary rules of the context I found myself in, supplying 'correct' information by speech when it was asked of me, no matter that my own responses also fit into a metaphorical reading and seemed to come from without me instead of within. It became effortless for a while to live in two minds that each seemed up to the task of the two foci, the literal or actual experiences in the world and the figurative and metaphorical interpretation that felt like communication. It was so, so very weird to participate in a conversation with a friend or in my class discussions in first year of university while concurrently registering an independent sphere of allegory and revelation resident to a sentient mind or minds that could somehow share causality and piggyback onto literal reality.

It's amazing I got nearly straight As with just a couple Bs while participating in the whacked out conspiracies of a chaotic spiritual education: props to the radical efficiency of parallel processing. I did "live my life" and participate in what sociologists might define as a "role" and/or "status," but I was always thinking on another level at the same time. It's still like that, really. Sometimes it was, and often still is, as innocuous "another level" as the curiosity about nature I had as a child. By that I mean I might often pay close attention to how I feel and to what the context of certain actions may be when interacting with someone or performing some activity by myself. I can "live my life" while at the same time I am thoughtful about dimensions of meaning and relation across multiple contexts.

In the time following diagnosis entering into my first year at university, I was very absorbed in my bizarre emotional, physical, and intellectual experiences, but I was fairly "high functioning." Between my INSANE 'telespiritual' experience of strange, powerful beings, on the one hand, and my ongoing refinement of philosophical and scientific ideas about the world and my place in it, on the other hand, I had a variety of bad habits of self-referential fixation on contextualization and communication. To speak for a moment about the writing of this chapter, I have with repetition through different and related wordings emphasized the bizarreness of my symptoms to give a rounder picture to those who cannot relate.

For those with a mind for analyzing beyond these words, I hope the multiple perspective detail of how it felt and what seemed to be going on will provide clues for more elaborate reflections. The functions of the mind (such as intellectual reasoning, abstract sense of communication and personality, as well as involuntary thoughts and sensations) relate to one another as the schizophrenic attempts to 'sort through and figure it out.' Of course there may be nothing very special to figure out.

I wouldn't recommend a schizophrenic westerner to run away to the deep South American jungle to join a mushroom cult. However, cultures outside the West have their own descriptions for psychological conditions that the West labels 'schizophrenia,' as well as their own methods of healing and integrating the affected individuals into healthier positions. They might not use a "mental illness" conceptual framework and "controlled normals" research methodology like Western psychiatry uses.

To try to get the individual into as "normal" a state as possible, and to consider that "healthy," attempting to make as "well-adapted" to an "abnormal" state as possible, may not be the focus or language in a non-Western framework. Another framework is possible, one that aims to transform the suffering schizophrenic into something like a skilled artist. I do not mean that all schizophrenics should strive to be artists, which is absurd. I mean rather that some schizophrenics would do well to *manage the unwelcome* perceptions, delusions, and social behaviours and *build on talents* like their ability for free association of thought and language.

I definitely recommend nourishing the intentional ability to construct perceptions. As an example of intending to modify one's perceptions, in case that is unclear: as a dabbling electronic musician since around 2005, sometimes I work with headphones late into the night on a single song, going over different takes and different parts of the song, tweaking them for a long time to get it just right. I laid down to bed once in late 2007 around 4 AM with a song more than stuck in my head. It was a bit like a tune stuck in pattern but it was very audible and sounding, and the music became very spontaneous and self-directed. The sound related to the music I was working on, but became much fuller than my notation or piano playing ability can translate. Imagination became the primary driving force behind pitch, timbre, and rhythm, of raw consciousness become etherial instrument, playing powerful, inner music.

This experience in 2007 was particularly intense,

primed after focusing consciousness for a long time on tangible sound waves. This inner instrument gets louder sometimes than other times, and is not completely disconnected from what makes me schizophrenic. While certainly "abnormal" in one or the other perspective or scientific discourse, it also feels completely healthy for me to hear music in my head. In short, all that is schizophrenia goes beyond the mere idea of illness. While hearing voices in my head who are angry will frighten and disturb, hearing music improvise in my head can relax and inspire me.

Experiencing the goings on of severe symptoms has indeed frightened, troubled, worked, and incited me in numerous ways which I can safely guess I would never have any sense of had I possessed "normal sanity." I recognize my personality traits have come to manifest my sense of self *as* schizophrenic, because schizophrenia has many peculiar characteristics which are rare enough that the experiences have composed a major aspect of my sense of identity. I know the medical profession has a motivated approach of "not identifying with the illness" so I am identifying with the basic strength and constructive abilities in my brain. Yes, all sorts of weird stuff happened *when* I did happen to be *ill*, but it feels like a cop out to say "I recovered and *now* I'm creative, open minded, and quick witted, and *no longer* schizophrenic." Now I feel like a *healthy* schizophrenic, rather than feel like I am normal or recovered.

However, it did take time to reel from the shocking experience of my first intense and severe psychosis and put together a set of healthier cognitive behaviours. After 2002, my delusions were very powerful regardless of my composure in day to day life. I had to slowly develop my powers of resistance toward the uncanny habits and patterns—which certainly were illness and abnormality—that were left in the wake of intense psychosis. Because the initial triggers of my particular anxiety and preoccupation never for a second went away, for a long time my taut heartstrings would ride stressfully between delusion and subtle hallucination weighing on one shoulder and the self-doubt and intellectual defensive mechanisms weighing on the other.

There were a few successful years of university after diagnosis, but clinging to barely enough sanity turned out not quite as successful. I would see another hospital psych ward in mid 2006. Again I would see stress forcefully pull psychosis out of me. Again the chaotic would throw me into the most intense impulses and hard to control emotions, thoughts, and perceptions.

Again I'd have to piece together a tough response, gather my senses and wits about me, and integrate new behaviours to work with new situations. In the next chapter, I will explore up to that second major hospitalization, covering the first half of my university education. In many ways it was ongoing tug-of-war between sensory perceptions and intellectual models.

The old irregularities of high school either remained or transformed into my time at university, so I was not in remission but had a fully chronic form of psychosis—a seasoned schizophrenia of great power, deceptively subdued and pushed to the background.

Chapter 9
On Reheating Leftovers and the Nutritional Deficits of Microwave Cooking

Why would anyone reheat a leftover word salad? They are not nutritious in any sense of a food, to begin with, and should be served cold instead of microwave-wilted, but I was a brand-new schizophrenic, living-on-my-own, with university student status. I thought I could make do on regular fillings of leftover word salad like some first year students away from home at school imagine a box of wheat, salt, and milk solids culture, with sugary ketchup, constitutes a square meal. The toxins of microwave-reheated word salad leftovers from my onset psychosis would of course accumulate and linger as a plaque of odd moods and thought disturbances in my conceptual arteries.

I'm glad I did eat and cook healthy real food for myself when I started post-secondary school. I might have been worse off and more susceptible to the normal stress I was facing going back to school and the strange stress of reeling from strange states while learning to manage the normal stress I had dealt with for, well, forever. Any scepticism I had was healthy enough that I was mostly able to keep together enough focus for each day, but underneath the gloss of everyday mental routine, a huge pile of leftovers chilled on the verge of putrefying. There were delectable arrays of delusion and half-pints of hallucinatory brew leftover from psychosis season's holiday partying, which were refried again and again in my private attention and reflection. I probably should have thrown them all out much sooner, but I didn't know how to.

I did keep my open mind, even if doubt was just strong enough to keep me from dwelling headlong into the delusion. I didn't know what to believe after having cycled through so many belief systems in the past few years before university started, except that as a new student I was very focused on my physical health, eating nutritious food and going to yoga classes when I could, and on my mental health, learning lots every day in class and meditating often. I was often contemplating past experiences of psychological weirdness and chaos, which provoked me to preoccupy to a large degree on promoting my mental and physical health. However, there was a rhyme to those preoccupations and contemplations: I was still stressed out, more or less, and still had persistent delusions.

Additionally, my delusional thinking was persistent because the narrative accounts and theories that I had for the strange beliefs were convincing. My perceptual experience often gave me the feeling I had evidence for the beliefs. Even on the medication, the susceptibility to 'think freely' was not eradicated. I may get headaches, but sometimes my mind would grow 'looser' and I would contemplate and revise the old weird theories. It didn't help the delusions, that my mind seemed to move either very excitably or very sluggishly, both of which are stated as my medication's side effects.

I think it is something about schizophrenia's aetiology of characteristics and symptoms that the conscious brain quite easily accelerates what happens. The conscious brain does this by putting before the attentive focus in compelling ways what are otherwise subconscious or unmade connections between ideas and perceptions. I believe the schizophrenic mind can sometimes work so quickly, integrating subconscious free associations and hard to understand perceptions into obtuse narratives, that even when the medication is 'working' as well as it can, the power of the conviction in the conscious, intentional system counteracts the 'balancing' or whatever happens when taking pharmaceuticals.

Thus, pairing the unhelpful side effects of medication with no intentional development of insight will only serve to intensify the energy and drive of the brain for chasing chaos. The therapeutic tactic of medication seems futile in respect to the nature of the symptoms. It takes something cognitive, intellectual, and emotional to really intervene upon the conscious desires for behaviour which corroborate with persistent and false, (or also true but obsessive), conscious beliefs.

I'll give the medication *some* positive appraisal for reducing the forceful habits my brain had for pursuing its strange paths and for helping me sleep and not strongly hallucinate. I must emphasize though that my beliefs and desires were never budged by the pills in any regard. I feel that my thought disturbance was always less affected by medication and more exacerbated by the emotional and cognitive habits I took on. Medication increases my zombie mood and replaces far-ranging thought with cloudy headaches, but reheating the leftover delusion and anxiety always feels natural.

That's because these symptoms emerge from stress and preoccupation concerning myself, society, and reality, as explored in earlier chapters. It feels harder than impossible to shut down my natural, voluntary inclinations. So in early university, I had to contend squarely with the old, very delusional beliefs and my rapid-fire mind, for the time being. I was still basically convinced. Like always though, besides the times I spent deep off my rocker in clinical psychosis, I kept the severity of my bizarre experience far out of sight. I think I had an otherwise outwardly "normal" beginning to my university education.

First year, I took a general assortment: two calculus classes, the first-year English course pair that most students are required to take, first year canadian sociology, first year physics, and some philosophy courses. The discussion-based classes were highly populated, but there was time for anyone who wanted to say something to have a small chance. I piped up most in the philosophy courses, during my first year. I loved the diversity of perspectives and personal histories that discussion-based classes exposed me to. It was easiest to keep focus on reality, and be the least delusional, in my philosophy and English discussions.

I had, since release from the hospital, been silently dealing with the hallucinatory inner sense of being communicated with by some spiritual agency when I would watch TV, listen to music, sit in the wind on a cloudy day, or when I'd talk to real people. University classrooms were no different and often felt like mystical poetry slams, although I did as students usually do, writing down notes and participating. The most INSANE discussions occurred in the math-oriented courses, where the symbols and theorems shared by the professors were interpreted in their literal senses but were also bent by my mind into the weirdest poetry. My brain exploded every day, revelling in the mysticism of derivative slopes or integrating areas with infinite domain and infinitesimal limit. I was a weird first-year student!

'Counting small stones' in math class, poetically understanding calculus, and waxing philosophically every day like a first year philosopher-at-large while *sounding* confident—while feeling at the same time like I was stoned on LSD and talking to God—epitomizes adrenaline thrill seeking (and endogenous DMT-seeking, according to some studies). It epitomizes a level of danger for having a total relapse and breakdown. I was potentially back on my way to hospital at any time, given a chance distorted plan that led me to, say, stop my medication for periods in order to amplify the effects I was only half-trying to block out and resist.

Every sentence or stimulus I encountered was a potent and deep reservoir of meaning I could explore in the back of my mind while simultaneously processing details of philosophical ideas or excelling at figuring out intricate mathematical ideas (really, beyond my craziest expectations, I did as well as I possibly could for my first semester calculus course, see below). I amazed myself at how adeptly I could course subconsciously thru word salad and the sense that my environment was channelling intelligent thoughts to me, while placing myself on the Dean's list of honourable mention for academic excellence.

I never indicated to anyone, I am totally sure, that often my response in philosophy discussion was half-inspired by the extraneous subconscious suggestions my brain created. I guess it really was my modicum of doubt that saved me... Or the tantalizing ideas that my brain was working at warp speed while the feeling was I might have been actually contacting some intelligence. In all those otherworldly experiences, I imagined I might have been in a strange afterlife, or I asserted the autonomy of the world remained under my extra perceptions. Sometimes I had complete doubt, but more often I actually just thought about and contemplated the raw and cooked meanings I was gleaning. I felt like I was learning twice as much as my fellow student peers, taking in the actual schoolwork and also feeling like participant in a whole other world of communication and profundity.

    I had an edge: It is probably because I had some skeptical inclinations, and was never paranoid in the typical ways certain schizophrenics typically become, I was able to relax and just let the various theories and delusions intermingle and pass through the attention like people appear when moving quickly and rhythmically in and out of revolving doors when looking from across the street. Sometimes, if you wait around the same place often enough, you begin to see some of the same people and the same activities, and even say hello or get to know the people who frequent that zone you are also frequenting. The belief system washout and leftovers of my sicker time was always like always catching the same bus route at the same time back and forth from home. I went around in circles.

    Waking up in the morning was most usually the clearest, most symptom-free time I had in a normal day. The very first 'INSANE' moment usually came into clarity at a random moment when I walked past a blaring TV, would walk past a group in a conversation, or be captivated by printed text. These were both common events in student residence where I was living with about 15-20 people on one floor of a three-storey house. The first slightest strange association, hearing people talk about whatever random thing was occupying their moment, would take over my linguistic thought. At some point in the day the 'thought associations' would totally take a life of their own, and I wouldn't be able to block out the sensation or hallucination of a real and coherent, external consciousness in dialogue with me through the environment of people and every other sort of signal that my mind could 'hear quietly talking in phase with me.' The rest of my day would be a diligent weaving between real life and INSANE life.

Interpretation Nurturing Significance *was* Apparently Near Earth for nearly the whole time, in varying degrees, between the beginning of university in Fall 2003 and my re-hospitalization in Summer 2006. At base it was a persistent symptom that I managed to manage, so to speak. Its severity fluctuated with numerous factors, stress being a major one, but it seemed ever-present. It also felt natural, except I knew it belonged in the classification of 'symptom' even if the underlying tendency was simply being too prone, or more than most, to understand through meaningful metaphors. In general, if stress and other triggers ever arise, it gets messier and busier inside my head but the feeling of self doesn't radically change in manner until I go over the edge into acute psychosis.

The pseudo-hallucination of feeling communication occur between myself and absent sources of sentience was not always a part of my personal nuances and idiosyncrasies, but it quickly became a natural way of going about my day. If I wanted to coax the experience, I would just sit and watch TV or leaf through books at random and quickly feel transported. Eventually, I became able basically to phase in or out at will depending on the nature of the sensory input.

I could attend to the metaphoric understanding or the literal as I wanted. One clear limitation was poor performance in shutting off the background sense of the metaphoric while wanting only literal.

I could struggle and generally pick up the meanings in what I came to think of as the shared and direct reality of the world that others knew and experienced, but I felt trapped in a solely personal and indirect reality of something totally weird. Aberrant meaning would often make me gap out and miss bits of conversation or warp the intended sense of the words in experienced sentences. Hard to get away from it at times, I condoned it most others. Mainly I desired to shut it out when I wanted to make sure I clearly understood people. Often I wanted to have a conversation be genuinely meaningful instead of overwhelmed by excessive, alien meaning so tough to resist.

If nobody noticed me behaving strangely, it's because of how intricately adapted and adjusted I was to the simultaneity in my head of different flows of thought. Since childhood in my memory I have had a lot going on in my head. In high school in particular with gaining social and political awareness that I didn't know how to communicate, I became accustomed to following through any given day's calls to action while consistently being focused on great internal ranges of thought and emotion. That "symptom" has always been a weird and busy time, wading through all of my life's activities while feeling intensely self-conscious and always driven by a separate guiding thought prerogative and awareness of a whole bunch of random personal or philosophical stuff.

On any "normal" day of interaction from early high school and beyond, until recently gaining some integration, multiple layers always formed the basis of my memorable conscious experiences. I've actually always had poor memory of what happened to who and when in my time and company. I think too much about the how and the why rather than what seems to me usually more memorable to others: What people say at which occasions, what people would describe responding to 'what did you do when...' and rather 'plot-based' details such as these more often than not evade the grasp of my retrievable memory. Even when reminded by someone's urge that I remember and when provided reminder of details, sometimes I have to piece together the information as though I'm doing forensics and reconstructing a model of events based on best facts available.

Aberrant psychological behaviour is not unheard of in everyday, non-schizophrenic life, as it just may be part of general types of common, occasional neurosis to sometimes dwell self-consciously on personal interpretations of some event or interaction, especially when a situation 'fires the nervous system' but memory sits with meaning more that plot matter. Some people of course due to various stimuli go deeper and farther in certain directions and tendencies, and situations and behaviour can go in the direction of health problems.

Some fluctuate across a diverse spectrum of function and ability in the light of their mind's many manifestations. Until the summer of 2006, I fairly comfortably coasted through university on the shiny surface of a deep, strong, and many layered soup of psychological compulsion, preoccupation, and strange reflection. I feel like I long lived in a very delicate balance of mind and worldly activity. Until the summer of 2006, I managed to just manage school and the large cognitive load of lingering psychosis.

A revolving-door mind of delusion filled empty space left over in my days, and hallucinating communication with independent intelligences eradicated any possibility of boredom. And, with homework to do, and everyday college kid socializing to keep up with, I had rarely a moment where hours would spread out before me, nothing and no one obviously there to interact with. It felt quite the opposite. As explored in the early chapters, though, I've never been much for boredom, preferring to occupy my attention on anything while maintaining a curious interest in the process of every experience. Schizophrenia has certainly engaged my time.

Philosophy class by far held the most interest. I started school intending to perhaps become a high school teacher. By my second and third year, my course selections alone proved I was in a clear direction to philosophy. My first real discovery of 'academic philosophy' came in a book called *Philosophy: The Basic Issues* which covered a broad spectrum of issues, from epistemology, theology, materialism, freedom and determinism, to ethics and more, divided into commentary and relevant excerpts and short essays from the canon. I found it in my parent's bookshelf and fell in love with the philosophical: the curiosity and thirst for many trajectories of contemplation about the good life and the nature of being. I grew accustomed to university level philosophy instantly.

Vancouver Island University has some excellent instructors; classes always had very engaged discussions. By having daily class content informed by student spontaneity as much as or even more than by single-pointed lecture, classes were always very dynamic, the concepts and examples kept diverse, and learning often involved personal reflection and consistent mental arm-wrestling with the core ideas of each course. Values were questioned, we assumed surely impossible logic recklessly for the purpose of thought experiments, politically relevant issues sounded to rooms of uniquely informed adult minds, and all the good stuff happened one could expect in a focused, critical study of ideas.

In all this excellent activity, I yet faced my delusions and hallucinations often. The most intriguing moments were when classmates in a course discussing general ontological, metaphysical, or theological issues (e.g. absolute nature of reality type questions) would try to deny the existence of reality. The 'extraterrestrial' or INSANE intelligence that I felt often sit in on classes with me had a heyday during outright speculation of classmates (sometimes sincerely, sometimes as devilish advocacy) that all of reality as apparent was perhaps some illusion compared to a higher spiritual reality populated by different beings, angels or demons, and so on, within it. My theoretical, open mind was often wild with such a proposition that various forms of my experiences may have been explored in serious theories and paradigms by various philosophers, mystics, and poets of different ages.

I must have taken Descartes' thought experiment of the Evil Demon much more seriously than indicated by my reverential arguments in those classes for the idea of a genuine, understandable, and knowable reality. I certainly wanted to understand my reality. Ancient mystic and religious lore spoke of God speaking through events and synchronicity in the world to those who would listen. What if something like that indeed was happening to me? I wasn't prepared to be an absolutely close-minded skeptic to the tenets of the lives of many a saint and mystic of much historical repute.

Too much akin to it was in my perceptual and conceptual field to not entertain at least the possibility of actual spiritual-sentient possession of the otherwise random signals in my physical and social environment. In actuality, the philosophical treatment of such possibilities may have been one of the best things for my wandering, wavering belief system. The bit of skepticism I did have likely allowed me to explore the ideas as speculatively as possible rather than to obsess on them. It was compelling to entertain the notion that my experiences were founded in genuine appropriation of reality by trickster forces.

Maybe what saved me from going all the way to a severe messianic complex was my continuing best hope that people were actually people and the brain was actually phenomenally powerful enough to actualize all manner of personal experiences. To this day I don't feel totally philosophically comfortable with the materialist theories that totally denounce the notion of any conscious, animate principle as belonging to the deepest nature of reality. However, my open mindedness for theories in new age literature is not twisted enough to close my mind to materialist possibilities entirely.

In a world of infinite possibility, a schizophrenic's unique brain and psychological dispositions could present auditory and visual hallucinations that have literally no other source. It could be the subconscious in some random yet perhaps somewhat meaningful dialogue with the conscious self. I have no reason whatsoever to out and out deny contemporary psychiatry to affirm my feelings that 'spiritual guides' may have shared something during some points along the way. If I yet steadfastly do not despair and preoccupy over it, I'm just being a free thinker and am not having a worrisome 'symptom' as the history of sane religious/mystical experience tells. I find to guard myself from some of those thoughts for the best balance, I never close my mind arbitrarily. I like applying reason in these matters and not going to wayward faith recklessly.

It did interest me to discover in one of my research forays into the history of schizophrenia theory that as late as the DSM current in the 1960s one of the qualifying characteristic symptoms of schizophrenia was, in paraphrase, holding a belief contrary to the conventions of your local and family social upbringing. That is so vague and was later obviously scrapped in the revolutions of psychology and spirituality in the mainstream West that a definitive mark of insanity was to have a thought in outright dissent or even somewhat contrary of the mainstream traditional belief systems 'you should have.'

Nowadays, it has become a mark of individuality to think for oneself and build a belief system through personal reflection and reasoning that needn't be borrowed from your mother culture. It has become a mark of freedom that religion not be maintained violently under external threat. Medically treating people simply for having certain beliefs is tantamount to an ideology suppressing cultural dissent, unless having those beliefs is clearly putting that individual at objective risk of harm (like he or she is verging on 'legal insanity').

School was a very good thing for me in my time of long term confusion. I was exposed to different ideas than I would have revolved on under only my own conscious stream. I encountered generally sound and strong arguments from my environment that my weird experiences were my own inner complexity presenting under its own power the variously meaningful sensations. Indeed it turned out eventually to be something I just had to learn to live with. But until the disruption in 2006, my delusions and hallucinations were only under control insofar as they were not disrupting the rest of my social life. It was half frantic entertainment, half chaotic torment, during that first half of my university progress.

One interesting story comes from my first year, at the end of first semester during exam period. I remember part of the night fondly. I was having a particularly INSANE evening, and my calculus exam was going to be at nine o'clock in the morning. I remember one point going to make some food in the floor kitchen in my dormitory, and housemates were playing Dungeons and Dragons in the living room. It was the first time I had ever overheard such a game, and I didn't understand it properly. They all knew how to play well, and weren't stuck on the rules, so they were fully into the role playing aspect, laughing and describing what their characters were doing. This kind of linguistic activity contains lots of rich narrative flow and metaphor-ready concepts (like phoenixes and fairy dust, maybe). It was always just the type of literary content to strongly activate my perception that an intelligence was conversing with me.

So I made myself a meal that one of my friends in the game commented was smelling interesting and disrupting his character's battle sense, all in the role played prose. I laughed at that point, naturally enough. Already having had a random high energy day that left me reeling in symptomatic magical poetry, this game and the allusions that were revolving in my mind sent me to my room with my prepared meal in a kind of conceptual dizziness. I laid in bed for a while after eating, but as my habit was to listen to the radio a bit before sleep, I did that. On the college radio station, CHLY, there used to be on Thursday nights an amazing psychedelic electronic music show, that often had songs featuring interesting and 'trippy' spoken lyrics. That was on, and it tweaked my brain's energy further. I have no clue now what they might have been talking about that night, but it was wild to my ears. I wasn't going to be able to sleep for a while, or at least didn't force myself to try right away after that priming.

I started writing and thinking busily as I did sometimes. After priming from enough linguistic sources, sometimes I felt like the communication or connection to a disconnected mind continued without that symbol stream to back it up. I jotted down random notes and remarks, like those that began this book. Eventually, around four in the morning, it dawned on me that I had five hours to both sleep and then wake up to get in metabolic and mental gear for a three hour calculus exam. My brain went yikes! I began to fret and under that duress, it seemed even less likely I would get to sleep and have enough rest.

I ended up scrawling on the small pages of a notebook a four page letter to my math professor, which to this day I haven't looked entirely through again and mostly because I can barely read it. In it, I described how I had been having a rough night with my symptoms and didn't think I would be in a proper state to write any kind of serious math exam. After I wrote it, I decided I would lay awake (thinking I wouldn't sleep) until time to go hand my prof the letter. I quickly relaxed and passed out in bed, amazingly woke up at about 8:40 am, felt very calm and refreshed and went and wrote a test that earned a hundred percent score...

I've always loved math, but that was ridiculous even for me. I ended up not giving my teacher the letter, which was a 'good thing' in terms of me not being met by ambulance staff upon leaving the exam room, but that also kept what I had been through the last night hidden from open view. I lucked out to be calm the next day and take my medication and not go even more crazy. That was the high point of fear during my school times at tempting fate with my condition, but it wasn't the only time I was up most or all of the night reeling in the INSANE. That was a fairly regular occurrence, really, but came and went in its severity. I missed morning classes or was nearly falling asleep in them several times, often strung out during the day if I hadn't slept at all but had things I needed to do.

Even if I wasn't totally tripping out, I often would be up in the night just doing my normal routines of creative time/internet time. Sometimes though, I'd be in bed by 9 pm. It seems I have for a long time not been able to manage a regular sleep schedule. I think I sleep enough, I just don't often go to bed at the same time each night or at all on rarer nights; it's hugely variable, even now years later. I am not filled with the same or as persistent delusions as that time, but still have some active tendencies to be sleepless sometimes.

I associate 'creative impulses' with restlessness. Sometimes it is the creations of chaotic impulse, sometimes I'm just geared for fluid conceptualization, able to process quickly what in retrospect is a great deal of information. For instance, I just told a story about being awake all night frantically thinking about weird things and inability to keep functioning, just to sleep a short spurt and awake to write a flawless calculus exam. I do find math an easily approachable subject, but that I could process that mathematical information so smoothly while so recently possessed by angst and strange perceptions is a startling example of the connective powers and spontaneity of a schizophrenic mind.

The mind can become so alert, and perform so many gigaflops per second of attention to cognitive processing, that it can get carried away entirely with creating the chaos. It still surprises me sometimes that I can manage to feel so weird and to hold on just enough to maintain my sanity to the standards and expectations of normal social events. I manage while quite involved mentally with *something internal and vastly weird* and represent haphazardly the appearance of a half normal fellow, probably just tired-looking and baggy-eyed on a regular basis.

My mind gets to feel heavy with inertia and to careen on its own course, while my body supports the shapes that the social day requests of me. I have to eat, go to school, go to work, relax at home—all with a dedicated and contemplative spirit. No wonder the philosophy education is where university pulled me. In such a field, one gets to deeply contemplate reality and gets to be readily accepted and promoted for communication patterns that contribute to growth in understanding for the self and others.

Sometimes in tense communication times I find myself enduring weird moods and very subtle though frantic anxiety, for which I get called out on 'thinking too deeply about it' or 'not listening well.' I see contemplation as absolutely bottomless, and without absolute peak—an ever-rolling field which I can walk around to get to many different angles on the landscape and to receive different reflections of lights and the sounds living between the related motions of Sunlight, Wind, Rain, and Dust. I love the ideas that resound and shimmer deeply in the echo chamber or maze of mirrors we call the mind. But engaging in the most vague contemplations and noting only the echoes of ideas while really lost in my own maze—I really do "think too deeply," especially when I don't remember to "listen well" to my real emotions!

Consciousness is a vast environment of myriad forms and life forms, and confusion can be the best friend of insight. I think that's how I've written this book about insights: I'm mostly confused. It's hard for me not to say this in such a wordy way, but I think what I look for in my reaching for words and what I will not find is simultaneous fluidity and solidity in my raw ideas. This could be my oldest and most dangerous symptom: I obsess and preoccupy myself with the "right way to say something" when "I feel I have a point to make."

A 'single whole idea' always fills a range of frequencies and has a particular timbre and amplitude, accentuating various rhythms and harmonies, kind of like a 'single whole song.' A good idea is something like a good song playing back in your headphones: it is simple or complex and you might like it, it sometimes gets stuck in your head and you might like that, and it has a particular 'feel' and you might like this feeling when you 'share' in it.

It likely has a diversity of elements, parts and motifs that get elaborated into a structured arrangement over the time of performance, while it may have been severely edited by a huge team, re-recorded from scratch umpteen times, and duly processed by studio magic before reaching your headphones in its mastered delivery format. It constantly shifts in form and aesthetic during live performance but it can also—to past tense this topic—exist in an *idealized* 'recording.' We acknowledge this huge intersection of art technique, celebrity persona, and collaborative works of effort under the umbrella term of 'one song.'

An idea I would argue even constitutes rhythms and harmonies, as most ideas fall out of attitudes, interests, and perspectives. These are reinforced behaviours in many ways, giving our unique headphone mixes their habitual (well practised and oft performed) character as the groove of any idea plays itself out under the stylus of attention.... Repetitions, resonances, and highlights are what we hear.... I can continue the metaphor easily: many ideas are connected to other ideas, of course, so much so it can be hard to differentiate when *one particular point* of *one elaborated idea* isn't a whole idea which could be elaborated unto itself or to differentiate where one idea begins and the next ends. There are even *relevant random associations* galore! Parts of songs remind people of other parts of songs and parts of feelings and of places.

Hence the 'concept' or 'loop-ready' album (The Wall by Pink Floyd an excellent example of both). I also love even more exotic audiovisual art forms like postmodernism-influenced interactive installations, with variously arranged, distributed, and modulated visual or sound sources and processes. People would create such art for two main reasons, I figure: it's inherently valuable for the audience to react and interact, and it is a rewarding technical and creative discovery and novelty. The unique requirement is that all involved including the designers and participants must cooperate to succeed in pulling off the creative process of the artistic vision, unlike non-interactive art process where once painted it is just looked at. My most excellent example for the preceding description of interactive art goes to <u>Steve the Robot H.E.Ai.D</u>.: 'Human Energized Artificial Intelligence Device… with lasers and generative sound.'

The link here to what I was talking about before is that music and art is as public and available for consumption as wild thought. It appears that thought is a private principle, but I found my internal weirdness resonating with the history of thought of philosophers and mystics going back thousands of years. Like music is created, the soul and heart are strummed into articulate thoughts during improvisation, theory, and revision. The 'ideas' are beyond language alone, like music.

They are lyrics, timbres, and arrangements that may change between performance or context of performance, but they always 'sound like it.' And ideas are communal in the sense that once one is shared or delved into with another, it is open game like a pin on a hat that wasn't seen, but is now totally public upon being revealed by just a turn of the head. They can be seen or heard again, replayed, and even remade from scratch and profoundly altered.

Any individual with schizophrenia that experiences strange thoughts and far-reaching associations surrounding a specific delusion might feel stuck in a perpetual skip of the record accompanied by live improvisation. Something repeats absurdly with new material reflecting and coexisting upon that repetition. It may deepen and build in some ways but will remain at the same time frozen in static persistence in other ways. That is how I felt when sitting in the classroom listening to a random topic under discussion while inwardly interpreting greater significance than apparent to anyone else, as the feeling of denial or confirmation of delusion would skip, skip again, and keep skipping around in circles.

What a precarious position it is to be in, the nether region of persisting delusion, recurrent hallucinations and aberrant perceptions, ongoing compulsion to continue the journey to some kind of understanding. Between my first in 2002 and the second hospitalization in 2006, I was more myself than during the intervening psychoses, but I wasn't totally together and collected in a clear stability of self. I was perplexed by lingering symptoms, by deepening systems of thought about my condition and those symptoms, and by trying to fit into that mess a regular life as a young adult in university.

Having to contend with the stress of having a mind that deviates in its patterns of ideas and develops randomly into processes of internal significance is a risky place if there isn't enough self-discipline and self-organization. When I couldn't help myself out of it and would plunge through social events in a half-daze of otherworldly sentience, I wasn't what one should call 'mentally healthy.' This is the case even if some aspects of that behaviour remain, today, and if I am healthy, today. I was thinking about mystical experiences, for years, but instead experiencing aberrant thought and enduring a kind of stress that just held on, under an outwardly stable demeanour.

It was stable at least until the summer of 2006, when I began to become more inwardly captivated by the symbolic significance that appeared to my mind. I withdrew from social activities, didn't work that university summer break, and spent more time online at night than with my girlfriend at the time, who I lived with. Then another load of stress hit me, and a bad move on my part infused with emotional duress finally derailed me.

I didn't get a job that summer and I failed to get on government disability support. I was bumming around smoking tobacco, trying hard to quit it, and I had smoked very steady since first hospitalization. I smoked during the end of high school, more and more, and just before first hospitalization was the only other time I was possessed with trying to cut out tobacco. It's a weird thing that some stats run as high as stating that eighty-eight percent of schizophrenics in North America are smoking tobacco. I was also spending a lot of time that summer of 2006 online. The residual INSANE feeling of direct communication with 3rd party minds in random anywhere perceptions started to grow stronger, to be more like when I had been closer to fresh out of hospital for the first time.

Watching random videos, stories, songs, poetry, I was warping my consciousness to a more prominent degree than in previous years. The change was: I decided that instead of trying to avoid what was happening with force anyway I should try to move into it and co-opt it or put it to use. It was a bad idea, I think, because my sleep patterns, economic patterns, and relationships were all disrupted that summer. I walked the streets listening to my CD player or stayed up late on the computer leaning toward the delusional suspicion that I was talking with God, Gaia, or something no one else could sense. I got into it a bit much, in hindsight.

A friend was dying, of cancer, and unfortunately was smoking crack in the last few years of life. I went one weekend to see him knowing he didn't have a huge amount of time and binged with him with others, and needless to say, my mind exploded. Smoking crack and doing cocaine have never been good for my extreme schizophrenic symptoms, and they were devastating at this time.

Midsummer, after I was invited by a friend to go visit the one who was very sick, I hoped they weren't doing the drugs anymore. When I got there, I quickly resigned that it would hopefully be my last binge ever, because I crumbled. I got severely delusional about the 3rd party consciousness broadcast I detected and interpreted. I did quite a bit of the drugs and it worked only to overwhelm my already fragile psychological condition. I returned from that trip in a complete mess, and my girlfriend was shocked at my state. She warned my family I was in a very hard time, and a few days later when my dad made the trip to see me, he asked me a few questions. Then he quietly and thankfully asked if I would come with him to the hospital.

At that point, I was entering my floral phase, where I was easy to go along with any plan, so off to the hospital I went, not really comprehending that I'd be locked in a room that night, isolated under watch. Times would be rough again for a while. So ends this chapter for the next to begin. It will be the tale of entering the hospital early in July and leaving it in August in time to go back to university! It was a rough month of learning a lot about myself, getting over some big obstacles in my psyche, and gaining more determination to keep my mind stable, dynamic, and free from this stress in the future.

Chapter 10
When Mind Opens ...

My biggest question stemming from the summer of 2006 involves the extent to which the relapse would have been avoidable. It seems to work either way to conceive the subtle and increasing deterioration of that summer as the cause of the return to hard drugs, as it is to conceive the hard drugs as what pushed me over some precipitous edge. I think back that I was riding on a thin sliver of sanity and losing clarity and calm, and then drugs came back into the equation—my brain altered states until it was like 2002, once again, in my head. I re-entered the old situation, reeling from a drug binge and thrashed by paranoia, struck with the feeling of altered reality and otherworldly communication.

That summer, I avoided getting a regular job and spent most of my time on the computer and walking around listening to music on my portable CD player. The residual framework of delusions that I never actually committed to rest was on the rise the months after that prior semester. My INSANE antenna were starting to pick up broadcasts. I was listening to lots of music videos and interpreting all the lyrics like a personal storyboard like I did that intense night before the television during my brief esplanade out of the ward in 2002, when they thought I was good to go, just before I was sent back in for further tests. For the longest time I could not get over the appeal of INSANE communication. It was a lot of fun and I seemed to be alert, and that summer, it built in strength as I became more stressed out and sleep deprived. I was on a very low dose of my med, and my tolerance to stress was starting to exceed the bounds of reason and the threshold of all might.

My mind opened too far to the possibilities of my perception, and I let it get away from me. Compounding that with the stress of losing my friend described in the prior chapter and the drug relapse it involved, my mind lost its lid entirely, and everything steamed away until the saucepan was smoking. I'm glad I recognized that I had made a bad move by letting myself slip away from rationality and composure, because that recognition allowed me to accept that I had become sick again. I didn't plan on it being necessary, but when my dad came to my door and listened to me speak for a few moments then asked me to come with him to the hospital, I had no problem with the notion of another ward visit.

Back in the psychiatric institution, I would ride out the storm, damages, and reparation of my mind. The first night was chaotic when I realized I was being locked in a room for isolated observation in the ER ward before being transferred to the psych ward. My mind was running and I yelled a lot at people until I finally tuckered out and the medication set in. I was quite sickened with myself that I had done the drugs and messed everything up, but I was also moving a light year a minute, and the following weeks would involve going in and out of trance states and hallucinations. I had a few incisive delusions and preoccupations. For the first week and a half, I was certain I wanted a helicopter ride to the other side of Vancouver Island. Once, I imagined that I was about to be taken to said helicopter, but apparently I was being very erratic. I followed the nurses and security dudes down the hallway, totally stoked, and was led into the solitary isolation room under lock and key.

It was a weird time for sure. I was happy enough after I stopped asking to be let out. I practiced my cartwheels and did yoga and looked around the room. The most fascinating aspect of the room was the presence of vicious scratch marks all over the fibreglass windowing. They were not random at all. There were symbols everywhere scratched in by prior tenants in their dazes and storms. The most profound of these to me was a two-sided image, the left half said Zeus and the other half was a lightning bolt, and this was superimposed upon a face with long, wavy scratched in hair.

This was profound because I knew of Julian Jaynes' work of anthropological psychology, *The Origin of Consciousness in the Breakdown of the Bicameral Mind* (1976), in which he makes an argument, to summarize briefly, that abstract self-consciousness has evolved only since roughly 1200 BC. Before that point, Jaynes claims that ancient people had "bicameral minds" where language and consciousness operated according to automatic habits more than out of individual self-reflection. Jaynes supposed that the reason the ancients mythified their world with gods and animate qualities was because the experience of consciousness and language wasn't necessarily thought of as created by the internal self. The idea was that their experience of their mind was as though the content were being created and transformed, indeed communicated directly, by the outer environment.

Meta-reflection, and a sense of perceptions as internally generated by influence from an outside, could at any rate be considered a phenomenon that had to have had a beginning, and perhaps a livelihood of only more advanced and complex life forms. It might be what humans received from the glory of Nature's long mutation, selection, and what obviously from shamanic rites to modern day coffee and cigarettes, has been steadily increasing environment modification and the intentional altering of internal states and our neural-chemical environment. Self-consciousness would blow someone's mind, to have it for the first time. Some shadow of it might be 'pre-living,' an aspect of Nature evolving and having the seeds of pre-consciousness and then in some forms eventually full-fledged and radically aware self-consciousness.

To that end, I am reminded of the times in my life that I have been 'absent without leave,' in the sense Antonio Damasio used in *The Feeling of What Happens.* Absent without leave describes the state of some seizures where after being lucid for some time, a person goes absent and unaware while the body moves, grabs a cup of coffee, kind of drinks it while pouring some on the floor, drops the cup, walks to the window to try to open it, then turns around to ask 'what's going on?' Some people 'black out' when they drink alcohol heavily or do other drugs, where whole spans of consciousness are totally obliterated from all memory, but others can attest that the person was talking, drinking, walking, acting berserk, what have you. I am reminded of the only times I have been absent without leave.

I've never forgotten where I was while on drugs or while drinking. Forgotten where I was... What a way to say what really is not forgetting as much as a shedding of self-consciousness and the absolute rupture between memory and the self. The mind is off, yet the self is autonomous and continues to behave. I 'forgot awareness' or something like that. Total oblivion of self-conception, but not the absence of perception and cognition.

The only time this has happened to me has been times surrounding my acute psychoses around both times I was hospitalized. My self awareness could phase in and out with intense effect, like the time in the desert I was unaware my own voice was speaking when I thought I heard "Jesus" speaking. Those moments were remembered as glimmers to the boy who only knew he was indeed in a hospital and being given pills and food to take. For the first time I was in a psych ward, I didn't know anything about where I had been, and didn't clue in until getting back to Canada with my dad. And after I had a sense of what was happening, I still went 'in and out.' I was observed interacting with invisible things and talking to nobody, but when I was aware I had only the sense of pocketed, transitory events that never seemed to line up.

This time in 2006, I had a similar intensity of perception and hallucination take over certain moments, although I generally retained more self-consciousness this time around. For what self-consciousness it was, I was still delusional and hallucinating. I didn't hear what people were really saying and I would see people I knew out my window, where those people certainly were not. I saw the person I was using the drugs with before being admitted, sitting in a wheelchair in the sun, and it was eerie. The light was so weird at the beginning of that hospitalization. My sensory gating was way down and everything was so loud, so bright, so full of smell and texture, deep colour. My own emotions were rampant and I was a bit hard to control at first.

Eventually I slowed down enough to take hold of myself, but I was off on a tangent and racing as is. I took it upon myself to write down math and physics and symbols on loose paper, and I wrote all sorts of weird things in a copy of a Calvin and Hobbes book. I haven't looked at that, since... When it came down to it and I was finally given a copy of the periodic table of elements that I had asked for, I found out I had remembered about the first 20 or 30 in very close to the correct order. My mind felt more vibrantly genius and memory seemed so superb for those weeks compared to how I feel at this point of writing and even fairly soon after the hospitalization until now.

I wouldn't say I prefer that state, because it was so chaotic and driven and agitated. I just know that the times after my psychosis have been some of the most rapid streaming consciousness I have ever experienced. I feel safe to explore my mind radically in the hospital. By the third week I was chilling out and enjoying smoking cigarettes and hoping I would get out of the ward in time to go back to classes the next semester. Exploring my mind with depth allowed me to focus on the reality I knew and to downplay the chaos that I know is counterproductive to my own feelings of stability.

There was one particularly intense moment that I could have been prepared for had I been more socially aware. There was a fire drill test, but the alarm went off when I was in the shower... I happened to freak out, drying as fast as I could and dressing a bit to go outside decently. I ran out of the showers which were by the locked doors to the geriatric ward. I ran to them and tried to open them, people on the other side waved me to go the other way. The dash I made to go outside was so surreal. Time and space opened up. I felt like I was moving faster than everything else and that the world was moving in slow motion. I got to the central reception/desk area and the nurse Richard, a good guy while I was there, saw my 'alarmed' state and pointed me to go out to the smoking area where the alarm would be quieter. As I ran and all the other bodies calmly puttered about in slow motion and without care and full awareness of the fire drill test, I was struck at their peacefulness. I got outside, caught my breath, and time returned to usual. I actually had a lot of time dilation experiences during those weeks. I still do on occasion, but not as severely. It happens now from music and mindfulness instead of reeling through psychosis.

By the third week, I was isolating the new and old delusions as foreign to my best reasoning, and I was coming out of the hospital in a better shape than when I had entered. I thank my family, friends, and own persistence to be healthy. I had let go that summer in a loose firing randomness. I let my mind obsess and struggle for tighter control of my mind, when I was not being wary enough about the delusional patterns of thought and impulsive cognition and perceptions. Angst was high that summer.

Basically, I got back into enjoying and satisfying my delusions. Between first and second hospitalization my delusions sat fairly dormant, only flaring up periodically, but increasingly early that summer they grew and grew until I was sleepless several nights a week. I was fighting with my girlfriend and probably being weird, and our relationship would be over by the end of the summer. It wasn't a bad thing, just a little subconsciously predicted surprise. The first night I was out of the hospital she told me again what I had let fly over my head when I was still incoherent in the hospital when she had visited and told me. She wanted to move out and move on. The surprise to me caused her to be alarmed that I might not take it well, but I was remarkably relaxed and accepting.

It goes to show what healing I had done in the hospital that I haven't yet had a day predominated by awkward delusional thinking or extreme rushing chaos or radically confusing interpretation or emotion. I sorted out a lot of confusions and tensions in my worldview and self perspective during that hospital visit. I behaved weirdly when I was first there, but I 'settled' quickly and surely enough that by 3-4 weeks I was about ready to certify for release. One of the things I learned before my first hospitalization during the events with the older man who had an obsession about me was that I was going to strive to be a calm, collected, fair minded, accepting, facilitating individual. So when it was sudden news to me that my relationship with my girlfriend was ending, I took it so readily that in itself that mildly shocked her.

I moved on from the second visit to the ward with a rejuvenated sense of stability and openness. I went back to school that semester and had time to contemplate where I had been. I began to write this book in early 2006, and didn't get very far before I was in the hospital. The early fragments were a random mess, but extended and refined in the fall of 2006 and through 2007 until the present undertaking of editing/revision through 2011 and 2012. I have taken time here and there when inspired and thoughtful enough to build on it, read over, and revise it. I am tempted to end the chronological and autobiographical journey here and continue with a last chapter regarding interpretation and symptom management, as well as an overall conception and summary of my sense of my schizophrenic identity.

My mind opened on exit of the hospital and back into 'normal' life. I've never been normal. As I began this story, I have always had a radical sense of involvement with the manifestations of my conscious experience. As a child I didn't have this structure of syntax and style, but I tell you 'I was really there!' When I was 14 or 15 and wrote a passage on a sheet of paper that was the very first wording I ever gave an introspective thought, I was incredibly startled by it and my mind was blown wide open. By 17 I was in the hospital for the first time. By 2006 I was 22 and out of the hospital for the last time and, seemingly, in the clear. Now in 2012 I am 28 and have never felt better in my life.

I've never been so free and with such a sense of eloquence in my interrelations with my environment. I feel like I know what my nature is to a tee and how to carry myself in confidence and aptitude. The only thing I've come to have any health concern about surrounding my schizophrenia is that stress does make me a little wacky. I remain medicated but as long as my mind flourishes, which means partaking in communication and sharing experiences with my friends and involving myself with my sprouting career as an audio engineer. I'm adjusted now to my schizophrenia, but in no way would I say 'it has gone away.'

I know I am still a weird, unique 1 in a 100 or 1 in a million kind of personality with a convoluted, heavily branching cognitive structure. I know I am smart in a particularly useful way, and I know that it was both broad and specific aspects in my approach to my situation which brought me to a better location with each hospital departure and why I haven't been in a ward more often. I'm so glad I earned a B.A. degree in Philosophy and English. It fortified an academic approach to the contents and structures of my consciousness, which as I began this book and want to emphasize clearly, has always been my interest. Consciousness is what exhilarates me in both intellectual and emotional ways. I do not take it for granted and 'just do it.' I pursue engagement with my own and the consciousness of others.

In a way, that's what my angst in high school was all about, really... I wanted more than anything to have contact with consciousness, so much so that my own mind manifested my thought-broadcasted friends and other hallucinations. Delusions were natural, because my mind moved so fast and I was willing to go wild and be as radical and exert even more difference in myself from my surroundings. That meant taking the weirdest conspiracy theories and stretching them more. One thing that never went away, though, at the deepest level of my mind, was something I had been smart about:

I felt the cosmic order was a scientifically understandable whole and I never much subscribed to the kind of paranoia about persecution or worldly matters. The sense that my essential self was a cosmic being of conscious energy, that I would ponder while sitting in my teenage room, prevented me from personalizing my experience too much or, on the other hand from externalizing too much of it. I've always at least felt myself to be living a frantic balancing act. The simultaneously personal and political cause of sustaining a balanced perspective and rational approach to my and our predicament is somewhat of a self-appointed lifetime task.

So be it. I will end this chapter with realization that I've basically been on a steady course toward chilling out and investing in my knowledge supply, since those days five years ago and prior. When I first learned the word 'enlightenment'—and I forget when that was—I had a thought: 'that's me!' It has only grown and been refined. If Buddha was right, 'life is suffering' whether you are enlightened; that is still the first Noble Truth. I feel lucky that I was brought up in a rural, coastal community, and that I had access to science, fantasy, philosophy, and spirituality at a relatively early age, at the home bookshelf and the local library, along with the reach of the internet which only accelerated the exploration when I was about 12.

I also feel determined to keep excelling at what I do best: to experience my consciousness. I don't do well in as many social situations if I behave as I do with those around whom I excel. I'm awkward and nerdy, and I stand out, but open up to me, and I might stretch your mind and let loose with poetic wisdom. I want to experience excitement in the consciousness around me. I want to share in the human self. I wonder if you have learned from the story I've gone through that wonder is afoot if magic is alive.

In the end of a rough day, we must guide ourselves in a way that supports our motive and orientation for living. We must fortify and strengthen the mind's ability to support curiosity and inquiry about living. That is the story of my life.

In a certified nut's highly subjective shell.

Chapter 11
Reflecting on Everything at High Velocity

So, what is schizophrenia, anyway? An answer to that question may have been why you read this book. It is the question I began with, but my preconceived notions, and states of being, have obviously distracted me from the same kind of objective and straightforward definition expected from people like doctors or psychologists. Luckily, I can rely on my first hand experience that many of the 'officially diagnosed' schizophrenics I have personally met have shared some of my experiences, but not every single one. Have you learned anything about schizophrenia by reading this book, or have you learned more about my character and wacky, out there thoughts, which are supposed to have been an account of schizophrenia?

Well, this book is kind of both. It is the account of a particular, peculiar schizophrenic. I am an individual. My own vocabulary and conception about my situation stems from an individual perspective, but what I experienced wasn't just the 'philosophy' or 'intuitions of consciousness' of some rare mind in the history of the world's enlightened, prophetic people. What I experienced was all that stuff in a very rich mix.

When I look through a huge list of potential 'symptoms of diagnostic criteria of the condition schizophrenia,' it is like I am reading a catalogue of my experiences. I am not of the variety of nut that I deny there is such thing as 'schizophrenia' even though I resist the simple 'brain disease' theory of what I tend to interpret to be simple-perspective doctors with a likely bias toward materialism and atheism. They don't often have a spiritual-philosophic understanding of humanity, so cannot understand anything other than giving a pill, as so far is the primary recourse in this century by the arbiters of psychological treatment, to eradicate the 'symptoms' of behaviour and cognitive structures that appear in healthy abundance to complexify the lives of about 1 in 100 of our nearly 7 billion.

I do believe there are other ways to treat my symptoms than medication, while they have tended to sedate the urgency of any preoccupation and sleeplessness. I'm sure the pills do what they are generally designed to do, but I think I'd be fond of the experience of going off my meds to integrate and work through my experiences and complexity. There's only one thing in the way that makes me accept the relative compromise, for the time being, of taking my meds to 'stay sane.'

Namely, I want to revise the story through which our civilization understands itself. I want a broader worldview to orient the people toward peace and intrinsic curiosity to explore experiential discovery. I want a more ecologically balanced life, and that involves human social ecology, not just balance, which is equally important anyway, for the conditions of the biosphere that is our evolutionary first cause and support system. Then, I think I could sleep easy and lighten up on myself. I think I could let go of my fears for the species going extinct and humanity's turn at the block approaching.

Then, I think I could go off my medication. For now, I appreciate that it slows me down and settles me down. There are enough people who are totally freaking normal that I think are absolutely culturally psychotic that to avoid so much more stress it is a good compromise to swallow a pill and sleep each night. That might sound radical, but indeed, a society is culturally psychotic that can justify the madness of our ecological collapse as not as important as maintaining a growing number of jobs for a recklessly overpopulated, thoroughly wasteful economy of finite resources and frustrated workers.

It is time for a talk with the children about how we've really fucked up. Don't mind the swear word, because its use is warranted to describe how badly our world needs changing because of deep errors in our thinking as a 'civilized race.' I began life with an openness and eagerness to explore, that turned into fear for the survival of intelligent life on Earth, a fear that is no paranoia. I tend to trust informed and educated scientists and philosophers before popes, rednecks, and hipsters, so I know it is no paranoia to feel eager to change human nature instead of keep putting up with it like our renegade environmental and social violence is "just a nasty part of ourselves" that is here forever.

It is certainly not here to stay forever. If we don't change our ways soon, we will go nearly extinct and the next step in our evolution will be painful. If the bottom of the ocean, which is currently very cool, warms up, then it will be goodbye totally, with almost certainty. 99% of species went extinct last time that happened. We might survive in artificial air-conditioned igloos scattered across the global desert, if we move fast enough even before the moment the ocean could turn precipitously.

1 in 100 people might do a lot better if we weren't all in a ship that is going down. Maybe my worldview and politics can shed light on the well known fact to all stripes of life that debt is on the rise, health is failing, violence is lashing, patience for governments is wearing thin, and wars and both legal and organized crime are basically unfettered on a global scale. Addiction and mental illness is on the rise everywhere that people are still civilized. We need a kind of archaic revival, to borrow the concept from Terence McKenna, and to keep our technology and science and forge ahead into an adaptive, survivable species on this planet rather than trillions of tons of dead poisonous weight in our dumps and chemical pollution.

I didn't talk about 'depression' in my book very much, but I think this 'civilization shtick' really sucks the life out of everything, the forests, watersheds, one another in the daily race to the rat grinder. *It is no wonder* that mass amounts of humanity have gone berserk in any number of ways, become suicidal, or taken to violent out-lash. That said, my book will hopefully impart some of the anger and despair that drove me mad in hopes that others as insightful and intuitive and alone as I began in my intellectual life will be spared from going completely mad. Maybe they will read this book.

That said, schizophrenia is to me a chronic form of peculiar and uniquely identifiable cognitive and social behaviour. To those who just see schizophrenia as illness rather than, when integrated and adjusted, a natural part of human diversity, it is chronic psychosis, which is an ongoing, lingering, or persistent disconnect from various established classes of ordinary social context and relationship. It is characterized by some or all of the symptoms of disordered thinking, auditory, visual, and tactile hallucinations, paranoia and anxiety, social withdrawal, delusional thought processes and strange beliefs, linguistic looseness and play that can be destructive toward coherent understanding and interpretation, and disregard to personal safety and hygiene. There is more than that when you get really specific too. There are sensory gating issues, which have to do with the ordinarily 'backgrounded signals' leaping to the forefront and becoming distracting. There are issues with appropriate functioning during ordinary social and conceptual situations, i.e. preoccupation, distraction, apathy, emotional disconnection. There are issues with lacking affect, the sense and 'feeling' of the emotions.

There are a whole host of ways the mind with schizophrenia has more or less of some kinds of cognition and more or less of other kinds of behaviours. Many schizophrenics have a 'big picture' mentality of their psychological predicament like I do, which can be an ambiguous influence on prognosis, the future of the condition. The big picture might reinforce the desire to stay cool headed. The big picture may drive one, sometimes, to dire paranoia and the exacerbation of hallucinations. Whatever the case, I believe that having a big picture that is positive and healthy is more helpful than not having any picture whatsoever, because a guiding framework and oriented approach to the unfolding of one's consciousness provides a path and habitual response, for the better, to the 'symptoms.' A guiding orientation provides a method of integrating the features of cognition and perception into healthy patterns, which allows a schizophrenic to be a healthy individual, as unique or as 'normal' as turns out to be. All in all, it takes persistence and learning to manage the complex of features called schizophrenia.

I hope that I have transferred more than only a glimmer of the insights toward sanity that I have slowly amassed and developed in my life so far. I also hope to amass and develop several more in an ongoing course toward greater and greater psychological coherence and experiential discovery. Farther than before, and within grasp of the heart, I steadily move on into the future—relaxed, nourished, and peculiarly me. I still have symptoms that put an influence on me, but I've come to be how the movie Beautiful Mind depicts schizophrenic mathematician John Nash and the life time he experienced of lingering symptoms. In the movie, Nash describes that he still sees his hallucinations, that they still follow him everywhere he goes, but he doesn't listen or at least doesn't respond anymore to them. The regular occurrence of certain symptoms become more like a habitual self-judgment or customary reflection and statement that goes through one's head when a common event occurs that bears similitude with all the others, all the other times it occurs. I have come to live with myself, as profoundly odd or as oddly profound as I continue to be.

To give an example of such 'regular occurrence,' think of the experience I have sometimes of watching a TV or internet video, when an interesting line tweaks a thought in my head and causes me to reflect on some idea of greater significance and beyond all capacity of the writer of the show to have wanted me to feel or think what I did. Then, habitually from long years of practice, my delusional ticker might just suppose and spontaneously throw at my verification subroutine the absurd and fully formed notion that a strange god is communicating across the airwaves. I simply cross my fingers in the direction of that thought, and simply reflect on the reflection, rather than the ridiculous and unnecessary conjecture that some of the thought in my head is too profound for me to have thought it under my own powers. I now accept that my mind moves light years a minute and I allow myself to free flow with ideas and align them to actual sources in the world's literature or to my radical, often fleeting imagination.

I have basically stopped reacting poorly to the emergent content of my mind. In high school, I was ill equipped and essentially flying solo at the helm of a high tech base of deep intuitions, fluttery emotions, and temperamental angst. I was smart enough to pay attention and trap inside my mind the methods of meditation and mindfulness discipline that could help me make it through each day. A few times I needed serious help to come back down to Earth, but for the main part, I've appreciated relatively quick recovery times and enjoyed my good prognosis as it turned out to reflect in my actual progress toward health. I'm not much for notions of religious salvation, especially that of my mother culture's traditions, but I feel blessed by the universe of ideas to have stumbled in due time onto the insights toward sanity and expanding worldview that have saved my life. And of course, I can't have gotten this far if it weren't for the timely and significant support of family, friends, and medical and social workers who listened, advised, and accepted me. You saved my life, too!

More than once, I am sure. Thanks for the compassion, knowledge, and ears!

Chapter 11.5
Harder to Back a Train Down than Up

Hold on, now in mid-October of 2012 as I first craft this sentence, I thought I had entered my "editing" phase when I wrote the last word of the previous chapter in... Hmm, was that even 2012? What a tricky last while. I am currently reeling from what I can no longer use a clinic to confirm was my third acute psychotic episode. This one was "brief" and "subtle," but was the longest coming... Or the one with a healthier prognosis, maybe. It feels hard to tell. I suppose this time has really clued me into why part of the definition of schizophrenia is "chronically persisting psychosis." But at any rate, I think I now understand, after this last month has gone by with so much weirdness, why I could not let go of a tension regarding the "end" of the story. I realize my story cannot end even with this chapter, because it simply has to be a summary and call to action.

No wonder I wrote the last chapter as the "final chapter" so long ago and have felt rather uneasy with the whole notion after the fuzzy "done!" feeling took a step back. Hmm...

I can truly imagine a poetry based culture, a tone based intellect. I esteem interactions of the most casual ordinary sort for all of us milling about in our daily, mundane affairs which stem from a deeply indwelling and intransigent earnest for exploring the exfoliation of consciousness to share transformation in musical playfulness of emotion. That's all I want in life, and I come full circle to my story's first couple chapters, wherein I esteem a view of my memory of my early human life, wherein I esteem a view of curiosity, desire, honesty, reflection, and compassion. I am more alike myself than I was, and doctors would be telling me to up my dosage and telling me to settle.

This is the thing: I'm having a quite legally sane psychosis—strange as it sounds. I've been through enough in the past months, while quitting my tobacco addiction and experiencing the variations of stress in my life and trying to help sort out the stress in my world, affecting almost everyone who is dear to me. A very smart girlfriend once suggested and often reminds that at face value my old explanation is unacceptable and unrealistic that "I don't really feel like I 'feel' my emotions." It's great of her that she never let me leave off the discussion there. It occurs to me that tobacco is a really powerful emotional sedative for some people. That is well researched, while I may frame the idea in nontechnical language.

It's related to "regulation" of routine and time and "stress" reactions. Go confirm on the internet with an academic materials search on "emotions and tobacco" or talk to a well read MD who has helped someone quit. That's how the Tobacco Industry markets it—"I smoke because of stress"—and is a good example of how little marketed seeds of ideas uphold by word of mouth the persistence of the second hand exhaust, from the psych wards in hospitals, to the streets. Tobacco is part of the schizophrenic psych ward experience, and for lots of people, there seems to be some kind of identifiable emotional character to the experience of smoking. I realize for 12 years I've wished I could cry some big tears. I also actually thought my smoking habit was a routine which locked me into a certain cognitive habit. At time of writing, nicotine has only been *not* pumping in for less than 2 weeks. It's chemical signature is slowly fading, the stress distraction via oral habit is fading, and I express "wow" at the instantaneous changes of a major sort.

It's hard to listen to friends saying "smoking is bad for you!" when the medical professional him or herself was telling my mom when I was first hospital admitted, "don't worry, smoking is good for him, or at least not that bad for him!" It's tricky. The research says, "you can relapse if you smoke and if you quit" so what do you do? For 12 years of smoking, I suppose what I did was to cling to a dirty habit which is otherwise well established to be an emotional suppressor (though the amount of research is relatively "news to me.") Emotional release and emotional honesty are sometimes what's required to facilitate the relief of stress and the adaptation of healthier reactions to stress—stress which often represents emotional and intellectual tensions, unresolved or unfulfilled needs, and so many other psycho-social issues that affect individuals.

Many people who know a tense schizophrenic will definitely understand the usefulness of relief from our anxieties and our quiet, withdrawal, and isolation! My girlfriend's attitude to my smoking was openminded, and while she shared in my own wishing I could quit, she did that without insisting about it either way or binding me in mixed, random messages. I think I personally transformed, by my own standards and at my own pace. This girlfriend also did so much being way smarter than tobacco company scientists and, rather than suppressing them, getting me to consciously address what the nature of my feelings really are.

I figure my immune system started to feel the tension in the predicament of a decade of varying emotional suppressions, and a wicked cold came on.

This was a serious cold, the kind that leads to pneumonia; one day, throat and lungs so clogged and sore and the thought in itself raspy of lighting yet another smoke, it occurred to me I had to quit. My mom said smoking cessation was very emotional for her, the research says so, and I can also confirm. It's been an amazing time, returning to a kind of psychotic state. I started the nicotine replacement patch a few hours after the insight to quit moment. After about a month, the patch started giving me steady increasing chest pain and throat flutters and I discontinued using it. The pain continued to increase in my chest and throat, until I took myself to the emergency ward and was sitting on a hospital gurney totally unable to relax as the tech said "hey, just relax," hooking up the terminals to record my heart's electrical current.

All the while waiting for results and feeling so much pain, I felt an abstract connection to the discussion in the next gurney behind the curtain which sounded to me like a group talk between friends about stressful conditions in the daily life of a young woman with an unspecified health issue. The issue sounded to me like a stress-related issue—especially when frustration about the stress conditions might often result in the outburst of "ow! This pain is so much, I can't concentrate on anything." My concern was that the history she described of doctors "not finding anything wrong" with her physiology, while she *was* stressed out, could be understood better another way. What may be an accurate assessment that psycho-somatic effects were at work in some way in this person's health problems became an intense mystical delusion suddenly.

I thought that fairly clearly, her stress and stress awareness were preceding bursts of pain. My chest pain continued to increase until I started to feel very disconnected from reality and remembered how INSANE I could get, to recall that older and now highly faded symptom of "external intrusions" of weird "conscious entities." In my fear of the INSANE delusion regarding causal connection to other minds and in a sudden recognition that "this is the tobacco-related relapse, right here," my heart felt like it exploded, but the anxious tension, that had (I think) been building over many years, sprung open with pouring, surging waterworks. The waterworks and sudden cessation of chest pain signalled that my primary problem was actually a nicotine withdrawal anxiety attack. Spanning 24-48 hours after stopping nicotine intake is the normal "peak" time of withdrawal anxiety.

I realized I wanted to join the discussion in the next gurney and offer the idea that psychological stress understanding may be a useful thing to consider in her health problem, even though the symptom seemed physiologically experienced. I didn't join in, I think merely for compliance to social norms and not that I have an opinion of default one way or the other about what's "my business or their business."

However, I did realize something about why some research says "group talk" therapy is good for schizophrenia and other psychotic disorder. It's always been more important to me that I resolve my tension regarding stress in my life, and much more of that stress is social and emotional stress, I feel, rather than the stress of brain disease or chemical imbalance. It's the stress of being a personality or brain type that is a likely candidate for early childhood and adolescent years of not fitting in, and perhaps thinking too much about distressing things like I did, which causes many varieties of emotional tension that need a lot of relief.

Marginalized and migrant populations are part of a subset that "do not fit in," traditionally, so theory aiming at stress understanding seems natural to explain the higher incidence of schizophrenic symptoms and many other health issues in such stressed people. As far as I have heard and read, on the internet and in discussion with nurses and other mental health consumers, a schizophrenic is commonly considered as often being the type who is creative, compassionate, communicative, critical, and sometimes more than a bit cranky. The fact that schizophrenics often fit descriptions of frustrated, stressed out cultural subsets like "outsider." "anti-authoritarian." or "spiritually focused being" totally makes sense of why "group talk" situations can be very productive for them.

I think every schizophrenic I have met personally would visibly de-stress, relax in their body, and be more verbally present and emotionally lucid, exactly when they feel free from stigmatizing judgment to explore openly the intricate and delicate sinew of their experience. This seems especially true in receptive, inclusive group settings of 3 or more people, roughly. Larger respectful groups do seem to have a more profound effect than one-to-one interactions in this regard. I have seen most schizophrenics go further—from comfort and motivation to engage in discussion—sometimes toward playful excitability with insightful spontaneity, when they get a chance to share in respectful, creative self-expression.

The heavily dosed patient in the brief intervention ward, recently recovered since escaping last night, may rarely hold a smile, or entertain the fancy notions demanded by normal congenial conversation. This patient may not shine with irascible glee or ease. I have seen the too heavily medicated and too emotionally stressed individual change in energy level from sombre, disconnected dazed appearances to the display of unlikely but masterful dopey grins and glinting eyes. It just takes a generalized conversation about the nature of the human mind, the stress of the world, the symptoms of schizophrenia, and ways we can get better and feel more like human beings.

That happened recently when I was invited to a psych ward with my good friend, invited by the patient freshly diagnosed schizo-affective, who sought out a conversation with someone her social group knew was schizophrenic. After meeting her, I'm concerned our psychiatry is far too mechanical and emotionally draining... And emotionally dull. It was intense to talk to a fresh patient of the hospital system, and not barely connect eye to eye when I first entered the room because of medication daze. However, after talking for a good while about what she thought she was going through and what she thought was happening to her mind, she then magically had the energy to look me in the eye, smile, and literally gently bounce in her otherwise exhausted bones with endearing and compassionate regard. She gave me a bouncy two thumbs up for my statement "yeah, I just quit smoking!" when she asked at one point about my friend and me if we smoked (big topic in the psych wards).

I'm not sure what to make of medication as a first response method to people's issues when stress seems to be the concern of the patient, and when alternate cognitive expressions and the engraining of appropriately adaptive habits seem to be what the patient wants to replace their experience with rather than endure side effects and psychological disregard. Basically, one of my primary concerns with the overarching "brain diseases" hypothesis is how weird the jump to totalitarian and unrelenting social materialism can make the "conditions" of our "persons" appear in our cultural metaphysic.

The patient I recently met in the "brief intervention unit" said the nurses and doctors treated her like all she needed was the medication and that she felt her concerns were not being understood. It angers me that medical professionals can do harm by forgetting on an intentional theoretical level that the psychosocial entity has an experience of being a person. A person continually engages in the construction of meaning, of decisions, which writes their lifelong neural-plasticity, over time with varied efforts, into interpretive, affective, intellectual, and sensory-motor habits.

What can in reductive, eliminative materialism be defined as "brain disease" sure does look like "a person with a vital experience" from the perspective of a realism which is physiologically- as well as psychologically-inclusive. This section of my book has basically been an open and reflective expurgation on the art of having schizophrenia. We all endure stress in a manifold diversity of forms, and we all develop a diversity of adaptations to overcome or manage stress. We have diversity in our bodily forms and our mental structure which correlate across different members of our species in diverse reactions to diverse stressors.

We are ineluctably members of the "same" species, too, so there is something of a "natural will" for solidarity in the acceptance of diversity in cultural and personal methods. That "nearly 1 in 100" people have schizophrenia-form disorders does not indicate to me that there are "genetic," "toxic," "developmental," and other kinds of "causes" to deterministically isolate. Instead, within the belief system which I gave in the last paragraph the name "inclusive realism," somewhat steady rates of incidence might indicate there are genetic, toxic, and simply all sorts of "contexts" and "experiences" to consider.

It definitely appears that "stress" is at least present in awareness, if not also the insistently self-specified cause of problems, in the lives of most people who have schizophrenia and other mental health issues. The standard supposition of theory may announce "brain disease causes a chemical imbalance that creates the stress." What makes a lot more sense to me, in the end, is to say that "stress in a person's thoughts and social situations probably play the largest role in expressing dis-ease, from troubling meaningful experiences to troubling brain chemical habits."

It's easier that way for me to understand my own stress triggers and needs, and goes to show why "group talk therapy" is shown to be more effective a method of treatment for psychotic disorder, and more preventive of relapse, than psychiatric medication has been shown to be. Robert Whitaker, in *Anatomy of an Epidemic*, suggests this from his review of research. It has been *felt* true, in my own case, that talking with others about what I go through and what I think about is way more effective in making me *feel* more sane and *actually act* with more calm, collection, and integrity. The side effects of medication, on the other hand, have felt much more like a hindrance to me being able to express my deeper feelings and really experience my experience of my being. Anti-psychotics don't just "stop" or "take away" the "bad symptoms" like hallucination and delusion. Rather, they are highly psycho-active in their own right.

The risperidone I take has side effects of sleepiness and it has side effects of excitability. Being dulled and tired sometimes while restless and emotionally or intellectually frantic at other times is no good for my composure or stress management. It has been wonderful to get quetiapine (or Seroquel) out of my system after being on it for six years, and a truly, superbly beautiful experience to cut out tobacco after twelve years of an increasing habit. My emotions have been up front, and I love it, even as dangerously apparent as my stress factors have become in this foregrounding. That's what I really think is the main issue as to why many people with schizophrenia have relapses after they remove emotionally dulling and agitating anti-psychotics—or also why they have relapse potential when they remove emotionally dulling and agitating tobacco. If our stress factors do not dissipate, or we do not initiate a pattern of healthy adaptation of stress management methods, then removing those drugs can spell disaster. That is my primary "insight toward sanity":

In a vein of theory comparable to Gabor Mate's observations in his book, *When the Body Says No—The Hidden Cost of Stress*, the mind also says no to stress, sometimes so loudly and violently that the individual is left totally scrambling for the capacity to respond for the better. We need to come together in moral and theoretical support for those in our communities who are stressed out for so many reasons, who are held down by so many pressures, who could use all kinds of help, who are misunderstood and unheard in their surroundings. We need to engender a great insight toward sanity as a whole culture, faced with impending ecosystem collapses and socio-political tensions on the verge of civil wars and despotism.

We need to tell stories that deepen the memories of history, and acknowledge the persistence of imperialism, patriarchy, and colonialism, when there is so much potential in reinvention and invigoration. And this is where I come full circle to the beginning of my story, and the vital needs I have for expression and understanding which have driven me mad and smart. What I have felt I must do is "surrender to experiential discovery" to "fly free" from "The Birdcage for Spirit." It's stress that did me in, and experiences of freedom from stress that I seek. For me, the emotional reactions in the philosophical intuitions I have—about social realities with ecological consequences—are prime examples of stress modulators for my brain chemistry.

I have to be the adult my childhood intuitions aimed for: there's no way I can finally pick what to be, now that I've grown up, and I must simply be more and am continually more than I could ever imagine in my most complex delusions. I am also more than the theoretical delusions dreamed up for me by drug companies, media companies, and economic "think tanks" whose centralized, internally memo-ed, and in many ways directly and overtly stated purpose is the for-profit management of the will and values of common people's purchasing power. The "lifestyle marketing" feels to me to be aimed toward controlling also the barest notions people ever have of the whole metaphysical and ethical reality we inhabit on this tiny planet Earth in this huge and sprawled out Universal Cosmos.

I would be more comfortable in a world where we continually dance in mutual respect and nurture the creative pursuit of sharing and giving meaning. To use a phrase and some concepts I learned from a website which has long interested me (www.organelle.org): I yearn to engage in "mutual uplift" with all of you who exist and who wish to assist the flourishing of cognitive animation on our living planet. I yearn to bask in the brilliance of the lack of the mundane which is the world viewed with social eyes and open hearts. I am reminded prominently here of a statement I made in the course of the "Very many really short poetic essays" included in Part One of this book:

"I am still containing a powerful, unresolved energy, evident if I forget my med for a day. I feel neglect. I don't like my basic perception of my experience reduced to terms...Again, I state, I feel misunderstanding abounds. I misunderstand too, and I feel this to be the actual source of my delusions."

So, I have in this book attempted to elicit some of the insights toward sanity I think have helped me be strong and as healthy as I can be. I hope you have learned something from this autobiographical conference I've held between the concepts of stress conditions, cultural adaptation, existential nature, and expressive needs. If you managed by reading this book to be spurred on in thought of something particular, which just happens to be tangible and actionable, then please by all means, I wish you the best of success in accomplishing some of the vital work that so many planetary particle histories have, jam-packed with really important jobs.

After that last sentence, I realize in a flash, finally, why it was, before first pondering Chapter 11.5, I already long decided on the present structure of the book's "parts." Because it feels proper to lead you into the final part of the book—the collection of essays—with this thought, I may as well tell you about why this book is the way it is, here and now at the end of the autobiography!! Because sentences and arguments are like words and ideas, and because organisms made of cells are like civilizations made of human beings—and because stress exists in the confusion, ignorance, awareness, habit, and spontaneity of every interrelationship—I thus conclude that I may safely, accurately, and wisely diagnose rapid association, word play, and so on as both creative skills *and* schizophrenic symptoms.

What I'm saying is that while it is a symptom of schizophrenia that "my ideas are all over the place," it is also possible, when healthy, to play a healthy game. I may be ill when I am ill, but it is still possible for me to use my odd brain patterns to weave complex and sound advice for my social surround. It is my intention that you try to charitably understand my arguments, but I also realize that my approach is inherently discursive. I seek that you ponder this book as a collection of some primary sources and some reflections aiming to gather into a set of insights. Hopefully containing a few kernels of relevant and useful insight, any advice I directly give for how to understand schizophrenia comes from both personal experiences and well-researched theories. What I seek to present is my gander at the manifold space of a suitable belief system for understanding the duress of schizophrenia.

The Nobel Economics laureate, mathematician John Nash, who is a diagnosed schizophrenic, was once interested in "manifold theory." I learned from the movie

A Beautiful Mind, and a small amount of online reading, that I have always also been hugely interested in "manifold theory." Something about the zoom and graphing problem intrigues me. When you zero in toward a limiting valuation in a region where your broader perspective had always seen 'smooth and flat' curves, indeed you may actually have and find, well, quite 'discontinuous and abruptly ranging' points of change. Zooming in on a situation may show you something very different than zooming out, but the really significant story seems to me in realizing that the actual reality actually permits both zoomed in and zoomed out perspectives and modalities of action. Rates of change *do* occur with 'manifold' variety. I can ascertain that the apparently slow, smooth motion of my "life" is *a span here*, and I must yet point out that identifying with precision the flow of one point to the next point involves telling an endlessly re-combinable "story" of things that are happening *at particular moments there, there, and there* as well.

There is a broad range of issues and situations which lead to illness in both individuals and whole societies. That's why I started writing this book as an autobiography and why it felt both natural and necessary at some point to include that beginning of scattered poetics and philosophy, as well as the essays which conclude my written portion of the book. Please connect the dots I dreamed up, by your own inclinations and motives.

I know I have strong ideas and that this is a longish book, but I mean to add to conversations and extend the offer to you to communicate with my ideas, which sometimes I've felt are urgent and forceful and necessary for world peace. I know that's a "messianic complex" but there you go. I totally feel in my bones and skin sometimes the logic endorsed by street-corner prophets, who yell and cajole at passersby who usually tend to fear eye contact. I have not done that, and I don't plan to start. My own tack was to write a book and hope you might read it or tell someone else to buy it. I may kind of feel and think I am "right" about what I have said through my stories, but I also know I am continually learning about life and human history.

Thus, I suspect only that my schizophrenic gaze will merely continue to explore many additional zoom levels and accept many additional considerations. Please, human brethren in this world of animate curiosities, speak your own stories of realization. Succumb to your expressive needs. Let's go.

It's time for lots and lots of storytelling. Ok?
So let's go.

Part Three

Journey to the Centre of the Universe: Coming to Terms with an Even More Radical Enlightenment

*Assorted Essays Collected over the Course of my
VIU Bachelor of Arts degree;
Major in Philosophy and Minor in English;
My studies took place between 2003 and 2009.
I dedicate this portion of the book to the professors
who changed my outlook and perspective,
who informed me and forced me to read so much,
who gave me continual feedback and provided
the much needed reality check on my loose canon quick firing brain,
and thereby contributed to the formation,
cultivation, practice, and evolution
of what became a cool-headed, thoughtful mind.*

I know you had to deal with a lot of ideas listening to me, sometimes, but take a look at and reread what you helped to be my best works:

ENGL 315—Advanced Composition Workshop
Fall 2005 originally, with revision until February, 2008

Essay 1
Insights Toward Sanity

My first psychiatric doctor told me I am an excellent case of schizophrenia, high-functioning and well-adjusted. She told me that I'm lucky for my ability to converse in psychiatric discourse at a somewhat intellectually matched level with her. She said she's never known a patient who was so knowledgeable and enlanguaged about his condition; in addition, before I got very sick, I had always done well at school, had been open to volunteering in my school and community, and had also possessed a healthy dose of teenage angst to change my world. Before I saw any doctor for it, I had already self-diagnosed and learned much on my own, feeling that schizophrenia intriguingly and weirdly challenged my mind, at least before I totally lost connection with reality.

Schizophrenia is a chronic form of *psychosis*, described by psychiatrists as a drastic disconnect from socially shared mental and emotional reality. The presence of delusions and hallucinations characterizes psychosis. Delusions are persistent, often destructive *beliefs* held onto in spite of any provided rational evidence to the contrary. For example, I had a delusion once that weather like the wind could be directed by my thoughts. Hallucinations on the other hand are *perceptions* that occur to an individual's senses, but which are not really based in an external stimulation of the senses. My delusion about the wind was not a hallucination because I really felt the wind moving. A dream, for instance, is technically a hallucination, because what we see in a dream is not really where one physically sleeps. For the schizophrenic, voices and strange objects might be perceived just like when one is dreaming, but these perceptions occur in waking life when there is no outer source for them. The difference between delusions and hallucinations is the same difference between belief and sense perception. The two relate as perceiving events through the senses provides material for a belief about events to form. This idea figures into my overall ideas on the subject of schizophrenia in a significant way.

  Before I was severely ill, my mind slowly filled with weirdness. I remember during teenage angst that I felt a need to express many views, but I felt none would listen to what I most wanted to say. I felt alone and developed a habit of imagining myself in conversation with the others that I really wanted to speak to. It was a tactic to test out concepts and simply explore by myself what I wanted to say, since I did want to say a lot. It occurred to me eventually that I almost literally heard speech of my friends and argumentative quarries when I imagined their responses. I thought in isolation about what exactly I might say if I were to open up and express issues important to me. I would go for a walk out back behind my house into the forest, find a spot, and pace back and forth while imagining and muttering under my breath both my words and the words of others. The experience gave me an eerily realistic sense of meaning that was exchanged and developed through the imagined dialogue.

This progressed until I could not shut off the perception of imagine-hearing others make statements, even when with them at school. I began to make up responses and follow-through statements in the direct midst of actual conversation. It happened when I would walk by a group that was talking, and the "sound" of these extra statements began to feel a lot like my own thoughts but attached to other personalities than my own. I had been reading ancient to new-age spirituality as well, and at the weirdest times, I imagined with some disbelief that I might actually share thoughts with others. The characters seemed consistent, and the thoughts kept appearing in my mind without any impetus or desire of mine to think about them, but I also didn't resist when I thought I could learn from it as I initially intended by testing out hypothetical conversations.

My last year of high school in 2002 went like this. Later that summer, however, a real trauma occurred[1], and I became even more disconnected from reality than during school. I gained so such emotional stress that while not going into the story, I can say a situation completely debilitated my already faltering psyche. I could no longer contain my already rampant imagination or maintain rationality. I started hallucinating extremely, totally blinking out with huge memory gaps and not noticing even several days going by—at that point I desperately needed help. And, it was at that crisis point that the struggle with my delusions truly began. How in high school I became prone to psychosis will elucidate the later points I make about schizophrenia. I think it is important to keep in mind that inadvertent ideations tend to confound schizophrenics; right before I got sick and in the midst of it, I felt I could not at all stop the flood of my thoughts.

In a state of recovery since becoming psychotic in the Fall of 2002, I attest to the following point: without many kinds of help, I would not have had the ability when totally convinced of my delusions and hallucinations to overcome them. A nightmare of horrors deeply daunts the individual who becomes severely schizophrenic. I happened to be watching TV the late night that the ambulance took me away, and at that crisis point, I thought that the television images and words were talking metaphorically about me. Around the same time, I experienced hallucinations of people that I talked with, so vivid that I could see colour in their eyes, feel their breath, and feel the touch of their hands and arms. With schizophrenia, an individual experiences profound changes in the function of his or her mind, and these changes have a potential to disrupt mental life by making it unmanageable and unbearable; they no longer share the reality had by everyone else. Luckily, the people I hallucinated were friendly and non-threatening to my emotions, which was a relieving way to experience the trauma that occurred within real events.[1] Talking to people who weren't there and unaware of what was happening, I was in a sick state. Psychosis intensely affects perception and imagination, leaving one susceptible to startlingly vivid hallucinations and intensely held delusions. Recovery must be guided with sensitive care, because insight toward sanity for a psychotic hardly derives from the distortion of insanity.

---

[1] A thorough enough account for understanding the events which took place goes quite beyond the scope of this writing, and exploring them would surely distract the reader from what I seek to emphasize. The events lacking mention do not pertain to what herein I have to say about schizophrenia and the delusional response.

All I can remember is one room and its two windows, a forest I sought out of the top of a mostly opaque window and a hall with desks around the corner out another. The door was kept locked unless I was given a pill to take. I was there a whole week, and I remember taking the med only once. They said (as I later heard) that I was often seen talking and looking around as though interacting with people. Although cooperative with treatment, I had no idea where I was. *A grounded mind supported by good knowledge is the essence of recovery for a schizophrenic.* I needed grounding alright. For the times I remember, I felt like I needed electrical grounding.

Recovery began for me as it does for most Canadians that become psychotic: I received the attention of a psychiatrist and then encountered psychiatric methods of treatment, beginning first and foremost with medication. Doctors, informed by science and not personally swayed by the torrents of a psychosis, have useful knowledge, and their help for grounding the afflicted usually begins in giving them a medicine. Anti-neuroleptics or anti-psychotics, as they are called, most directly aid schizophrenia by controlling what has become the chaotic chemistry of the brain, full of processes that doctors can associate with hallucinations and delusional impulses. Different drugs help various individuals by offsetting their brain chemistry, thereby helping to balance their minds by controlling and limiting what manifests to perception. This medical knowledge is still growing and improves the chance of recovery for schizophrenics who have access to the most effective drugs.[2]

---

[2] Different drugs work with varying degrees of success. My doctor says sometimes a mixture of various medications is necessary for some. My contention herein is that cognitive treatment is bound to help a lot.

Medicine at least allows recovery to begin and maybe should only be intended for short term remediation, but the afflicted individual *must*, I believe, attain also a coherent mental framework to make chemical treatment effective. No schizophrenic individuals will be okay if given only adequate doses of some pill but are then deposited in the street before *working through* their onset and lingering psychosis. I responded well to medicine and my hallucinations faded. Medicine indeed helped to settle my teetering mind, but much was yet amiss.

After my initial hospitalization and "settling" closer to sanity as the nurses and doctors described, I was still convinced by some strong beliefs that I only later learned referred to the unreal. I realized at some point that real people had not seen the things I hallucinated, but I still thought the visions were more substantive than waking dreams. Delusions still swayed my judgment to a bad end, for example discontinuing the stabilizing med. Utterly convinced by my experience right before the first ambulance ride to a psych ward, I consciously supported my delusions. After watching TV that time feeling so powerfully that it was about me, I readily convinced myself any image through my senses could carry a metaphorical message like the TV had seemed to. In the hospital, medication ended the strong and active hallucinations that had onset during severe psychosis, but an inclination to form delusions remained. I did not yet doubt the hallucinatory images or feelings that had occurred, so like ghosts in my memory, the response lingered of looking for a message like the one imagined from the TV. Choosing to stop taking my med and spending a whole night watching TV again like that, I required a second hospitalization to "settle" again, but I started to recognize the presence of persistent delusions. They did not dissipate even as my heart and mind grew calmer and as my thoughts composed some measure of reason. Exploring the confused, I entered confusion, unable to understand. I needed more help than a pill, because even on it, I could inappropriately desire the alternative to its settling effect.

Where pills do not and cannot reach, I have found the mind can easily respond to aberrant perception by intentionally creating and maintaining delusions. In recollection, many delusions and strange concepts came to me directly from trying to figure out or think through the weirdness of various hallucinations and feelings that invaded my unadjusted and untreated, schizophrenic mind. In the period during high school, feelings dwelled in me and led to preoccupations, which I think might have advanced the neural pathways needed for powerful hallucination, my mental future at which the spontaneous inner conversations hinted. In the period during my hospitalizations, the perceptual symptoms grew more hallucinatory, and the near-delusions from high school evolved and shifted with my changing perceptions. The conversations and thoughts of others I imagined happening inside me during high school were overridden during psychotic onset by more intense feelings that a worldly separate thinker was communicating straight into my thoughts. The base perceptions underlying my beliefs changed drastically, in the nature of how thoughts appeared to my mind: the thoughts coursing through my mind grew even more intrusive and automatic. My explanations kept changing in a struggle. Instead of fake-talking in my head to my friends, or thinking I maybe heard my friends' thoughts telepathically, I began to think my mind totally invaded by a foreign communicating entity or spirit.

Consider another case of strange perceptions: most people who ingest psychedelics to create hallucinatory images tend to avoid strange beliefs that persist after the chemicals are flushed from the system. When a person using a drug forgets that the drug causes what they perceive, they may become prone to cognitive disorder. Doctors describe "toxic psychosis" as a result of some drug use where the user "does not come down" as anticipated. People are susceptible in this way because they usually try to explain and understand objectively what is happening to them, which will not likely succeed for an experience not based at all in objective reality. Being literally convinced of a hallucination can prolong it chemically in the brain, I figure. I see an analogy: not knowing oneself is dreaming prolongs the perception of dreams or to say that more familiarly, discovering that oneself is dreaming often immediately rouses one from slumber. The brain works in mysterious ways and can make the mind strange when creating representations to the mind that are not based in sense stimulation.

Hallucinations for the schizophrenic generally occur over a far longer period of time than for a psychedelic user or a dreamer, so one afflicted tends to struggle a long and arduous time trying to reconcile a coherent worldview. Memory and thoughts of a drug user or dreamer can turn into specific albeit loony perceptions that are sometimes incredibly meaningful to the experiencing mind, and the long-term experience of schizophrenia fills a mind like some dreams do with meaning to comprehend or think about. The biggest problem I believe exists for schizophrenics in thinking the 'waking dreams' are real and in working on with 'the faculty of reason' to reinforce the imagined but inappropriate ideas of some principles or facts that are supposed by the schizophrenic to explain intrinsically bizarre or hallucinatory perceptions. I believe the delusional response requires deep psychological and cognitive treatment to offset perhaps years of intentional but unbalanced thought tendency. This is my best sense of my own case with schizophrenia at the very least, but I know it'll hold to some others.

Because delusions are an active mental response[3], any treatment can have little lasting effect until one is convinced of the truth despite being also swayed by feelings. For schizophrenics, some kind of truth or some insight must develop before they possibly clarify or abandon what is untrue and insane. Coherent thought breaks down when one believes totally in a different reality than the one shared, and reparation in logic and in understanding needs correct and true ideas as well informing the ill mind.

Faulty beliefs seem to me to form in articulate and rational-like streams of thought. They appear more verbalized into language and actively put together compared to odd feelings just bubbling up or absolutely bizarre hallucinations presenting themselves suddenly. For example, some people have intense paranoia and work hard to ideate complicated conspiracies because of a recurrent, unintentional feeling that they are being strangely stared at by complete strangers. After the peak of my own disarray, I continually perceived

---

[3] I allude to in discussion of my "high school conversations" but never explicitly state that sentences and words can appear in a hallucinatory fashion like when hearing voices in the head, but I do hold an important distinction between sentences that might pop into mind as hallucinations and between delusions which I primarily conceive as statements consciously derived by meticulous, reason-guided articulation about what might first pop into the mind unabated as raw perception or feeling.

creepily profound meanings in ordinary statements, or built strange meanings myself into what I witnessed. After almost six years, I'm beginning to comfortably watch TV without seeing at everywhere the potential for the meanings that used to flow in with clear meaning to my mind as directly as I hope these words communicate my experience to you.

I thought for a while that every word I received could metaphorically convey a message, and this intense feeling gave me the reason to seriously speculate about an entity or aliens directly communicating with me. I thought some entity could reach through time to coordinate events to enfold me in a rapture of symbolic learning. No kidding! Reading, radio, TV, and conversation with others—these seemed to flow in a continuously meaningful and never-ending message to myself. Sometimes what people said took on such significance in my mind that I felt the extreme meaning I gleaned in some statements could be rationalized through the existence only of powerful, indeed omnipotent beings. I transferred at various points between the angst-ridden desires in high school to speak up on toward the unavoidable perception of an intangible entity's speaking of its mind through my consciousness. I would not imagine that the profound meaning could simply be in my mind, so I made up pseudo-theories that aberrant perception seemed to validate easily. I did not accept my own mind's inner work, disposition, or personality, what have you, as the possible source for these *feelings which were so strong.*

Mine was a breakdown of interpretation. To understand what happens during the perception of events, people use language, or to say it another way, if asked we can usually give some words that clearly convey the sensed meaning of our experience. Similarly to ordinary speech, delusion formation in schizophrenia involves mentally active expression, but about a strange perceptual world. I've hinted consistently at a distinction between communicative expression and passive perception, and I find it is an essential distinction for me to investigate in my ongoing recovery from untruth. I keep clear to myself that there is a big difference between having a spontaneous thought or perception and then deciding which thoughts to nourish with faith in an external to me (like the entity). A schizophrenic must, to overcome, not only question whether what they actually see or actually hear is also actually real, but question as well whether they are thinking as clearly as they could be. Philosophy class makes me laugh when someone asks "what's this thing people call reality? What if, *really*, all life is but a dream?" Hah, I've questioned that, but it dug way deeper.

In my mind I know that mainly good ideas, some given by friends or my doctor and some gained myself, have helped me sort through the surrealism and hold on to some sound reason. I attribute my recovery to many factors, but I want to emphasize the overcoming of delusions, reiterating it was hard because they stuck around far beyond medical treatment and awakening from hallucination. I'll speak of one delusion I overcame and of how I overcame it: to avoid believing in higher beings (or whatever) to explain strange encounters of strange meaning with ordinary people, I held instead to the idea that my mind can quickly glean profound meanings. These meanings once seemed to specially arise for me, but genuinely, they arise from my mind. I now imagine a hyperactive subconscious in conversation with itself to be my mind when I get a little schizophrenic. This idea is so much more comfortable than thinking seriously and mysteriously that you (someone, anyone) are not truly yourself at least for a moment that another being, one interested in me, speaks through you. Weird, eh? With a mental choice I offer a weird part of my experience a poetic response instead of a delusional response. Luckily, I still get the old feeling of wonderful and exhilarating meaning sometimes, but a few insights toward sanity help me have these interesting experiences and also keep sane inside them.

Not every schizophrenic is so lucky with their course through the disorder. The Public Health Agency of Canada released *A Report on Mental Illness* in 2002, the same year I was diagnosed. In the relevant chapter, it says "the chronic course of the disorder contributes to ongoing social problems. As a result, individuals with schizophrenia are greatly over-represented in prison and homeless populations." Further, the report says between 2 and 3 out of 5 schizophrenics attempt suicide and about 1 succeeds. As a rough average, about 1 in a 100 individuals in the general population faces a life of schizophrenia. If Malaspina (the school I attend) had 8000 students, anywhere in the range from 45 to 140 individuals with the illness might walk by me daily on campus. My doctor asked me once to tell her if I had delusions that would not go away so she could consider raising my dosage of meds. She worries for me, because she knows from trying to help them that many schizophrenics never get over their lingering psychosis. I shared more of my own perception of how I've done so well because I consider my own mind more invaluable than my meds for stopping delusions.

I told my doctor this summer more thoroughly that the medicine never surely stopped the delusions, and she seemed sort of aghast for just a moment wondering if I had been lying to her about feeling better. The meds have stopped the most vivid hallucinations as well as allowed me to sleep, but the crux of my recovery conjoining these vital parts of it are recurrent choices of how to respond to strange feelings, and the delusional response weakens gradually. Sanity is with- in -sight, to play a little friendly word salad! Ah, I find so much joy when characteristics of schizophrenia, like a far-reaching imagination and play with language, two abilities which used to hurt my mind as symptoms, can now be used for beneficial expression. I would like more people to have a general knowledge about how delusions form, because I find the process so integral to individual suffering. It would be good for more people to know better how to engender that grounded mental framework that guides the disrupted and distorted individual to inner peace. We schizophrenics need real help out of illusions.

English 321—Modern Literary Theories
Wednesday, November 28, 2007

Essay 2
Truth in Critical Theory and Simulacra in the World: From Language-Games to the Defence of Meaning and From Ordinary Language to Ideology

> *The best that I could write would never be more than philosophical remarks; my thoughts were soon crippled if I tried to force them on in any single direction against their natural inclination.—And this was, of course, connected with the very nature of the investigation. For this compels us to travel over a wide field of thought criss-cross in every direction.*
> –Ludwig Wittgenstein in *Philosophical Investigations*

> *All ideology represents in its necessarily imaginary distortion is not the existing relations of production (and the other relations that derive from them), but above all the (imaginary) relationship of individuals to the relations of production and the relations that derive from them. What is represented in ideology is therefore not the system of the real relations which govern the existence of individuals, but the imaginary relation of those individuals to the real relations in which they live.*
> –Louis Althusser in *Ideology and Ideological State Apparatuses*

When saying "the term 'language-*game*' is meant to bring into prominence...that the *speaking* of language is part of an activity, or of a life-form" and exploring this idea in depth in the *Philosophical Investigations*, Wittgenstein brings into prominence an idea integral in any adequate 'critical theory' which attempts to deal with some aspect of the production of meaning from language (§23). We are alive and it is part of our living that we produce meaning and *speak* language. A central 'problem' of literary theory over the previous century has been what I will call the defence of meaning and truth. Regardless of the certainty people usually have when they speak and perhaps have when they write, a lot of literary-critical talk in the 20th century suggested a lack of certainty in meaning or in truth existing for any kind of text.

In his essay "The Death of the Author", Roland Barthes suggests a reader's "only power is to mix writings, to counter the ones with the others, in such a way as never to rest on any one of them...words only explainable through other words, and so on indefinitely" and that "[t]o give a text an Author is to impose a limit...to furnish it with a final signified, to close" it (149). In his essay "Structure, Sign, and Play in the Discourse of the Human Sciences", Jacques Derrida suggests that "the entire history of the concept of [any linguistic] structure, [before 'play' began], must be thought of as a series of substitutions of center for center, as a linked chain of determinations" and that "[t]he absence of the transcendental signified extends the domain and the play of signification infinitely" (90, 91). These two writers, among several 'postmodernists", promoted ideas that assess the interchange-ability and depth of meanings within any kind of sign, and extending these ideas, they *can* seem to suggest the impossibility of finding clarity and truth in the projects or discourses of supposedly knowledge-generating discipline.

There is a lot of skepticism and\or relativism floating around today about the defence of meaning and truth that is to an extent justified, because it's easy to see two different people taking totally opposed meanings from reading the same text and because it's hard to accept the dictums, for example, of religious or scientific discourse that God decided the fate of everything or that Physics decided the fate of everything. When confronted with various truth claims, anyone can surely see that at least truth is hard to come by, hard to verify, but is that enough to say a text just cannot have a certain meaning intended by a clear-headed author which represents something either actually true or actually false? Personally, I think the simple fact that some of my readers understand what I am talking about means people can relate accurate meanings.

Our life activity of speaking, given the success we usually have in conversation (whether ever agreeing), entails that the meaning of ideas often come across clearly in particular language acts, so the results of some discourses might indeed be reliable, too! At least, it seems we must nullify extreme relativism and assert that reality does contain real states of affairs whether we know and understand them. Truth exists, but it's up to us to articulate it if we can. Abandonment of meaning and truth is not what all literary theorists had in mind when debunking and deconstructing the prevalent 'truths'. Arguably, they focus on lies.

Edward Said in writing about Orientalism (the imperialist discourse of the 'West' over the 'East') draws attention to "the disparity between texts and reality" (285).

Not that finding truth is impossible, it is the prepostering of conclusions such as 'all Muslims are terrorist enemies' from evidence like repeated news coverage of car bombings which is so ethically and logically reprehensible to the 20th Century thinkers who question and attack the reliability of some symbolic structures of meaning to accurately portray reality. Respect for "the human ground…in which texts, visions, methods, and disciplines begin, grow, thrive, and degenerate" calls for us to understand the difference in the various grotesque and dishonest symbolic footholds on unaware minds from the intellectual efforts of 'deconstructionists', 'postmodernists', and other so-thought rejecters of structural truth (Said 285). I take it all as fleshing out the nature of the connection between our conceptions about the world and the thrust on our psyche of symbolic meaning and its associations; I think these thinkers were developing notions about the living nature of signs.

By encouraging the idea that our life form simply and complexly consists in knowing, understanding, communicating, and creating meaning, the Wittgenstein of the *P.I.* tried to debunk the stringent analytic and positivist philosophy that declared truth was a refined and lofty ideal that entails we could never find accuracy and universality in any deep metaphysical or applied ethical claims. The Wittgenstein of the earlier *Tractatus-Logico-Philosophicus* propounded the view, much revered by some analytic philosophers, that certainty of truth was a function of the structure of propositions in relation to their contents in some empirical, logical sense, which seemed totally to leave out ethical and metaphysical claims from possible articulation and verification. In the *P.I.*, Wittgenstein only makes seven references (according to the index) to certainty, and in the final brief look at it, he bitingly says "Am I less certain that this man is in pain than that twice two is four?—Does this shew the former to be mathematical certainty?...The kind of certainty is the kind of language-game" (p. 191). Wittgenstein's philosophic concerns were always more linguistic and psychological and almost never overtly ethical, but I guess that his later views would not suggest it impossible to find valid truth in matters of ethical significance, such as the examples of Orientalist delusions about the distant (terrorist) "other", the perspective of people that are just "it" and "them" to "ours" and "us".

Apparently to many as ideologically backed, some news coverage tells blatant lies by prioritizing the association of some images with absurd claims and downplaying or entirely neglecting coverage of relevant 'opposing' voices and situations. The media system of the news, sitcoms, "reality TV", and commercials in their tattered ideological simulation of life "corresponds to a betrayal of reality by signs…to a short-circuit of reality and to its reduplication by signs", to borrow a phrase of Jean Baudrillard from his essay "Simulacra and Simulations" (411). The mass media routinely repeats the same messages which carry a similar set of values, and it is oriented toward grandiose complicity with the agenda of traditional civilization against unheard opposing voices which are so many. The repetition and endless reconnaissance by blind-to-the-world, capitalist-friendly media represents "always the aim of ideological analysis to restore the objective process" in its favour to propound falsehoods and complicity in the enemy other or the repressed, unheard other (Baudrillard 411). I think of the way the phone-in section of news stories is often so brief and rapidly paced that many voices will never have an ample venue for discussion before the time limit is up and the sitcom or neutral business report comes in which prevents voices which aim "to restore the truth beneath the simulacrum", leaving us in complicity with the media rolling on the next *show* (Baudrillard 411).

A simple example consists in the fact of how much coverage topics like global climate change and social issues like weapons of various degrees of destruction and terrorism actually gets in the whole slew of media and how urgently we are being told by some political thinkers, scientists, and others that there is too little time to waste flaunting consumerist-ecological tendencies. Steven Hawking said for example that "as citizens of the world, we have a duty to alert the public to the unnecessary risks that we live with every day, and to the perils we foresee if governments and societies do not take action now to render nuclear weapons [including depleted uranium weaponry!] obsolete and to prevent further climate change", recorded in the ABC-News article "Doomsday Clock Now Gauges Climate Change". Clarification of such issues could result if people had more knowledge of the "other side" and gave more priority in attention to hard social issues, but we'll never know while the schizophrenic psychosis rages of SITCOM REALITY TV© mentality with its 'news', commercials, and Orientalism. As a diagnosed schizophrenic, I feel justified in making this claim. Honestly, the experience of watching television and an idea of its production psychology is one of the only and indeed the most profound analogous experience compared to the torrent of my worst schizophrenic bouts.

Proof that the media is VERY selective in what gets regularly presented comes in the following example: Adbusters: The Media Foundation, based in Vancouver, has offered up to twice the dollar value for, say ABC-TV perhaps, prime time commercial slots than what, for example, Gillette for girls or macho machine Mitsubishi for men are asked to pay for their commercials. I feel obliged when presently writing to give an example of ideology-complicit advertising which happened recently and is locally relevant to where I am living and studying, in Nanaimo, an hour and a half ferry ride from Vancouver. I guess it will be easy for anyone to guess my position on this issue as I present it, but I'll just say it:

The Jim Pattison Group owns a local radio station (it owns twenty-five in BC, two local) which presented a brief "news segment" in which a friendly, happy-go-lucky voice announced that the official website for the 2010 Olympics, which will take place in what I will agree is unceded traditional Sechelt and Coast Salish aboriginal territory, had officially announced new "mascots" for the event. The evidence of explicit ideological motive comes in the fact that besides the people who just like the idea of the Olympics happening, there are a LOT of people who are upset and some who are protesting the plans for the event. By glossing over ANY aspect of the 2010 Olympics with joy and humour while a respectable portion of the British Colombian and global population has strong to radical feelings on the subject, the radio station indicated the intentional exclusion of some perspectives and the endorsement of complicity with other perspectives. So "The mandate of the Jim Pattison Group is total customer satisfaction" except for those customers with a social conscience in solidarity with the 2010 resistance (quote from Jim Pattison official website). Yeah, right! I feel I should go on, particularly to talk about the nature of these brand new branded mascots for the 2010 Olympics, "dedicated for all children and critters with a dream" (from the official Olympics mascot video as of November 27 2007).

According to "www.vancouver2010.com/mascot/", we have little Miga, "a young sea bear who lives in the ocean with her family pod, out past Vancouver Island near Tofino", living in my place of birth, aggressively advertised for tourism; "Sea bears are part killer whale and part bear", two arguably poor off species, whose favourite food is "Wild salmon", which is VERY arguably poor off, in the form of "(salmon jerky, BC Roll, smoked salmon, etc)." which on the market is mainly farmed, drugged, GM salmon, actually. We have Sumi, "an animal spirit who lives in the mountains", whose "dream" is "[t]o share his forest and mountain home with the world", which reminds me quite of NAFTA, SPP, and the construction industry but I won't get into that. There is also "a young sasquatch who comes from the mysterious forests of Canada" named Quatchi whose hobbies are "hockey, photography, travel", three likely pursuits of a creature from deep within a mysterious forest. He likes what a 'good Canadian' might be prescribed by the mass media to like, I think. He "loves to try all kinds!" of food, meaning he's probably multicultural, "always encouraging his friends to join him on journeys across Canada"! And not least, curiously introduced later the same day as the first three, there is one actually real animal mascot for the 2010 Olympics, Mukmuk the Vancouver Island marmot, "an extremely rare and endangered species" which as a cartoon is simply adorable! Its "dream" is "to tell the world about his fellow island marmots". I hope before they go extinct because of industry and highway building like that going on for Olympics!

With numerous inter-textual weavings with the ecological, spiritual, and linguistic traditions of the aboriginal peoples in Canada, these mascots support the industries of tourism, construction, and of hockey. These symbols, whose basis is profit motivation, are language sequestered for ideology. The symbols are Canadian complicity with post-colonization, laughing in the face of First Nations groups who are actively protesting the excessive development of highways, accommodations, and sport facilities for the event that some argue will just open routes for unwanted, excessive tourist, resource, and construction based industry in the future. I think it is impossible to find a link from the official website to any of this resistance movement, but that is sadly to be expected. Arguably, the pros of a mere athletic competition plastered with corporate brand advertising televised with commercials world wide hardly outweigh the cons represented in the First Nations groups. It is the official declaration that "the International Olympic Committee Session *awards* a city the *right* to organise an edition" of the games, but it seems odd the idea of 'awarding' something unacceptable (my emphasis, Olympics website FAQ). Ordinary language powerfully orchestrates ideological exploitation.

The way they write is how they imagine they live. A story of Gerald Vizenor's, a Native American writer, *Heirs of Columbus* feels just as true a story as the idea that First Nations groups have been 'awarded the right' to experience further Canadian complicity with the destruction of ecosystems and the economic imperialism associated with the current undertaking of 'progress'. In the *Heirs of Columbus*, Vizenor tells several short stories thematically aligned with a revisioning of the history of the 'founding of

America'. In "Stone Tavern", Vizenor outright parodies the supposition of founding fathers that wrote long ago about the 'beginning' of the history of the 'New World' and the aspirations of currently funding fathers that now write the 'future' of the history of the 'New World Order' when he mocks "[c]ivilization started right here in our stories at the river we named the gichiziibi" (13). "Civilization" likely began long before even the first historicized cultures in our history books. 'History' used to begin with an account of the kings names written in the Sumerian times; writing and leadership were associated with civilization. No wonder oral First Nations cultures were originally seen by "civilization" to be "savage" and our political leaders say things like "Canada is the greatest country in the world, a nation of enormous potential built through the imagination and dedication of ordinary Canadians" like the Chinese who worked on the Railroad and the Indigenous who have been directly intentionally harmed throughout history (Throne to the Speech 2007). Some folk who reject the view of the throne assert that Canadian history is in part intensely forced colonization by diverse forces acting way beyond the scope of what Harper or whoever wrote this gibberish deems the symbol of an "ordinary Canadian".

I've now gone through example after example of highly structured and profoundly meaningful messages purporting around as beacons of truth and proper civilized society which seems from one subdued perspective incredibly corrupt while from the dominant perspective of the power structures in today's world seem just fine. That powerful ideology deems the perspective I share to be that of a delusional rabble-rouser or as too far leftist. To get back to where I started in this essay, I introduced the idea of relativism as a consequence of judging truth in queer manners and introduced meaning generation as a part of our life activity. I hold that the school of thought loosely called "deconstructionism" never intended to destroy truth and misplace certainty in interpreting literature or social worlds when theoretically attempting to mediate what is true and understandable with what is false and misleading in language.

They mostly pursued this endeavour by taking apart and overturning traditional and ideological linguistic structures. It might seem easy to go from a critique of the adequacy of certain forms of language to a feeling that language is futile in all matters of identifying relevant matters of fact in any domain or discourse. However, one could argue that in the time of these thinkers and still to this day, there sense of futility stems from fatigue of active traditional or ideological paradigms endorsed and acted on by several people that want to discredit the critique of their structures as unqualifiable and disregardable, as patently untrue. I think it was easier for defenders of the old and increasingly seen as faulty truth claims to describe the postmodern era as extremely relativistic. As for analytic philosophers of language in the early 20th century that restricted truth to a property of perfectly ordered linguistic structures and their empirical correlations, they irrationally restricted truth claims to matters of hard science and mathematics, disallowing truth pronouncement on matters such as important ethical issues. On the contrary, such "pompous scientism and appeals to rationalism" (to borrow a phrase from Said) disrespect the fact that many voices have been forcefully silenced and intentionally ignored throughout history by the regimes of material and psychological power (285).

However, through the work of some good thinkers in the 20th Century, the global casino (dominant ideological voice) has lost its anchor (transcendental signifier) and moorings (associations of tendency that many now disallow to tie up their mind) like "[t]he *Santa Maria* lost her anchor and moorings as a sovereign casino" (Vizenor 12). "[T]he spirit catchers, macaroni, and polyurethane" of the ideological sovereign are "lost on" the unimpressed and stifled voices; the simulacra of the fleet of ideologies has burst open (Vizenor 12). The somewhat small but louder growing voices of the colonized, the orientalised, the lied to, and the made complicit are less and less putting up with psychotic symbols that have no basis in reality and are hostile to their life-form. The simulacra of dominant ideologies have been spilled open, on and on through history, as revolutions in political, religious, scientific, and literary discourse take place. The theories dubbed by some as 'truth denial' have really aimed, like me with my examples, to deconstruct and deny destructive illusions rather than affirm relativism! These methods of post-analytic philosophy of language have sought to go beyond the so-called limits of language in order to relay adequate ideas about the real structure of our imaginary symbolic relations with ideology and to relay adequate ideas about ethical and philosophical issues.

Works Cited

"ABC News: Doomsday Clock Now Gauges Climate Change". ABC News Science and Technology. 26 Nov 2007 <http://abcnews.go.com/Technology/wireStory?id=2801776>.

"About Us". The Jim Pattison Group, Signs, Outdoor, Auto, Media, Food, Entertainment and Export official site. 26 Nov 2007 <http://www.jimpattison.com/corporate/about_us.htm>.

Althusser, Louis. "Ideology and Ideological State Apparatuses". 1970. Marxists Internet Archive. 24 Oct 2007 <www.marxists.org/reference/archive/althusser/1970/ideology.htm>.

Barthes, Roland. "The Death of the Author". Ed David Lodge. 1977: (146-150).

Baudrillard, Jean. "Simulacra and Simulations". Ed David Lodge. 1980: (404-411).

Lodge, David and Nigel Wood. *Modern Criticism and Theory: A Reader—Second Edition*. Edinburgh Gate: Pearson Education Limited, 2000.

Said, Edward. "Crisis (in Orientalism)". Ed David Lodge. 1978: (272-285).

"Speech from the Throne—Strong Leadership. A Better Canada." Government of Canada official website. 27 Nov 2007 <http://www.sft-ddt.gc.ca/eng/media.asp?id=1364>.

"Vancouver 2010—Meet the Vancouver 2010 Mascots". Vancouver 2010 Olympics official website. 28 Nov 2007 <http://www.vancouver2010.com/mascot/en/meet.php>.

Vizenor, Gerald. *The Heirs of Columbus*. Middletown: Wesleyan UP, 1991.

Wittgenstein, Ludwig. *Philosophical Investigations: 50th Anniversary Commemorative Edition*. Trans. G.E.M. Anscombe. Malden: Blackwell Publishing, 2001.

English 214—Themes in First Nations Literature
Wednesday, March 30, 3005

Essay 3
To Inspire an Adequate Response...

Joseph Dandurand's play, *Please Do Not Touch The Indians*, conveys a dark history in Canada that many do not fully conceive the extent of. Cultures of colonization historically accepted and sought to legally justify the forcing of most indigenous cultures in Canada into conditions today deemed deplorable, which writers like Dandurand explore. In his play that inspires respect for those impacted by past and present conditions, Dandurand subverts both colonial as well as contemporary patterns of oppression by exploring Canadian history from the telling perspectives of characters who received the dark side of that history.

The characters of the play are one white tourist, three animals—a wolf, a raven, and a coyote—and two wooden Indians with an appearance "not quite traditional but more of a Hollywood taste" (7). The overt plot of the play consists in "Tourist" emerging upon stage to represent the others in a medium like photography, painting, or film while ignorant that when offstage, the others communicate and reminisce upon events in their past. The characters other than the tourist are the tormented ghosts of devastated Native individuals who were deprived of peace by murderers of an oppressive culture. Throughout the play, the characters fondly remember bearable parts of their lives and later in the play painfully remember the events that ended their mortal lives. Via characters whose memories are archetypal of real abuses that occurred toward Natives, Dandurand teaches to his audience a dark side of Canadian history such as terrifying experiences that happened in residential schools and army-perpetrated massacres.

In his essay "The Hearts of Its Women: Rape, Residential Schools, and Re-membering," Ric Knowles comments on what he interprets as a primary focus of First Nations Literature, noting that many Native playwrights have quoted the traditional Cheyenne saying that "[a] nation is not conquered until the hearts of its women are on the ground" (Knowles 245). Knowles comments that

> [the] most pervasive feature of current Native writing ... seems to be the impact of "Residential schools—past, present, and future" (18) on Native Children. These are the Christian-run schools to which First Nations children were taken by force, removed from their communities, and denied access to their languages and cultures, by government decree for over a century from the mid 1800s until the 1970s. (Knowles 245).

That means some people currently alive have living memory of this disservice, but Joseph Dandurand is young enough that his knowledge of the greatest material abuses in Canadian history come from the memories and stories of others. Perhaps, the greatest value of Dandurand's writing comes in the very fact of his continuing to tell stories of abuse in history even when personally beyond it, for unless people continually retell these stories of past colonization, some may lapse and hurt others again. In an essay that talks about the impact on children of colonization called

"The Children of Tomorrow's Great Potlatch," Ernie Grey writes as a member in the Cheam band of the Sto:lo nation that "[we] dream of the day when First Nations people and whites will sit together to take part in a great potlatch. Before this happens, the whites must learn more of the First Nations history, because understanding is essential to create solutions and harmony" (Grey 150). Immediately following this statement, Grey includes a quotation from Chief Joe Mathias that "[the] Indian Act of 1876 shattered the lives of the aboriginal people of Canada," and Grey continues to state "those most profoundly damaged were the children of the First Nations people" (Grey 150, 151). Colonizers strove hard to disrupt healthy human growth.

Sister Coyote, a character of Dandurand's play, represents this history as a child taken from home and put in school. Her heart stomped hard to the ground, Sister Coyote relates her experience in the school, "being beaten and kicked around," and then she describes a priest viciously raping her while telling her frighteningly gross lies: "he hurt me real bad, all the time telling me I was his gift from the lord and that I should never tell anyone. He raped me and then he smacked me across the face and told me to never tell anyone or else God would punish me" (49). This priest attempts to conquer Sister Coyote's heart by crushing her to subordination by his desires and reduces her to such a state that she kills herself with a belt discarded by him while exploiting her.

Grey informs his reader with a quote from Dr. Neil MacDonald of the University of Manitoba that when children were when taken from their parents' shelter, they were "assigned a number and unceremoniously herded into cattle cars for transport to the residential school" (Grey 151).

Values of the kind pervaded in real life that in the play allowed the priest to attack and dismiss the importance of Sister Coyote. Dr. Neil MacDonald wrote about an incident at one "Fall round-up" of children when they were taken to go to residential school:

> The women ran alongside the cattle cars until they found their child or children. They grabbed the hands of their children and refused to let go, thus preventing the train's departure. The RCMP constables responded by climbing up the sides of the cars and stomped on the hands of the mothers, breaking their grips and some of their hands and fingers. (Grey 151-2).

All sorts of horrors abound in the colonizer's historical treatment of First Nations people, horrors whose diversity and quantity forces upon one the realization that Canadian history involves entrenched systematic oppressions. "Real, material technologies of colonization," the phrase Ric Knowles uses to describe rape and sexual violence, exist in many forms as shown by the preceding story and the story of Sister Coyote (Knowles 245). Spiritually dismissive attitudes—the kind acted upon Natives by the various modes of destructive colonization—run together with assimilation, "ethnic cleansing[,] and cultural genocide" (Knowles 246).

Nothing but spiritually dismissive attitudes could result in a whole society systematically oppressing, injuring, and attempting to assimilate another. Wooden Woman, another tormented ghost of Dandurand's play, relives her memories of being a Native mother at a time when "battle" went on—when dressed in "blue US cavalry" purposefully hunted Native groups to scalp and massacre any dark-skinned man, woman, or child they could find (42). In a culturally autobiographical vein that also imparts visceral emotions, Wooden Woman tells that "[the US cavalry] slit their throats, the youngest of the children, slit their throats and tossed their small harmless bodies into the hole" (48). She relives an attack as she hides with her child waiting for the dark-hearted men to find her. The attackers annihilate her sanity—frighteningly stomping her heart to the ground: "They were coming to kill me and take my hair. My child wouldn't stop screaming so I took some dead leaves and gently pushed them into her mouth" (51). Eventually the crying child suffocates, which itself most powerfully torments Wooden Woman's soul while in limbo with the other characters.

Colonial patterns of oppressors must include delusional self-rationales for acting out these torments, rationales which I refer to with the phrase spiritually dismissive attitudes. Colonialists needed to strongly imagine their Native hosts as worth very little in order to have the moral ability to so mercilessly ravage and malign. To feel sane while murdering or raping someone else, people who deem themselves "good and civilized" or at least "right" must force their minds to contort reality into severe delusions of dichotomy between self and other. Such a colonial dichotomy surely lent philosophical support to both the "legitimized" abuse upon Natives by Canadian law and the preservation of residential schools until the 1970s, within 35 years of today. Dandurand subverts colonial dichotomies of worthy human versus denigrated primitive by relating to us compelling first-person perspectives of innocent, intelligent Native people impacted and devastated by savage colonizers.

By informing his audience in a carefully symbolic way about this side of Canadian history, symbols which I'll explain in the next paragraph, Dandurand also subverts something he perceives continuing to happen now. I have noticed a phenomenon that some people do not fully conceive the extent of a dark Canadian history, tending to believe Canada to be a forerunner of international peace with nothing under its belt but innocuous good will. A look within, however, such as the look given by Dandurand and the critics I have mentioned, reveals a great deal of social decay that festers under the surface of everyday contemporary life. The most desperate colonial actions thrum in a time just now behind us. Today, our governments renounce such cultural decay, but I suggest contemporary values have not instantaneously and easily changed between generations. No reason other than to merely recite the past exists for Native playwrights to go back, again and again, to the subject of lingering suffering unless hazy, decayed contemporary values provide such a reason to tell stories that instruct societies away from destructive behaviour.

Whereas life memories of the Native characters in *Please Do Not Touch The Indians* primarily express the emotional hell perpetrated upon Natives by colonialism in the past, the character simply called Tourist most vividly symbolizes the contemporary persistence of sick values behind past atrocities. The title of the play is the same statement that reads on a sign initially hanging around Wooden Man's neck, a kind of sign to tell tourists not to touch, because they might damage what they touch. Tourist spends much of his time onstage taking images of the Native characters while not knowing or touching at all upon the horrific lives they lived before becoming spirits in limbo. I think Tourist symbolizes intended efforts of the colonial project and can provide insight into the strange phenomenon I discussed concerning Canadians not fully understanding the extent of suffering perpetrated through their history. I feel the presence of an analogy occurring somewhere between Tourist's ignorance of the Natives' deeper lives while striving to have a beautiful image to keep of them and the way contemporary Canadian society carries forth its history. I think Dandurand subverts contemporary social prerogatives by making a damned fool of Tourist, especially when at the end of the play he stunningly directs the Hollywood-ized enactment of the horrific massacre that Wooden Woman lost her life and child to. If elements of contemporary society genuinely are as negligent as Tourist in their evaluation of history and of cultural identities, then Dandurand subtly presents a strong case for a re-evaluation of contemporary social agendas.

As example of how contemporary Canadian society responds to its history, I have my own experience to offer. I went through elementary school instructed by teachers that Native culture was a) interesting to know about, b) worthy of respect, c) as good as other cultures and d) important to my Canadian heritage. Beyond seeing examples of art and technology and beyond doing crafts, I do not recall an equivalent amount of sincere discussion about highly problematic values that currently linger from a dark history of systematic cultural attack. Elizabeth Mary Furniss wrote her thesis dissertation for a doctorate of philosophy in the department of anthropology and sociology at UBC, and its name is *In the Spirit of the Pioneers: Historical Consciousness, Cultural Colonialism and Indian/White Relations in Rural British Columbia* (1997). She claimed "the power that reinforces the subordination of aboriginal peoples in Canada is exercised by 'ordinary' rural Euro-Canadians whose cultural attitudes and activities are forces in an ongoing, contemporary system of colonial domination" (ii). On Vancouver Island having grown up in the rural town of Ucluelet (with a population around sixteen-hundred, a couple hundred of which are Natives mostly on a reserve) before living in the city of Nanaimo, I attest that I bear witness to more "subordination" in everyday racial attitudes in Ucluelet than Nanaimo and in Nanaimo than Vancouver, and I also attest that 'both sides' often construe their ideas as perfectly "ordinary" and "reasonable." Issues of subordination sometimes entered secondary school classrooms, but I mainly remember being told dates of armed conflicts and being told about the activity of trade routes in distant regions. Although the official mandate is that Aboriginal and Euro-Canadian culture should peacefully coexist in Canada, I think the current state of moral affairs and the current state of public education lag and do not adequately supply the data and testimonial—such as Native authors like Dandurand convey—that will expose to youth the real problems opposed to a cultural peace.

I think we still linger near the beginning of a transitional period toward peace, considering residential schools ended only within 35 years of the present day. Canada is still discarding the oppressive, destructive values and learning the constructive, compassionate ones, and as long as stories keep spinning, we will learn. Luckily, First Nations Literature grows in popularity, and I see only Native writers that, like Dandurand, well know history and intentionally work with constructive goals in mind toward a peace for those impacted in various ways throughout history and to this day. The history of our land and people reveals its shades, both light and dark, to us upon our today reaching—striving—beyond the causes of suffering through literature and charitable remembrance. ...Please do not forget the Indians.

Works Cited

Dandurand, Joseph A. *Please Do Not Touch The Indians*. Candler, NC: Renegade Planets Publishing, 2004.

Furniss, Elizabeth. *In the Spirit of the Pioneers: Historical Consciousness, Cultural Colonialism and Indian/White Relations in Rural British Columbia*. Ottawa, Ontario: UMI Dissertation Services, 2001.

Grey, Ernie. "The Children of Tomorrow's Great Potlatch." *In Celebration of Our Survival: The First Nations of British Columbia*. Ed. Doreen Jensen and Cheryl Brooks. Also BC Studies no. 89. 1991.

Knowles, Ric. "The Hearts of Its Women: Rape, Residential Schools, and Re-membering." *Performing National Identities: International Perspectives on Contemporary Canadian Theatre*. Ed. Sherrill Grace and Albert-Reiner Glaap, Vancouver: Talon Books, 2003.

PHIL 362—Philosophy of Mind
Wednesday, April 19, 2006

Essay 4
The Physical Future Awaits
Our Conscious Contributions

A lot of us want scientific truth about the structure of our reality, truth about the cosmos observed around us. For a majority of thinkers in the contemporary era who pursue rational, natural explanations of the world that we observe, physical theories take centre precedence in explanatory accounts. In particular, the idea that all matter behaves independently from human choice has heavily influenced empirical science and materialist philosophy for the past three hundred years. Mainstream scientists traditionally discount any possible effect of mind upon matter in any context, including the physical motion of the particles in our body. *However, today's science shows that physical outcomes are not always physically predetermined.*

One should question what the old science says about our conscious choices. Stapp et al. (2005) wrote a paper called "Quantum Physics in Neuroscience and Psychology" in which they criticize the stagnant "classical physical theory" that proposes "the complete history of the physical world *for all time* is mechanically fixed by contact interactions between tiny component parts, together with the initial condition of the primordial universe" (their emphasis, p. 19). Mainstream neuropsychology believes

325

this "causal closure" to include the matter of our bodies and brains, such that "you are a mechanical automaton" of blind brain physics (Stapp et al. p. 19). In the mainstream science, all "mental aspects are *causally redundant*" compared to nature's presumed blind choices (their emphasis, Stapp et al. p.19). The incredible experience of the meaningful involvement of conscious beings with their life activity is *deduced* from classical notions to be an entirely "false and misleading illusion" (Stapp et all, p. 19). Even if newer physics describes the future of any physical system as truly open-ended, mainstream perspectives insist that the nature of indeterminate openness is utter mindless randomness.

There is no way around the fact that if the universe of matter behaves with absolute causal independence from mental action, then consciousness has no efficacy in governing our mental or material behaviour. Our conscious experience of making effective choices is just a meaningless mystery of delusion if our physical bodies do every necessary causal job without conscious input. However, such a "classical mechanical" view of life has actually been firmly falsified by contemporary science, namely by quantum theory. Classical mechanics, the view that matter always behaves independently from the choices of conscious agents, has been demonstrated as plainly false, but experts in physics, psychology, and neuroscience stubbornly and irrationally refuse to admit it. They won't admit the empirical evidence from actual, repeatable experiments that physical processes can definitely require the input of conscious choices in a non-physically determined way.

"Free choices" underlie today's "orthodox" science, regardless of the belly-aching of experts. Physicist Henry Stapp wrote an essay called "Quantum Interactive Dualism" in which he explains "[t]he most radical departure from classical physics instituted by the founders of quantum mechanics was the introduction of human consciousness into the dynamical and computational machinery" (Stapp, p. 3). Unlike the picture of the independent universe held by Descartes and Newton, quantum theory *in principle* depends on consciousness to explain the physical world. Stapp talks about two prime obstacles to such an inclusive theory: 1) the vehement opinions of some non-physicists that blind matter "provides an entirely adequate foundation for understanding brain dynamics, in spite of the physics calculations that indicate the opposite" and 2) the backward opinions of certain physicists that science should simply do away with "the hugely successful orthodox quantum theory, which is intrinsically dualistic", just in order to satisfy materialist philosophy (Stapp p. 18). Stapp says "[n]either of these opinions has any rational scientific basis" (Stapp p. 18).

To common, scientifically ignorant materialists, these words sound simply absurd. It is very troubling for several philosophers and scientists to accept that human choices possess a genuine capacity to cause physical effects or accept that matter is neither classically nor randomly determined in every instance. In the physics laboratories, consciousness has verifiable causal efficacy, and many scientists now rationally suppose that it is only a matter of time and experiments before neuropsychology has actual empirical proof that causal efficacy exists between our minds and our brains and not between just our minds and subatomic phenomena outside our bodies. One would be thoroughly irrational, given the experiments, to argue on the grounds of "what makes physical sense" that the claim "consciousness has a causal role in physical events" is *a priori unscientific*.

Entirely on the other hand, the best available physical evidence and the most parsimonious, coherent theory require that consciousness be deemed an essential element of nature's causal mechanisms. There is no way around this idea of basic freedom, unless we abandon scientific principles and accept a fundamentally irrational universe that lies to us and gives us the illusion of free efficacy. Freedom of choice to affect matter is already empirically verified by physical experiments, so before throwing out all our intuitions and best predictive science, perhaps philosophers should straightforwardly accept that consciousness might affect the brain. If one would still, after learning about the quantum experiments, find it untenable that our consciousness alone can govern physical changes, then that one had better accept as most scientific the perceptual illusion of Rene Descartes' Evil Demon. I insist again that laboratory experiments have already proven beyond possible reasonable argumentation that a human mind is no "causally inert witness to the mindless dance of atoms" (Stapp 18).

Karl Popper (1902-1994) contributed to philosophy of science, and one concept he discussed was "promissory materialism", which accepts that materialism has big explanatory inadequacies in its present form but believes that mere physical mechanism will eventually explain consciousness as scientific understanding grows. Materialists can only prophetically promise that one day far from now our knowledge, decisions, and efforts will be successfully interpreted as contributing nothing to the causes of our physical behaviour or of the behaviour of any objects in the physical universe beyond us. However, (Stapp et al. 2005) write that this

> *"reductionist demand that the course of human experience be determined by local mechanical processes is the very thing that is most conclusively ruled out by the structure of natural phenomena specified by contemporary physical theory.* To expect the mind-brain connection to be understood within a framework of ideas so contrary to the principles of physics is scientifically unsupportable and unreasonable" (their emphasis, p. 60)

The hardest part of this proposal for most people is letting go of the principle of complete bottom-up causation from merely third-person entities. "In the first place the idea that all causation is *fundamentally mechanical* is dropped [by the quantum approach] as being prejudicial and unsupported either by direct evidence or by contemporary physical theory" (their emphasis, Stapp et al. p. 61). Unlike the math of classical physics, the mathematical rules of quantum physics "directly specify the causal effects upon the subject's brain of the choices made by the subject, without needing to specify how these choices came about", which provides an empirically testable method for seeing the effects of our choices (Stapp et al. p. 62). Instead of seeing conscious choices as totally automatically emergent from a third-person ontology of classically conceived brain connections, "[t]he form of the quantum laws accommodates a natural dynamical breakpoint between the *cause* of willful action, which [is] not specified by the theory, and its *effects*, which are specified by the theory" (their emphasis, Stapp et al. p. 62). It is within the reach of science to empirically verify that voluntary action can affect the brain. Science has already falsified that matter does all by itself in a blind way.

There is a particularly common objection to this material accommodation of free will. It says, "Quantum mechanics gives us randomness but not freedom." This is misleading and actually indicates the interpretation of "some theory that re-converts human consciousness into a causally inert witness to the mindless dance of atoms" (Stapp 18). The concept of randomness needs to be explained. It stems from Heisenberg's uncertainty principle, which entails that measuring one property of a physical system has the effect of "randomizing" future measurements of complementary properties. For instance, measuring the position of some moving particle will change in a non-classical way the possible future measurement of its momentum. The momentum could randomly be a high or low value, and the range of uncertainty depends on the accuracy of measuring the position. In other words, when a human becomes consciously aware of certain aspects of some physical processes (a measurement), nature makes a choice in a probabilistic way of what the human will become next aware. The choices of nature have been shown by empirical methods to be "random" in the precise sense that all processes have fairly "statistical" yet "uncertain" outcomes. Nature makes a "random" choice for the system to evolve along one path and no other, and each path will have a relative probability (with 50-50 chances or yes-no occurrence, etc) while the actual path is truly physically indeterminate. Significantly, the act of measurement *is not* random in this same sense.

That a human measures and becomes aware of some property is in no way trivial to the physical dynamics under question. One quantum theory founder, Niels Bohr, said the experimenters "make a choice between the different complementary types of phenomena that we want to study" [1], so physical uncertainty really exists in addition to conscious efficacy. Random things occur in laboratories, but we also consciously affect what occurs. Niels Bohr also said "we are both onlookers and actors in the great drama of existence." [2]

The real clincher in these experiments, which the reader must intend to study and acknowledge for him or herself, is that *when a human develops awareness* about certain aspects of some process, *nature makes a different kind of behaviour*, and the experiment turns out different. In the laboratory, IF someone A) shines a beam of light through two openings in a barrier, B) has a computer record through which openings each photon passed, and C) deletes half the record while becoming aware of the other half, then to our amazement *two unique patterns* of light are left on the detector screen. These patterns demonstrate the capacity of human awareness to *create different physical realities*, and the detected patterns change even if one deletes half the record and looks at the other half weeks after the light beam was turned off. Distinct patterns physically created by some process depend on when and how a human consciously accesses different aspects of it. The difference in the light pattern never depends on mechanical interference of any of the equipment. See www.bottomlayer.com for

---

[1] Niels Bohr. 1958: Atomic Physics and Human Knowledge. New York: Wiley, p.51
[2] Niels Bohr. 1961: Atomic Theory and the Description of Nature. Cambridge: The University Press, p. 119.

great run-downs of these experiments and their classically counterintuitive results.

The scientific task of understanding the experience of free will in human behaviour involves, then, a rationally coherent endeavour toward understanding how conscious awareness might "make the choices" of our brains, which in principle are composed of processes that are physically indeterminate and require at least the probabilistic choice of nature. In terms of scientific rationality, philosophers just cannot base their theories on a brain that is a lumpy mass of goo that inexorably automates for itself what will happen next. Certain laboratory experiments well support the thesis of physical indeterminism offset by strange effects of human awareness, and time and research could make sensible the effects of minds in the brain.

Neuroscientists might eventually correlate subjective human decisions with physically indeterminate processes in the brain that have, in principle, a nature that necessitates the making of some choice or another. Perhaps unconscious behaviour belongs to nature's statistical randomness, and voluntary behaviour belongs to our conscious choices. Such a reality has both an intuitive and scientific sensibility, and materialism can never make as much sense. Really! The scientific and philosophical climate has come to this question: will we accept the evidence, if it mounts, that speaks directly to the involvement of consciousness in the outcomes of our brains and universe made of matter? The science and math enables us in principle to literally see the effects of consciousness on a physical system like the brain; moreover, the cause of our choices could never occur as result of a deterministic brain, because such a brain does not exist. If we believe no causes are unnatural and want to keep the best scientific theories we have (to keep our lives away from the reaches of a domineering god or demon), then free will might be the only rationally scientific way to understand the apparent link between choices and knowledge, on the one side, and the future-open brain processes that facilitate and inform our behaviour.

Materialists want to see individual living cells, slugs (which have about 16 neurons!!), and all the molecular mayhem before human emergence as occurring absolutely independently from all conscious whim whatsoever. This seems to me the antiquated residue of philosophical tradition against Descartes' last ditch effort to unite God and physically objective science. I think the real trouble for materialists is accepting the premise as a principle for argument that matter might exist only amidst conscious whim, and they cannot accept such an openly conscious reality as having any rationally conceivable merit. The materialist usually objects: how do the stars exist in such a pan-psychist world, and does this not presuppose an absurd vitalist teleology with respect to ordinary matter?

The Ancient Egyptians believed Ra the sun has consciousness like them, many indigenous cultures believe nature to embody unseen minds, and contemporary science now begins to unearth facts about our role in nature: we know that we in part establish physical reality because no "ordinary matter" exists. This *spiritual* conception of human nature as causally effective fits well with the scientific view that physical systems need non-classical mechanisms to evolve, so the notion of an ultimately independent physical reality is irreparably compromised. That doesn't mean I hold that gravity does not cause rocks to fall when we drop them!

It just means the existence of life in the universe primarily involves our kind of consciousness instead of conceiving life as being just a mere result of forever absolutely blindly guided matter. Regardless of what "scientific understanding of matter" traditionally entails, sensitive reasoning about actual facts might eventually lead us scientifically to view the universe no longer as a bunch of blind particles and waves but instead as a swarm of causally influential, intelligent beings. It turns out in quantum theory that only freedom of will can adequately secure our scientific conception of the rest of the physical universe. If that sounds strange, keep in mind that the quantum theory of physical nature both allows minds to have influence on matter as well as it mathematically accounts for every classical physics prediction. Causally effective consciousness in no way implies an absurd physical universe! A physics that entails conscious agents never direct their own behaviour is what seems absurd.

Works Cited

Schwartz, Jeffrey. Stapp, Henry. Beauregard, Mario. "Quantum Physics in Neuroscience and Psychology: A Neurophysical Model of Mind/Brain Interaction". Philosophical Transactions of the Royal Society, B 360(1458) 1309-27. 2005.

Stapp, Henry. "Quantum Interactive Dualism: An Alternative to Materialism". Journal of Consciousness Studies, 12 no. 11. 2005.

Additional Resources

<http://www-physics.lbl.gov/~stapp/stappfiles.html>—The above cited works and more writing by Henry Stapp can be found here.

<www.bottomlayer.com>—See for discussion of quantum theory's underlying "weird" experiments that may be demonstrating consciousness to interfere with processes in physical systems in a manner vastly unique from ordinarily conceived physical causation. Pursuing empirical experiments is basically the only satisfactory rational way to start to theorize these strange immaterial powers of the mind.

Phil 370—Philosophy and Social Science
Monday, November 24, 2008

Essay 5
Worlds Apart from the Same World

I will begin by exposing the "illustrious postmodernist fallacy." It goes something like this, to use the words of John Searle, eminent philosopher, in *Mind, Language, and Society—Philosophy in the Real World*: the "postmodernist challenge" consists in saying (of any discipline, humanistic or scientific) "our discourse is a series of mutually untranslatable and incommensurable language games...in which there are [no] universal standards of rationality" (Searle 4). Face-painting freckles with a double-wide roller just ain't pretty.

He somewhat accurately groups the postmodern challengers with the theses of "relativism" and doubt in "the Enlightenment vision." The fallacy is named thus for the illustrious attitude of the "postmodernist" who would fledge a whole scale barrage upon not only the recently established edifices but also any mere notions of enlightened truth and reason. Searle thinks "that the universe exists quite independently of our minds and that... we can come to comprehend its nature" in supposed contradiction with what postmodern paradigms uphold. There may be a *few* renegade Western-raised Liberal-educated students of "the" postmodernists who run a line of extreme, across-the-board relativism, but I would hardly say the truly influential writers of this zeitgeist of a movement deeply oppose theses such as that reality or the universe does have a comprehendible and independent systemic organization.

The postmodern field may still have a different approach than Searle's so-called-by-me Enlightenment methodology, but this approach need not deny the possibility of "epistemic objectivity" about "ontological objectivity and subjectivity" which is the real position Searle seeks to defend. Some postmodernists take the position that science is fairly right on about the truth, but they still doubt the moral and intellectual will of political systems. Some think "ontologically subjective" human experience of "epistemically subjective" aspects of reality, for example choice and effort to create by definition and rule-process labels like "(gay) marriage," are simply more important socially than a straightforward scientific, shall I say, Enlightened account that not many people can relate to without great hope that one day some kind of magic exists. I refer to biological and physical explanations and the insistence that these operate beyond conscious intervention, while some like Searle also insist or at least strongly imply that we probably intervene somehow. The tension in such theoretical, metaphysical arguments predisposes some thinkers, surely many in "the postmodern group," to argue perhaps validly that some science and believers in science have definite dealings to make with some apparent deep contradictions between some of their theories on the one hand and their living, daily principles on the other hand. A critic can make an argument along several of these lines and properly belong to the recognizably vague label of postmodern school, most importantly all without denying *that we can know about reality* and without a jump on board with raw "idealism" and the abandonment of mind independent, mind knowable phenomena (Searle 16).

That's enough about the illustrious postmodernist fallacy and a taste of other potential ways to doubt the so-called Enlightenment vision without throwing out reality with the bath water. Let us get on with a constructive criticism of Searle's positive argument for "How the Mind Creates an Objective Social Reality," which he makes in chapter 5 of his recent book. To make my case in basic agreement with Searle, I will use a hopefully controversial example of "social reality" that Searle may take odds with given some of the premises and passing points of his overall perspective. I will discuss the social reality of physics. "[W]e have turned to physicists to find what the world is really made of, and they have told us" says Bruce Gregory in a chapter titled "The Last Word" in his book *Inventing Reality: Physics as Language*. What they have told us, however, has "hardly reassured those of us looking for certainty" (Gregory 196). His book chronicles some epistemological debates, amongst physicists, about the fundamental nature of reality. Basically, we don't know squat about 'what that there' *really* is in terms of anything independent like a bunch of microscopic billiard balls in somewhat bent space. The important point Gregory makes, is not that such a claim in some way reduces the plausibility of the thesis that we can accurately predict and model how physical systems will behave.

His point is that in their social practice (of trying to articulate truth and increase control about the physical universe) "physicists choose the language that allows their predictions most closely to fit their observations" (Gregory

199). In general, the physics-based scientific method may have been successful most of all "by *letting the agreement* between prediction and observations tell them *which ways of talking to keep, and which to discard*" (Gregory 198, my emphasis). The move in Gregory's argument is not the blatant postmodernist effort to depict, as several key founders of contemporary physics like Einstein and Heisenberg concluded, that "despite how it may seem, physics is not an undistorted picture of an already-made world but a way of talking about the world" (Gregory 201). He does say, averse to Searle's ears I would suppose, that we can still "choose" to speak of "given realities" (Gregory 201). But, this is still a twine into language and, at least according to some of the great minds of modern physics, not clarity in our exact knowledge of facts of physical reality as they "really are." However, the interesting move is that all we can "say" really is are oranges and humans and assemblies of cells—which are assemblies of molecules which if you keep shrinking are ultimately, by one *worded* interpretation, regulated assemblies of potential for systems of spatial form and conduct.

The key revelation of modern physics, according to Gregory, is that molecules are as real as observations of oranges and humans are real objects of inquiry for hungry kids and social scientists. One way to frame it would be to talk about how microscopes and Geiger counters are ultimately ways to give us information about how we interact with the world; physics is thus a language game, which improves powers of prediction and technology precisely by clarifying concepts and methods of interaction. The lack of ability, to say what an atom and an orange "are" in final terms of structure or substance, gives no problem to the postmodern philosopher of science. Basically, as I would articulate it, physics as essentially a mentally constructed "objective social reality" in the sense Searle takes provides us with knowledge, which Searle would not disagree with I think, that takes the form of a consistent language of models based on observations which do entail accurate predictions of and interesting explanations to certain questions about physical systems. However, to go postmodern on Searle, seeing an atom with a microscope thru our optic nerve is "identical" in some sense with holding an orange in the palm of our hand. A physical system mediated by language and experience of observations exists, answering "what is it?"

This discussion should only slightly unsettle Searle's conceptual roll, and his basic thesis that we can have knowledge of a world either independent from mental construction or "not a matter of (epistemically) subjective opinion" is obviously not set out to be damaged, and if he were to think such an argument about physics as language does so, I have one response (Searle 45). It's not that physics as an ontologically subjective and mind-dependent social reality negates the possibility of epistemic objectivity about 'the world.' On the contrary, the move in question is one more of recognition that all knowledge is mediated by language and still rational and acceptable as knowledge. What modern physicists might say we know are the mathematical relationships between different aspects of the experiential field from which we linguistically transcribe our observations and descriptions. What we know, with obvious limitation, is something like 'the order and connection of metamorphosis undergone within the substance of experience' rather than 'the actual substance of a human being or frog or photon.'

Really, I don't see the point to the trouble or fuss that Searle takes in rejecting the "postmodernist challenge" or see the trouble he seems to perceive in making a case for socially constructed objective realities. Part of Gregory's *Inventing Reality* articulates the social formula or "institutional facts" at play in the phenomena of physics (Searle 121). He points out that physicists conduct their activity that plays several functions (broadening understanding and knowledge for the curious and procuring technological finesse; two good examples) by agreements to articulate observations and predictions about the real world of structural motion with finer and finer language. We got so far with robots and into outer space by learning to talk about the world in undeniably better (more accurate, useful, sophisticated, etc) ways, hence we can say we verily know objectively aspects of the world better than we used to. Physics, even though it's constructed by minds for minds, is still an objective social reality, and even though the world is a certain way regardless of our opinions, language in experience is the mode of our being and hence entails the shape of our knowledge of the world. Just think of the line from Quantum Theory: one particle goes thru both slits at once—is simultaneously in two places.

Therefore, while Searle may feel worlds apart from postmodernist views of social constructivism, relativism of the sort Searle rejects is the least likely of sophisticated postmodern responses to the idea of objective science or, for that matter, morality. That language and perspective shape our knowledge, the real harbinger of postmodern critique as Searle gets right, does not anywise *a priori* delimit the ability to construct objective social facts. For example, marriage may be subjective in being, essentially arbitrary in form, its value culturally relative, but the reality of what marriage or physics means and what we can know about marriage or physics consists in a *kind* of certainty! What function we assign into and procure from our institutions and our subjective language constitutes the objective reality of what we create in our role *as* subjects.

Works Cited

Gregory, Bruce. *Inventing Reality—Physics as Language.* New York, New York: Wiley Science Editions, 1990.

Searle, John. *Mind, Language, and Society—Philosophy in the Real World.* New York, New York: Basic Books (Perseus), 1998.

English 300—Backgrounds to English Literature
December 1, 2008

Essay 6
Shifts of Focus: Encyclopedia in Dante's Divine Comedy *and in Niven and Pournelle's* Inferno

> *O sages, standing, in Gaia's holy fire*
> *as in the shining golden mosaic of a wall.*
> *Beheld exotic soma, threshold reality;*
> *and be the singing masters of my oversoul.*
> *Consume my heart away; drunk with desire*
> *and fastened to a dying, primal, screaming animal.*
> *It knows not what it is, but gathers*
> *me up*
> *into this artifice of eternity.*

—"Icaro Ayahuasca," by band Catal Huyuk on *Nature Loves Courage*, a rare, discontinued release; contemporary adaptation of third verse of W.B. Yeats' "Sailing to Byzantium."

There has circulated for cultural eons the idea that humans are in need of much guidance, support, purpose, correction, or whatever term fits the bill as the motivation for acts of education. Stories often mean to guide how people see themselves and the world and see their relations with others and the world. *The Divine Comedy* of Dante

Alighieri tells of a midlife pilgrimage of a poet through Hell, Purgatory, and Paradise in order to save his soul. Literature also happens in specific historical, cultural, and intellectual contexts of an author. In the words of Joan Ferrante in her book titled *The Political Vision of the Divine Comedy*, "[b]ecause neither the empire nor the church was functioning as the guide God intended it to be, the poet had to fill the vacancy" (43). New times call for change as it were, and writers leap to the task.

This essay will explore the ways in which Dante's epic and a contemporary rewrite share purposes and literary structure while a shift in the rewrite focuses on contemporary concerns. To rewrite famous works new attention must be given, as my epitaph indicates in the update of Yeats' "God" to more new age "Gaia," among other changes. One can read the first canticle *Inferno* as a warning of what eternal damnation pursues a lifetime of sin, and knowing Dante was a Christian may impose on a contemporary reader that something like a real, eternally damning Hell might have been Dante's actual, deep belief. Regardless of biographic detail that would be hard to pin down, however, there are many possible manners and paths for a reading of Dante's text that do not require a reader to impose the categories the text overtly provides, even if we know Dante is Christian. Instead, we can elicit glimmers of those categories while making interpretation withstand a tension of potential meanings, including following simultaneous paths through the thick of the text.

There is the encyclopedia of Christian sin, but Dante also catalogues the political and social attitudes of his day by including Florentines and others from the actual world in his fiction. Encyclopedia or bodies of knowledge, instruments of guidance, are evoked in the text ranging in topics from physics, political philosophy, and psychology, to name a few that I will mention here. Dante's legacy lives on as a profound influence to many authors since his time. Authors approach the *Divine Comedy* through their new texts very diversely, choosing elements and themes to explore and develop. Larry Niven and Jerry Pournelle are contemporary science fiction authors who have collaborated in writing more than a couple times.

One bout of cooperation led to *Inferno* in 1978, a rewrite of the first canticle of *The Divine Comedy*. Instead of a pilgrim basically having a vision with half his life yet to lead on Earth, Niven and Pournelle's *Inferno* begins with a jolly drunken escapade of a mediocre science fiction author that leads to him falling off a roof during a sci-fi convention and ending up in Hell. There are numerous obvious to subtle variations in the story compared to Dante's version of Hell, but reminiscence is plentiful along the journey through it by "Allen Carpenter." I want to argue in this essay that the new *Inferno*'s unique encyclopedias of modern physics, sci-fi literary forms and motifs, along with a plethora of contemporary sinners allow contemporary readers of sci-fi literature to dialogue with and ponder Dante with a contemporary refocus of concerns.

A brief discussion of one concern of science fiction would be useful. Very relevant to *Inferno*, sci-fi tradition both in literary and critical work has revolved around aesthetic and metaphysical issues in the portrayal of believable, possible worlds. While some discuss the aesthetics of being focused on plausible (and artfully twisted) scientific physics-based details of a sci-fi universe, there is also recognition of the need for care to other regions of detail. Jerry Pournelle wrote an essay titled "The Construction of Believable Societies" wherein he remarks at a relative paucity in some sci-fi writers to details regarding what he holds to be "the obvious importance of social order to science fiction" (106). For one precise reason, "fiction is about people" and thus in creating a serious exploration of a human or alien world authors should take care to pursue "examination and presentation of the society that produced the character" (Pournelle 105). Allen Carpenter the fictional science fiction author injects firmly this mood of inquiry about possible world aesthetic and metaphysic into *Inferno*. As a sci-fi author, he easily questions along material and ethical lines what he finds "to be artificial…a construct, a design" that he as a writer might have imagined (Niven and Pournelle 108).

Allen did not expect Hell, and he finds out that his being "an agnostic" and not a dire sinner is the reason his journey began "in the Vestibule" of the First Circle of Hell (Niven and Pournelle 108). He was well meant in life, and quite a nerd or buff of physics and sci-fi literary form. His particular agnosticism and scientific knowledge are a pertinent embodiment of contemporary secular attitudes and approaches on nature that are neither passionate nor irreverent to notions about "higher power" or the idea of God. Allen flips between thinking "I had to be dead" to "I couldn't be dead" on pages 12 and 13 and wrestles through the whole book with recognition that his "hypothes[e]s needed more work" if he was going to make his post-death experience part of a rational world (Niven and Pournelle 18). The possible world in New *Inferno* takes something like Dante's Hell as literally real, and the telling of Allen's descent to the bottom of Hell is at once an encyclopedia of theories about physics and sci-fi literary form as it is a vehicle for bodies of psychological knowledge and of contemporary doubt and analysis about theological matters. By a shift in focus, wrestling with the secular impulse becomes as central to the structure of Niven and Pournelle's *Inferno* as the belief in punishment for Christian sin is to Dante's *Inferno*.

To give some concrete examples, Allen presents an aspect of the theory of relativity, the fact that the observed speed of light is constant regardless of observer velocity. His guide, the good "Benito," allows him to try to get out of Hell by walking toward a wall far in the distance instead of following Benito down to the bottom-most point of Hell. Allen narrates that "[t]he wall was like light speed. We could get arbitrarily close, but we couldn't ever reach it... like nothing else in the universe I knew...just where were we?" (20-21). A few pages later Benito confirms for Allen that they are indeed in Dante's Inferno and his hypothesis is further developed: Allen narrates "I'd been dead a long time. Centuries? What kind of civilization would build an exact copy of Dante's Inferno? An Infernoland" (23). In essence, Allen echoes in his curious nature Pournelle's final words in his essay: "the writer's questions will be more important than the answers he assumes" but in Allen's case, he is a character in a world who supposes thus that there must be a reasonable explanation of its possibility (Pournelle 118).

This question echoes and reiterates through the text, especially in response to the "moral superiority" of judgment and punishment on sinners rendered "in the hands of infinite power and infinite sadism," a phrase used a few times by Allen to describe what he calls the builders of Hell (109). Some iterations of the question are "Was my loony-bin theory right after all? Psychodrama on the grand scale?" on page 64, "I'd seen enough atrocities already. Were the builders the crazy ones?" on page 66, "In what way do Big Juju's abilities differ from God Almighty's?" on page 108, "How could I worship a God who kept a private dungeon called hell?" on page 109, and "What if it had been built by interstellar conquerors for their own amusement?" on page 157. The questions draw the contemporary sci-fi reader into sharing Allen's predicament of doubt and eventual revelation. He cannot square in his mind the metaphysical possibility of Hell, and it takes until the end of his journey and takes a lot of elucidating to get Allen to the conclusion that "Hell was the violent ward of a hospital for the theologically insane. Some could be cured" (237).

This guiding principle for Hell starkly contrasts what at length is accounted in the first canticle of *The Divine Comedy* as the eternity to be suffered by the shades. That dead souls are bound in Hell permanently, while living souls are temporarily sent to Purgatory before they enter and remain forever in Paradise constitutes a wide theological difference from Niven and Pournelle's take on the Inferno, where there dominates the ever-presently subtle and eventually clearly framed hope for the dead to overcome their "theological insanity." Such a theme obviously reflects contemporary concerns with the Christian vision of *The Divine Comedy*. As Niven and Pournelle yet plan to write a sequel[1] to their *Inferno*, I would hesitate to make haste in comparing the second two canticles of the *Divine Comedy* to the sci-fi rewrite of the first, but I think certain literary critical questions that have arisen from *Purgatorio* and

---

[1] Interview at <http://www.alternatehistory.co.uk/niven.htm> accessed Nov. 25 2008.

Paradiso have a place in reading the version of *Inferno* by Niven and Pournelle.

The drawing from *Purgatorio* is evident as a broad psychological internalization into the updated Inferno, in the sense that "purging" and conversion seem to be a process in Hell implicit in being under punishment and explicit in Benito's work. Nearing the end of the book, and echoing prior passages of varied emphasis, the question of Purgatory seems to be directly addressed: speaking of six souls that Benito had previously rescued and brought to the bottom of Hell, Allen challenges him for never having gone all the way out of Hell to see where it goes; Allen says "Dante's been wrong a couple of times. Admit it" and Benito responds "I belong here, so long as there are lost souls to be rescued" which progressively makes Hell, even in its extremes, a sufficient locale for some moral-theological bootstrapping (223).

Relation to themes of *Paradiso* and overarching issues of *The Divine Comedy* may be found in a deeper, more subtle internalization into the writerly structure of Niven and Pournelle's *Inferno*. A look into Christine O. Baur's reading of Dante presented in her essay titled "Dante as Philosopher at the Boundary of Reason" will help elucidate what I have to say about Niven and Pournelle's vision and articulation of Hell. Part of her argument involves critiquing the pair of Freccero and Barolini who argue along the lines that the difficulty expressed by Dante the poet in rendering Paradise into language represents an intractable defeat to a problem. Barolini said Dante tried "to render a condition defined as beyond space and time in a medium that is intractably of space and time" and in the words of

Freccero he was "attempting to represent poetically that which is by definition beyond representation" (Baur 196-7). An example is Dante's description of the final vision of Canto XXXIII of *Paradiso*, "for now my vision as it grew more clear/ was penetrating more and more the Ray/ of that exalted Light of Truth Itself./ And from then on my vision rose to heights/ higher than words, which fail before such sight,/ and memory fails, too, at such extremes" (52-57). An infinite experience of reality can not be conveyed in terms of human memory, understanding, and language, as Freccero and Barolini argue in their work according to Baur, but she argues that

> Dante's aim is not only to give an account of what he saw in the afterlife—it is also to give an account of his own account-giving of what he saw, and to persuade his reader to become personally involved in the issue of his own freedom and salvation. Accordingly, while memory and language are not the same as the experience of Paradise, they are also not just inferior substitutes for some prior 'seen in itself' (196).

Baur has a particular interpretive strategy or prescription for reading *The Divine Comedy*: the reader is dialectically implicated in "the 'simultaneous self-perfection' of reader and text…by means of the mediating nature of language" (194). Her evidence is that the dialectical relation is made by force of the developed distinction in Dante the poet recounting for readers the journey of Dante the pilgrim, which is a similar attention-grabbing distinction as the one made in framing a sci-fi writer in a sci-fi novel. Dante wants to contend with words with a reader what words most regularly fail at and which only a reader can complete: he asks "O Light Supreme, so far beyond the reach/ of mortal understanding, to my mind/ relend now some small part of your own self,/ and give to my tongue eloquence enough/ to capture just one spark of all Your glory/ that I may leave for future generations" or in other words, leave it to readers to capture the spark of Paradise and nurture a flame, to move *beyond words* in the manner of *direct realization of experience* (*Par.* XXXIII, 67-72). To help Baur's case by making a modest suggestion from personal reflection on the meaning of the inability to transcend the limitation of word nature to convey a matter of deeply significant experiential nature, I would say that stating a vision of Heaven without recognition of limits to language would be untowardly precocious for the reasons that follow.

In contemporary slang, if it is not standard yet, "being in heaven" is as practically relative to individual journey and interpretation through life as it is relative to disambiguated and precise statements of "a paradise." For some, self-subsistence on a tract of land is "home in heaven," or it's being part of a meaningful, peaceful family or having a beneficial impact on the lives of others. One can say such things in words, sure enough, but the importance and actual meaning takes on experiential dimensions that simply go beyond the containment of words: they are meanings contained by the living soul alone, to be poetic. As such, they are meanings that need to be realized by a dialectical process with the reader that involves "passing beyond the human" into direct experience (Baur 196). Dante tells his reader, " '[t]ranshumanize'—it cannot be explained/ *per verba* so let this example serve/ until God's grace grants the experience" (*Par.* I, 70-72). "[T]he poem is itself the kind of event represented" by allusion to the unspeakable which thus points to the experiential: the poem is "a recapitulation of the pilgrim's *trasumanar*, which can in turn be reenacted by each reader in his own journey 'beyond the human'" (Baur 196).

Larry Niven wrote an essay titled "The Words in Science Fiction," in which he argues that how sci-fi authors use language will reflect much about the thought process which lies behind any story. Ideas "take root in your brain… [b]ut the words keep tripping you up" because "[it's] there in your head. You can describe it" but the word does not come (178). Niven's hope is to help authors of sci-fi to write better, but some of what he says informs my discussion. He writes that a "language is a mapping of the way people think, of the way they believe the universe works, and of what they consider to be important in that universe" (189). Language is that part of a story, even as Dante questions the limits, which provides people with a narrative account to follow, so words openly intended not to circumscribe an experience but point to it may by skill provide a map to but not a territory of experience, so to speak. As Niven points out, a simple word like black can point to a skin colour or a feeling of evil, or both at once, so doubly difficult will be the task of words for hard to explain, hard to identify features of reality. He goes on: "Science fiction writers, and readers, have this in common: the sense that there are other ways of thinking than their own" which alerts me to what Baur notes is the purpose of Dante's dialectic, being the synchronous perfection of reader and text brought about in the relation, mediated by language, between our limited ability to understand a text and the desire or need to transcend that text toward "other ways" of personal guidance and meaningful experience.

At least to me, Dante's depiction of the limitations of language applaud the fact that language is what *mediates* experience, not what *constitutes* experience, and by giving a vague picture, he also applauds the open nature to a sense of Paradise. Given the shift of focus in Niven and Pournelle toward the contemporary question of faith in what is for Allen the unimaginable suffering or "infinite sadism" of Hell, the dialectic between reader and sci-fi author in doubt of theology shifts from "self-perfection" of sinful nature to a more basic "self-realization" of it, which is Allen's and by dialectic process if he or she follows along, the reader's attempt to think though a theodicy. The sense of "being in a hell" has a similar sense, in today's secular new age, as "being in heaven" does: The new age has given to the sense of Heaven and Hell a relation to personal experiential discovery as most relevantly to be contemplated in terms of *conditions found on Earth when alive, which matter now.* This development of the notions of Heaven and Hell bear importance not only to how we read a theological story, but also to Niven and Pournelle's and Dante's bodies of knowledge about the psychology of personal salvation, about sin, and about political philosophy. These distinct encyclopedias can be explored by allegorical reading, and I will do so in turn with an interest to combine them. Doing so will expand the conception of Dante's Inferno as simply representing the eternal damnation of the shades inside a Christian ontology and make firmer the analysis I am making.

Baur offers a psychological interpretation of *The Divine Comedy*, which informs her conclusions about the text as a dialectical object and which I find useful for getting at Niven and Pournelle's *Inferno*. She describes Dante's *Inferno* as "a situation in which the incarcerated have no hope, no possibilities, because those in hell do not have the *ability to see* themselves in any way other than the way they *literally are*" (198, my emphasis). They "interpret themselves…on the basis of categories derived from things in the world" in a Godless way, stopping them from performing acts of "self-interpretation, and [to accept] gradual movement beyond a merely literal understanding of the world" to that of a connected whole of divine purpose and order (Baur 198). In other words, they are stuck in a mindset of evil. In its depiction of "the 'landscape' [that] is made up of artwork, which derives some of its meaning from the way the penitents interpret it," Baur argues that *Purgatorio* "represents the self's gradual but always incomplete self-perfection through the self's interpretive making and choosing of itself" while the artwork is interpreted as "partly the results of one's own making," which is the unknown nature of self that obscures to the shade the poignant contrapasso of punishment in *Inferno* (198-199).

Without the ability to see how their "sin" or imperfect nature creates the conditions of *a* hell, the shades are doomed to have their creation shoved in their faces, as it were, forever. What I spoke of as internalizing *Purgatorio* into Niven and Pournelle's *Inferno* signifies the contemporary hope in hope, to be frank, that they articulate as follows: the "only one *possible* excuse for Hell" is that it is "the final training ground. If nothing can get a soul into Heaven in its *life*, there's still Hell, God's last attempt to get his attention" (235, their emphasis). This rewrite of *Inferno*'s psychology informs a contemporary allegory of Hell, which is bringing to light the nature of being trapped in a hell, which for the contemporary secular reader is being trapped in Hell on

Earth. It leads to Allen's final conviction that for the reason "[s]ome could be cured, [he] would have to return to hell" while sending Benito on finally to Purgatory (237). If one gives sinful nature and consequences due attention, there comes a desire to help sufferers in some hell that may be close to realizing the truth of their role in constituting evil. In the words of Madison U. Sowell in the essay "The Niven-Pournelle Dante: A Twentieth-Century Odyssey Through Hell," a contemporary American like Allen "can fathom divine justice only if the pain inflicted is viewed as a final attempt to redeem a sinner's soul; hope springs eternal" (77).

A brief look at Niven and Pournelle's and Dante's encyclopedias of sin behaviour and of political matters will brighten the current discussion of taking the role of an activist or advocate in the world toward the nature of faulty will and morally appropriate behaviour. In Dante's *Inferno* as well as in Niven and Pournelle's, there is shared much appreciation of the dynamics of personal, spiritual involvement with a material, social, and political life. From the tripartite structure of violence, we learn that individuals can afflict violence upon God, the self, and neighbours (*Inf.* XI, 28-33). While violence to neighbours is the first round of the Seventh Circle, per Dante one sees that violence to the self puts people as "self-*robbers* of [the] world," which is linguistically reminiscent of the *loss* experienced by the community (*Inf.* XI, 43). One also sees clearly that violence to God consisting in being "hypocrites, flatterers, dabblers in sorcery,/ falsifiers, thieves, and simonists,/ panders, seducers, grafters, and like filth" can leak over to affect along with spiritual value the condition of self and human community (*Inf.* XI, 58-60). God cannot be affected, anyway, so this leak makes sense in the ontology of sin and Hell as something which allegorically pronounces on the hellish conditions lived in life. The Eighth Circle further contains people who committed various sorts of fraud, deception, and other evil to self and to others. In the words of Ferrante in *The Political Vision of the Divine Comedy*,

> the issues raised…are complex…but the lessons are simple: greed and selfishness are destructive to the public good and to the individual soul, whereas love, concern for the needs of others, and a sense of social responsibility bring personal rewards and strengthen society (42-43).

So many Florentines are in Dante's Inferno, to elucidate trouble for the community due to individual disorder, because he supposed "Florence…[was] destroying itself by its selfishness and total lack of moral order" (Ferrante 195). Ferrante echoes one of my claims quite directly: "Dante shows, through the cantica of Hell, that we choose in our acts to inhabit the city of Hell, to turn our own city into Hell" (194). In Niven and Pournelle's *Inferno* in the second round of the Seventh Circle, the "wastelands" of Hell's self-violent take quite a departure from Dante's vision. In Niven and Pournelle, the Wood of Suicides has shrunk to a small patch as new sinners have moved in and developed the area extensively. At the boundary of the wasteland, Allen, Benito, and some companions picked up along the way pass over a filthy ground full of "erosion gullies" that are filled with

> water filthy with broken bottles and bottle caps, used condoms, floating grease, occasional bursts of brightly colored dyes, chemicals that burned our sandaled feet. Nothing grew here; there were dead stumps of trees….

Strange smells moved on the air: incongruous whiffs of automobile exhaust, acids, burning oil and rubber (133-4).

The urban-industrial junkscape and little emphasis on the evil of suicide highly figure Niven and Pournelle's *Inferno* as a "product of late twentieth-century American culture" (Sowell 75). Without fail, Hell has been updated and expanded (and contracted in the case of so-called obsolete sins) for a contemporary audience, with "topics alluded to or discussed [that] include ecological problems, blacks and the Ku Klux Klan, a bureaucratic government, oil slicks, and nuclear power plants" (Sowell 75-76). These themes, in their depiction of the ecological, social, and political health of the current age as full of "sin," are clear examples of shifts in focus of encyclopedia to promote timely purposes of writing a tale of guidance.

To speak of one final, major point of interaction between the science fiction *Inferno* and Dante's *Inferno*, I will rely on Robert Pogue Harrison's analysis in "Comedy and Modernity: Dante's Hell" where his overall argument attempts to show that Dante's damnation of the deceiver Guido da Montefeltro is actually a critique of "the modern era['s] single theme: man's attempts to ground himself in the law of his free subjectivity," which refers in part to the modern impulse to rely on self-constructed interpretations of reality rather than on master traditional narratives (1056). According to Harrison (with no pretense to authorial intentions), Dante damns Guido for his "modernity [which] lies in…psychological selfhood" (1051). Guido performs an "act of willful self-deception whereby the self freely persuades itself to believe what it knows is not true" as in holding with his contract with peer sinner Pope Boniface, while he is "deceived only by his own willful self-deception, motivated by fear" of damnation (1051). The connection to Niven and Pournelle, in light of an analysis of the force of modern acceptance of subjectively constructed motivations, speaks through the final scene of their *Inferno* when Allen breaks from all conventions he relies on throughout the story, from his sci-fi author doubt to his dedication on escaping, by suddenly deciding to be the one to stay in Hell as he frees Benito. Such a move intriguingly presents the modern impulse of relying on self-directed purposes, a modern departure Dante might approve: the overtly theological realization of Allen is that his subjectivity should respect nature's larger-than-human ontology. Like the freedom enjoyed by Niven and Pournelle to write, in light of a slew of contemporary assumption and sentiment, new interpretations of Dante's story, Allen demonstrates his modern sort of freedom in freely matching self-motivations to the constraints of the situation, in a path of honor even if Hell is where he remains for the next part of his "life."

Works Cited

Alighieri, Dante. *The Divine Comedy*. Trans. Mark Musa. New York: Penguin Group, 1995.

Baur, Christine. "Dante as Philosopher at the Boundary of Reason." Proceedings of the American Catholic Philosophical Association. 76; 2002. 193-210.

Bretnor, Reginald ed. *The Craft of Science Fiction*. New York: Harper & Row, 1976.

Catal Huyuk. "Icaro Ayahuasca." *Nature Loves Courage*. Icaro Records. 2000.

Ferrante, Joan M. *The Political Vision of the Divine Comedy*. Princeton: Princeton University Press, 1984.

Harrison, Robert Pogue. "Comedy and Modernity: Dante's Hell." MLN Comparative Literature. 102 (5); Dec. 1987. JSTOR. Nov 3 2008. 1043-1061.

Niven, Larry and Jerry Pournelle. *Inferno*. New York: Pocket Books, 1976.

Niven, Larry. "The Words in Science Fiction." Bretnor. 178-193.

Pournelle, Jerry. "The Construction of Believable Societies." Bretnor. 104-119.

Sowell, Madison U. "The Niven-Pournelle Dante: A Twentieth-Century Odyssey through Hell." Studies in Medievalism. 2 (3); June 1983. 73-78.

Philosophy Directed Studies
Submitted April 14, 2009

Essay 7
Imaginatively Fancying Nature from Spinoza to Romanticism

> *We see therefore that all the notions whereby the common people are wont to explain Nature are merely modes of imagining, and denote not the nature of any thing but only the constitution of the imagination...For many are wont to argue on the following lines: if everything has followed from the necessity of God's most perfect nature, why does Nature display so many imperfections, such as rottenness to the point of putridity, nauseating ugliness, confusion, evil, sin, and so on?...For the perfection of things should be measured solely from their own nature and power; nor are things more or less perfect to the extent that they please or offend human senses, serve or oppose human interests.*

From the "Appendix" to Part I of Spinoza's *Ethics*.

> *The Giants who formed this world into its sensual existence and now seem to live in it in chains are, in truth, the causes of its life and the sources of all activity, but the chains are the cunning of weak minds, which have the power to resist energy.*

—Blake, In *A Memorable Fancy* [A Printing-House in Hell] (Wu 212).

> *There are laws of sustainability which are natural laws, just as the law of gravity is a natural law. In our science in past centuries, we have learned a lot about the law of gravity and similar laws of physics, but we have not learned very much about the laws of sustainability. If you go up to a high cliff and step off it, disregarding the laws of gravity, you will surely die. If we live in a community, disregarding the laws of sustainability, as a community we will just as surely die in the long run. These laws are just as stringent as the laws of physics, but until recently they have not been studied.*
> —Fritjof Capra, director of the Center for Ecoliteracy, in a short paper titled "Ecology and Community".

Baruch Spinoza's *Ethics* (1677) employs the ancient geometrical method of argumentation, whereby one takes a set of clear and self-evident definitions and axioms and proceeds to derive, prove, and explore the propositions that the initial principles entail and build up into. By this method, he upholds several claims, making his *Ethics* a theory about the metaphysical foundations of God (or Nature absolute) and a theory of the ideational structure and emotions of the human being. However, he intends for his readers to have more adequate understanding of reality and human nature, not only for the sake of simply knowing, but also that this knowledge may open a path to liberation from emotional passivity and harmful bondage to the delusions of imagination. In short, Spinoza intends for readers to achieve blessed lives. Of course, in the concluding remark of the *Ethics*, he advises that "all things excellent are as difficult as they are rare" (*Ethics*, Pt 5, Scholium to Pr 42).

The path to excellence in the human condition can be elusive, and the direct goal of Spinoza is by no means to achieve an absolute and unending utopia for all but to help individuals become more "wise" so that one "suffers *scarcely* any disturbance of spirit... but always possesses true spiritual contentment" (ibid, my emphasis). In coming to an inner core of peace and blessedness, we do not leave behind the world of pain and desire but instead acquire a spiritual power akin to Eastern notions of enlightened detachment, which is the self's evolving beyond habitual compulsions of the mind that lead it to suffer so deeply. In the present discussion, I explore Spinoza's perspective on the relation of the human mind to Nature with special regard to how understanding Nature in certain ways will affect our emotional condition. Toward this purpose, I will demonstrate Spinoza's sustained influence and relevance for important issues of today by connecting parts of Spinoza's thought to Romantic era concerns, which also have prefigured current strains of philosophy.

Robert J. Richards, in *The Romantic Conception of Life—Science and Philosophy in the Age of Goethe,* reminds students of literature that while "[w]e usually think of this group as forming a coherent movement" of poets, philosophers, and theologians, the Romantics "often appreciably diverged from one another in their conceptions of the operations of sensation, imagination, and reason" and even frequently reassessed their own views during ongoing intellectual development (18). Nevertheless, "[i]n conformity to our usual understanding of Romanticism, [some individuals] turned decisively toward the night of cloudless climes and starry skies, under which beauty revealed a more intuitive, emotionally marked, and even mystical path to reality's inner core" (Richards 19). In a usual understanding, being *un*romantic might be akin to turning decisively toward reason-driven, method-bound knowledge expressed in clear thought and orderly representations, not art inspired by the vastness of a starry night. Some thinkers contrast the Romantic activity with that of the equally radical "Enlightenment," scientific, political achievement born from scholastics and law, not the poetics and dreaming of rivers and faeries. Figures espousing rationalist approaches to philosophy over romantic approaches have also differed amongst themselves.

Personally, I like drawing parallels and relation rather than division and exclusion between the directions and pursuits of the epochal, critical periods of human thought. Michael Scrivener, in his essay "Inside and Outside Romanticism," asks "have we so far removed ourselves from the assumptions of Romantic texts that we are finally outside of Romanticism?...Is it possible to get outside of Romanticism?" and he answers no to both (152). He mentions that romanticism sourced ecocriticism (which I will focus on later), and suggests an argument he attributes to Hans-Georg Gadamer, a German philosopher of the twentieth century: Romanticism "has shaped our pre-understanding, [...] has inscribed us with meanings we cannot disentangle from our lifeworld" (Scrivener 152). Romanticism persists in the manners and methods of Western mind.

The canonical Romantic figures had new ideas and modes of expression that arose in the intense revolutionary and intellectual fervour of Europe in the late 18th and 19th century. This fervour includes political upheaval in the instantiation of modern democracy and of rights movements, an up-and-coming scientific-industrial-capitalist culture, and in the Romantic awe and curiosity about natural settings the precursor to still-emerging ecological paradigms. Scrivener calls the "periodization" of Romanticism "always a risky enterprise", giving modestly the era a fifty year span and reservedly a hundred year span (151). What constitutes the history of Romanticism must really be diverse cultural phenomena on time scales perhaps transcending millennia in both past and future directions as some potential perspective to history might give the "Romantic" impulses.

Stretching this impulse a bit further back, I have come to identify what is (at least pre-)Romantic impulses in Spinoza, whose widely influential "rationalist" philosophy was written in the 17th century. Many scholars place Spinoza as a member of Europe's "Radical Enlightenment", but interpretations of his work have always varied with some broad agreements but also huge gaps in the understanding of what he was getting at. Is he a pantheist or a materialist? Does he believe will is "free" in any common sense? Spinoza has also been read by 20th Century feminist and ecological philosophers, who have found very new readings for his works. Romantic works such as Mary Wollstonecraft's *Vindication of the Rights of Woman* set the foundation for "feminist theory as a modern intellectual enterprise" (Scrivener 152). As well, the nature writing of Romantics set the Western foundation for ecological paradigms, so if Spinoza is interesting to these discourses now, there will be ways to re-read him in terms of Romanticism and as well the Romantic figures in terms of his work.

I shall start with a seeming contradiction of terms involved in what Richards identified as part of Romantic thought, "conceptions of the operations of sensation, imagination, and reason". A profound poet of the Romantic age, Samuel Taylor Coleridge wrote in the nineteenth century about "Nature" and "imagination" in a very different manner than did Spinoza. Coleridge is also no exception in a long line of Spinoza interpreters who have read him in a certain way; Coleridge saw him as a revisionist of Descartes' dualist philosophy and as a precursor to Leibnitz' materialist philosophy. Needless to say, this is contentious. Close readings by various schools have also related Spinoza's metaphysics and philosophy of mind to pantheism, animism, and other spiritual belief systems that compare the body and mind very differently than Descartes or Leibnitz did. For instance, in the *Ethics* Spinoza holds that "God" or "Nature" or the necessary and all-creative power of existence is a "substance consisting of infinite attributes, each of which expresses eternal and infinite essence" (*Ethics*, Part 1, Pr 11). Later when identifying the limits of the comprehending human mind, Spinoza claims that we indeed have clear and adequate insight into only the attributes of extension and of thought, but no others, which is a potential source of traditional notions about Spinoza's tendency for dualism and materialism (*Ethics*, Part 2, Pr 1-2).

As he claims in Proposition 7 of Part 2, "the order and connection of ideas is the same as the order and connection of things," and this can appear to be a resignation to dualism of a materialist causal basis. However, Spinoza is careful to qualify in the Scholium to Pr 7 that "a mode of extension and the idea of that mode are one and the same thing, expressed in two ways," once under each attribute but of the same thing, i.e. a coherent being of Nature with more than one manner of existing or experiencing. Spinoza elsewhere qualifies that there is an infinite number of attributes expressed in infinite ways, even if we have no ideational access to their modal features and associations with the two attributes that we are aware of. There is a lot of mystery inherent in Nature according to Spinoza, but decidedly humans are limited beings in an indefinitely large system of expressive powers.

When Coleridge in chapter VIII of *Biographia Literaria* upholds that "the system of DUALISM introduced by Des Cartes--Refined first by Spinoza and afterwards by Leibnitz into the doctrine of Harmonia praestabilita—Hylozoism—materialism—None of these systems on any possible theory of association, supplies or supersedes a theory of perception, or explains the formation of the associable" (Representative Poetry Online, U of Toronto 128). By "formation of the associable" he means the nature of the bodily vehicle's association with consciousness. Coleridge believes the association is not explained but later in talking about the materialist system writes that "Spinoza...had himself taken the hint from Des Cartes's animal machines" (RPO 129). Hold on, Samuel! Maybe Coleridge did not read Spinoza thoroughly enough to see that there are stronger interpretations which override notions of the philosopher as being a simple materialist.

In *The Ethics*, Spinoza either directly or indirectly critiques much of Rene Descartes' philosophical positions. If they do agree on anything, it may only be on some very general characteristics of the project of rationalist philosophy, such as appeal to self-evident and indubitable, or clear and distinct, ideas; Spinoza hardly "refined" Descartes as much as he continually exploded his ideas. Descartes may have indeed attempted to *explain* the "associable" in terms of a perfect God-system who governed the mechanical body according to the soul's inclinations, but Spinoza seems to work out the self-evident connections between the mind, body, and God. However, to Spinoza is it likely that God is to be understood as Nature itself and the mind and body as complementary aspects of Nature's expressions of existence.

I read Spinoza as *assuming* "the associable" rather than trying to explain it; Coleridge may be considering passages such as the definition of emotions as "the affections of the body by which the body's power of activity is increased or diminished, assisted or checked, together with the ideas of these affections" or such as propositions like "[t]he body cannot determine the mind to think, nor can the mind determine the body to motion or rest, or to anything else (if there is anything else)" (Spinoza 104, 105). Spinoza does seem to try to explain emotions through the body and seems to claim also that mind and body are logically independent from each other, which Coleridge may find "absurd... [and] too repugnant to our common sense" to consider as a viable explanation (RPO 129). Spinoza seems to intend no formative explanation of the mind and body's association; he claims rather that Nature is necessarily just that way: "man consists of mind and body, and the human body exists according as we sense it" (*Ethics*, Part 2, Corollary to Pr 13). *As we sense* our body should surely be contrasted with *how we conceive* it, which may be imaginative fancy and little more.

Spinoza regards the imagination as the progenitor of "inadequate ideas", or spurious universals of the ungrounded ideational structure that comprise the thoughts of an unliberated, passive emotion-bound human mind. In chapter XIII of *Biographia Literaria*, Coleridge articulates what he calls "primary" imagination "to be the living power and prime agent of all human perception, and as a repetition in the finite mind of the eternal act of creation in the infinite

I AM" (RPO 295-296). The difference in terms may at first glance seem to be the contradictory views between rationalist philosophers versus romantic poets. Worse yet, someone may just decide that Spinoza and Coleridge, as rationalists and romantics probably using their words differently and independently, should not be compared. In the *Ethics*, Spinoza deeply investigates the system responsible for inadequate ideas, and this system is translated plainly as "imagination." Thus it is understandable that Coleridge—a crafty poet who enjoyed intoxicated trances, who wrote explicitly about the human imagination, and who deemed it a part of our beauty—would take issue with Spinoza's frankly wordy and logical exposition on the nature of Nature and of the human being.

Coleridge has the conviction that "body and spirit are… no longer absolutely heterogeneous, [as in the materialist philosophy] but *may* without any *absurdity* be supposed to be different modes, or degrees in perfection, of a common substratum" (RPO 128-129, his emphasis). Quite similarly, Spinoza holds that "mind and body are one and the same thing, conceived now under the attribute of Thought, now under the attribute of Extension. Hence it comes about that the order or linking of things is one, whether Nature be conceived under this or that attribute" (*Ethics*, Pt 3, Scholium to Pr. 2). Spinoza's position might be confused in Coleridge's philosophy of mind as materialism or hylozoism, the view that mind is nothing more than what matter is or that matter is life's fundamental basis, and Spinoza surely does base his philosophy of mind around the nature of the body. However, Spinoza refers mind and body both back to the underlying "Nature", which as he describes in the first part of *The Ethics*" is "substance consisting of infinite attributes, each of which expresses eternal and infinite essence, [and which] necessarily exists" (37).

The nature of the body is unity with the nature of mind, and when Spinoza says that "the order of the active and passive states of our body is simultaneous in Nature with the order of active and passive states of the mind", he is not saying that the order of states of the body occurs before or mechanically causes the order of states of the mind (*Ethics*, Pt 3, Scholium to Pr 2). When he says that we conceive *substance* now under one attribute, now under another, he means that what essentially exists is the unified totality of Nature's expressive powers or, as Coleridge might call it, the "infinite I AM" (RPO 296). To Spinoza, mind and matter are complementary attributes or aspects of our deep and fundamental being, which is neither fundamentally mind nor fundamentally matter, but rather profoundly powerful existence. Coleridge is close to sharing his ideas, but harder to compute are their differences concerning the powers and consequences of the imagination.

For Spinoza, the *passivity* of emotional states can be seen in how socially acquired habits can cause the fanciful mind to act upon desires and memories that are divorced from reasonable or adequate ideas about human nature and big Nature. That's why Spinoza says that imagination limits virtue. Spinoza is claiming that *how* we understand, describe, and behave within reality tends to be obscured, disturbed, and made passive by imaginative processes lacking sound reason. Coleridge gives a more hopeful account of imagination, but the language differences obscure what at the surface seem to be conceptual disagreements. It is prudent to consider Spinoza's basic definition of imagination before considering its consequences: with "the affections of the human body whose ideas set forth external bodies as if they were present to us…when the mind regards bodies in this way, we shall say that it 'imagines' [but]…the mind does not err from the fact that it imagines but only insofar as it is considered to lack the idea which excludes the existence of those things which it imagines," i.e. the mind errs insofar as it has the potential to be deluded about the reality its ideas intimate (*Ethics*, Pt 2, Scholium to Pr 17). To go back to Coleridge's language, the pure power of imagining that need not err but likely may seem indeed to be akin to "repetition in… the infinite I AM" (RPO 296). Spinoza may than have no special word that equates fully with Coleridge's imagination, but Coleridge does use a certain word that seems to fit Spinoza's sense of error, and it is "fancy."

I will directly discuss Coleridge's fancy, but will take these ideas slowly. Dr. Timothy Brownlow (writing in an essay about Romanticism called "Only Connect" that was published online in the University of Maryland *Romantic Circles* web journal) distinguishes between jargon that is just the specialized vocabulary of a certain discourse community and the jargon that is used in a way to "obfuscate the issues and intimidate the reader" intentionally, and he suggests that "whether the [Romantic] writers were up to mischief or not, they are often obscure" (Brownlow paragraph 5). Both Spinoza and Coleridge could be employing jargon, whether mischievously, and both aim to elucidate sounder understandings and experiences. Coleridge, being a poet in the foray of philosophy, may be more inclined to linguistically play to his desired meanings than Spinoza the geometrical rationalist. Whatever the case, Coleridge and Spinoza were both jargon users. Had they regarded William Wordsworth's advice and spoken not jargon but language "which is uttered by men in real life under the actual pressure of those passions", they may have realized that "no words which his fancy or imagination can suggest will be compared with those which are the emanations of [the] reality and truth" whose understanding they both sought to articulate and share with readers (Wu 526).

I think of Spinoza's rejection of teleology and insistence on the chains of Nature's organization. Coleridge writes: "We might as rationally chant the Brahmin creed of the tortoise that supported the bear, that supported the elephant, that supported the world, to the tune of 'This is the house that Jack built' " (RPO 134). Coleridge quite satirically relates a determined chain of foundations to something as arbitrary and contingent as a house being built. He seems in these words to say that a story like Spinoza's about necessity in Nature's expression falls short of the common sense world of human needs we live in, regardless of intricate Nature's non-teleological determinacy. A house seems to be a product of human-borne purpose, or just an intended *telos* (or goal,) not a result of some infinite chain of connections in a world of absolute order and causation. What sense does it make, Coleridge asks, that arbitrary human choices are the outcomes of a Nature with connections only of necessity?

Spinoza is keen to this critique: in the preface to part IV, he writes about human conceptions about the perfection of some objects, and I think back to the passage I quote at the beginning of this essay: "if anyone sees a work (...not yet finished) and knows that the aim of the author is to build a house, he will say that the house is imperfect...but if anyone sees a work whose like he had never seen before, and he does not know the artificer's intention, he cannot possibly know whether the work is perfect or imperfect" (*Ethics*, Pt 4, Preface). However, "when men began to form general ideas and to devise ideal types…and to prefer some models to others, it came about that each called 'perfect' what he saw to be in agreement with the general idea he had formed of the said thing" and when they foolishly apply this kind of standard to natural phenomena, "they believe that Nature has then failed or blundered and has left that thing imperfect" (*Ethics*, Pt 4, Preface). Spinoza believes the world is perfect the way it is, regardless of what people do, whether they build a house, go to war, or spoil and waste valuable nature. In other words, what Nature's necessity has entailed is that Jack indeed endeavored and sought after an ideal for a house as shaped by his imagining intellect.

Spinoza means "by 'good' that which we certainly know to be the means for our approaching nearer to the model of human nature that we set before ourselves" (*Ethics*, Pt 4, Preface). While we are firmly grounded in Nature's chains of order, virtues orient to the stipulated models we set forth. Spinoza insists that our knowledge of determinations and causes in Nature is forever incomplete and hence that "those who believe that they speak, or keep silent, or do anything from free mental decision are dreaming with their eyes open" (*Ethics*, Pt 3, Scholium to Pr 2). However, "by *virtue* and *power*" such as a human could have in order that he or she build a house, Spinoza means "the same thing; that is…virtue, in so far as it is related to man, is man's very essence, or nature, in so far as he has power to bring about that which can be understood solely through the laws of his own nature" ((*Ethics*, Pt 4, Definitions). I think Spinoza's fairly complex notion of "virtue" and "power" if any of his terms do, may subtly relate to Coleridge's imagination as the prime power of human perception, the cognitive iteration of Nature's fundamental being. Coleridge's view on nature and human power does not differ too fundamentally from Spinoza's, albeit in different articulation and emphasis.

Reminiscent of the preceding discussion, Mary Shelly wrote in her introduction to *Frankenstein*: "Every thing must have a beginning…and that beginning must be linked to something that went before. The Hindoos give the world an elephant to support it, but they make the elephant stand upon a tortoise. Invention, it must be humbly admitted, does not consist in creating out of a void, but out of chaos" (Shelly viii). No teleological reason for the animal support of the Earth, the Eastern reference elucidates simply that an immutable (while animistic) order provides the set foundations of human reality. *Frankenstein* explores a perversion of the given 'natural' order of life, of what happens when the chaos of passively driven imagination is exploited to inventing—birthing—a creature not human anymore but one of the living dead. I think *Frankenstein* provides a good Romantic source for comparing the evils Spinoza associates with the passive qualities of imagination and Coleridge's assertion of an imagination with active, powerful qualities.

The creature gives his Dr. Victor a request for making a companion female creature: "My vices are the children of a forced solitude that I abhor; and my virtues will necessarily arise when I live in communion with an equal. I shall feel the affections of a sensitive being, and become linked to the chain of existence and events, from which I am now excluded" (Shelley 106). This language reminds me of the Spinozistic picture of modes of being as linked in infinite chains of temporal existence with the "order and connection" of things and ideas as the source of all emotions: the affections of sensitive being leave one prone to states that are either supportive or debilitating toward the achievement of "virtue." According to Spinoza, we love more who we can relate with and share commonality and community with, and we hate more those parts and entities of our world that we regard as posing a risk to our joys and destruction of our natural power. The creature and Dr. Frankenstein (and most of Shelley's fictional cast of humans) abhor each other to great extent for the regarded differences and divisions between their natures. The fears and judgments of the society upon the creature are more illusory than warranted, especially in regard to the creature's eventual literary intelligence and potential for compassion, among other so-called all-too-human qualities.

On the thread of "equality", the creature in *Frankenstein* eerily reminds me of what Mary Wollstonecraft, Shelley's mother, wrote about women in *A Vindication of the Rights of Woman*: Wollstonecraft notes that physiologically speaking women are the carriers of beauty but "in point of strength[,] in general, inferior to the male" (Wu 279). But Frankenstein's creature is much uglier and stronger than an ordinary man. Another relation comes in Wollstonecraft's statement that "[women] are only considered as females, and not as a part of the human species, when improvable reason is allowed to be the dignified distinction which raises men above the brute creation, and puts a natural sceptre in a feeble hand" (Wu 279). The creature possesses that "dignified distinction" but for bodily difference, is outcast, rather than like woman who is outcast for her mentality.

If *Frankenstein* offers a feminist reading, it may be in the binary relations of *Frankenstein's* creature to the female creature under patriarchal perspectives, deemed sinister but nonetheless a reasoning creature forced into layers of "conduct and manners," in Wollstonecraft's phrasing (Wu 279). Spinoza brings something relevant to such a discussion because of the bodily emphasis in both *Frankenstein* and in feminist theory and of Spinoza's emphasis that emotional liberation from false ideas (such as the inferiority of women) are significantly tied to the bodily nature of the emotions and imagination. Specifically we see how aversion and ethical exclusion follow from habitual ideational patterns that ingrain inadequate knowledge about our relations to others and that obscure peace and the flourishing of our inner and common connections. The development of prejudicial attitudes toward *Frankenstein's* creature can be fleshed out in this way by a reading along Spinoza's views of the passive imagination. The creature had no stable community of adequate ideals.

The creature's relationship with the family in the cottage in the woods, his reading of significant literature, his innocent if misguided desire for Victor to redo the original work with the parts of a woman's body, and of course his rejection from society all represent the creature as curious, desirous, and as bearing a burden of alienation due to a faulty and sinister notoriety. It is the "inadequate idea" of the people in the creature's world that he is deemed evil when blameless for his creation and unrequested nature. The negativity which results seems unavoidable given the faults of the social community of the creature, i.e. the lack of a community of active, inclusive love, which could arise to replace the hatred toward what most feel is antithetical to nature proper.

Coleridge might say that in "the living power… of all human perception"—in the chance of an active imagination—there is the potential for the creature's society to find a way to see and respect his commonality with them instead of manifesting fears based in passive and disconnected imagining, which I better relate to Coleridge's account of "fancy," "a mode of memory emancipated from the order of time and space" (RPO 296). The fanciful mode of memory is emancipated from the order of time and space (quite poetic language, I think) in a sense that Spinoza well captures in remarks on the usual functioning of memory: "everyone will pass on from one thought to another according as the habit in each case has arranged the images in his body" and not according to ('emancipated from') the real 'order' of the world, adequate cognition of Nature with its modes situated in 'time and space' (*Ethics*, Pt 2, Scholium to Pr 18). *Frankenstein's* creature by his strangest of origins is emancipated from inclusion in the fanciful order that objectifies and exiles him. The living can relate to the mind of the creature, but do not to his body, and they cannot take him as a respect-worthy equal.

Spinoza may well, having had a serious political philosophy, have forewarned had he thought about it against possible advances in cloning and genetic engineering experiments. He might have described the desire to breed by scientific manufacture smarter or less destructible bodies to be wrought by the spurious imagination obscuring more "natural" potential. To want to ward off death or perfect our bodies by force seems to represent a great fear toward the more established methods of growth, learning, evolution, and dying ingrained in the chains of biological and social existence. Victor might have succeeded as a human had he gone back to his wife-to-be, Elizabeth, instead of forsaking the immanently active role in life—he could have had a life spent enriching the self and others he could bond with—for a passive role in life, a life spent passively obsessing to control the mysteries of death unto his own personal ruination. People lose their freedom and learn to hate when their lives become wrecked in recklessly pursued and unreal ambitions.

Think of the potential cultural problems with people changing genes to change skin colour to retrofit our bodily image according to social images, or with people striving to eradicate mental illness traits by brain, genetic, and chemical modification, which both have a possibility of making the species boring. These sorts of things are already beginning to happen in various regards. There is a very worrisome potential inherent in practices like near-compulsory chemical medicines as the first-tried and usually the only technique psychiatry uses and in practices like socially inspired selective abortions. When we disregard as undesirable or harmful the diversity of nature's expressions which has built us into how we are, we run the risk of losing valuable differences and important limits and of excluding people just access to a quality life and to social opportunities. Of course people may claim to pursue these arguably destructive activities only to better their life. The central principle of any living being is its endeavour to persevere in its own being. Spinoza formulates his concept of *conatus*, the principle of each self to endure in itself, in the beginning propositions of *Ethics*, part 3, but the potential for any being to self-endure requires going beyond the passively imagined to understand the real conditions of organismal continuity: If we twist our body and mind grossly out of our naturally evolved balance of proportions, then we could easily destroy ourselves. The same goes for balances of social organizations and of ecosystems, which informs Spinoza's contribution to political philosophies and to Deep Ecology. Spinoza's physics provides a strong base for any discussions one could have about the nature of systemic balance and of a life form's endurance.

While *The Ethics* primarily aims to teach about the deep nature and about ethics for the human mind, imagination, and emotion, as the Romantic writers I've sampled seem also to take as an aspect of their projects, I will emphasize another connection of Spinoza to Romantic impulses and conceptions (that are still very with us, to remember Michael Scrivener's claims). Numerous aspects of Spinoza's thought shine interesting light on Romantic and contemporary ecological philosophy. One of the links is found in the physics in part II, "On the Nature and Origin of Mind". The most interesting axioms are about composite bodies, which are united formations made from the physics of simple bodies, which very closely relates to Newton's basic laws of motion for ideal point masses. I think it is valuable to have Spinoza's careful and precise words to ponder (*Ethics,* Pt 2):

> **Definition**: When a number of bodies of the same or different magnitude form close contact with one another through the pressure of other bodies upon them, or if they are moving at the same or different rates of speed so as to preserve an unvarying relation of movement among themselves, these bodies are said to be

united with one another and all together to form one body or individual thing, which is distinguished from other things through this union of bodies.

Lemma 4: If from a body, or an individual thing composed of a number of bodies, certain bodies are separated, and at the same time a like number of other bodies of the same nature take their place, the individual thing will retain its nature as before, without any change in its form.

Lemma 5: If the parts of an individual thing become greater or smaller, but so proportionately that they all preserve the same mutual relation of motion-and-rest as before, the individual thing will likewise retain its own nature as before without any change in its form.

Lemma 6: If certain bodies composing an individual thing are made to change the existing direction of their motion…and keep the same mutual relation as before, the individual thing will likewise preserve its own nature without any change of form.

Lemma 7: Furthermore, the individual thing so composed retains its own nature, whether as a whole it is moving or at rest, and in whatever direction it moves, provided that each constituent part retains its own motion and continues to communicate this motion to the other parts.

This could be a list of ideas pulled right from a general description of biological structures and of homeostasis, the balancing act or "same mutual relation" of an organism or ecosystem's structure relative to the chemical components of the biological form of that "individual thing" that exchange between the thing and other things or between the thing and the environment, such as eating 'food' or breathing 'air'. Spinoza articulates the ecological character of his physics clearly in the fourth postulate which follows the lemmas: "The human body needs for its preservation a great many other bodies, by which, as it were, it is continually regenerated" (*Ethics*, Pt 2, Postulate 4). These claims present Spinoza as possessing a very profound and intricate talent for scientific reasoning about the *ecology* of organisms and systems of organisms. If his "intention had been to write a full treatise on body [or biology, or ecosystems, for that matter, he] should have had to expand [the] explications and demonstrations" (*Ethics*, Pt 2, Scholium to Lemma 7 of the physics). What falls out of these notions is that the actual history of an embodied being, and thus its knowledge and its powers of action, relate to a mind's idiosyncratic ecological development and interactions within larger systems.

Some of the Romantics were keen to note within their industrializing societies that basic, stable, and necessary patterns in the living networks of Earth's diversity were threatened by human activity, i.e. by the activity of our imaginary, erroneous, and emotionally driven goals. Some were also aware of the amazing, wondrous interdependence of living things. Dorothy Wordsworth, in her journals, spoke eloquently of nature: "…so divinely beautiful as I never saw it. It seemed more sacred than I had ever seen it, and yet more allied to human life" (Wu 585). She felt intimately connected to nature's beauty, which is just the expression of itself, ultimately. It was 'perfect,' in itself as itself, and not because of any desire or ambition of her fancy to exploit it for her own ideals. She also demonstrates that people in this era must have been starting ever more to notice, virtuously, the networks of life's bounty and to notice, sadly, the sick advancement of human industrial economy: "an old man almost double…said leeches were very scarce partly owing to this dry season, but many years they have been scarce. He supposed it *owing to their being much sought-after*, that they did not breed fast, and were of slow growth" (Wu 586, my emphasis). This reveals an understanding and compassionate attention to the mutual relations of living things with humanity interacting, a desire to preserve the beings of nature and to "hear the *peaceful* sounds of the earth" (Wu 587, her emphasis). Spinoza and the Romantics alike demonstrate links between the risks of human imagination upon individual, social, and ecological conditions, which Western civilization tends to overlook when pointing fingers at the causes of various conflicts and crises instead of reflecting on its own involvement with perhaps radically fanciful ideologies about humanity and Nature.

William Blake wrote poems with ecological and other philosophical relation to the thoughts of Spinoza. First I will express the philosophical relation: the "giants" in Blake's quote in the epigram of this paper remind me well of Spinoza's overarching "attributes" by which we fundamentally understand the "chains" of interconnection which express being. Any particular body or mind of "sensual existence" is a particularization and instantiation of giant, all-originating and encompassing aspects to nature, which are named by Spinoza extended and thinking substance. Blake's title for this poem is "A Printing House in Hell", which makes me think of an analogy from printing technique, with giant plates (or attributes) that "press" onto an open substance to produce readable texts, or in other words, actual modes of being in the chains of sensual existence (Wu 212). Reminiscent of Spinoza view that God is Nature which is only fundamental substantial existence, Blake holds that "God only acts and is in existing beings or men" (Wu 213).

Some of Blake's poetry also has an ecological dimension to relate to Spinoza's though. In "The Tyger", he asks "Did he who made the Lamb make thee? … What immortal hand or eye/ Dare frame thy fearful symmetry?" (Wu 198). This poem calls to my mind Spinoza's relation between "reality" and "perfection" and the relation between "good" and "evil". To Spinoza, perfection and reality are names for the same thing, ultimately, while in common use "perfection" mainly describes *perspective-laden judgments* while "reality" mainly describes our *judgment-laden perspectives*. In his poem, Blake notices that one idea of God, creation, perfection, and good implies that there is a paradox in the creation of a Tiger, which is an evil to the Lamb. As an even simpler question, we could ask why bodily pain at all exists if the origin of the whole world is perfect good. Blake, however, isn't really asking this question; he always means much more than he says, often the opposite of what his words seem to point out. I think Blake's interpretation is like Spinoza's: the "Tyger Tyger burning bright" is simply a resilient expression of Nature's ultimate power to infinitely express forms from the godly "hammer… chain… furnace… [and] anvil" of all existence (Wu 198). I think Blake's answer to his question about the Tiger is resolutely that no one would ever dare to create such a dangerous beast, but that regardless Nature exerts its primal power of expressing diversity.

I wanted here to talk about Spinoza's connection to the Romantic era. I think I have succeeded in demonstrating some significant parallels between threads of Romanticism and Spinoza's system. I have connected him to Romantic philosophies of mind, intellect, and imagination (in Samuel Coleridge), to Romantic notions of emotion, human value, and community (in Mary Shelley), to Romantic ecological sentiment (in Dorothy Wordsworth), and to Romantic ecological philosophy (in Blake). As I mentioned earlier, contemporary movements of thought have taken Spinoza further into the future, relating Spinoza's keen insights to fields as diverse as feminist theory, biology, and Deep Ecology. I touched on that in my discussions, such as those surrounding *Frankenstein*, but much has already been done and still can be done by many other thinkers connecting Spinoza's philosophies to twentieth century perspectives on pressing links between social, metaphysical, and ecological issues. I aimed here to demonstrate several possible ways to interrelate the impulses of Romantic thought and Spinoza's philosophy, because I believe Spinoza and the Romantics have offered ideas which will always be and are now very important for human existence.

The insights of Spinoza and of the Romantics will be of utmost importance as long as passive imagination continues to distort knowledge about Nature and the self, distortion which entails that we obscure human and ecological potential with ideological fancying. A deeper understanding of Nature's hanging together and the processes of human ideation should lead us to respect and to seek to nourish each other, to find our common Nature instead of be lost in the mean flight of reckless passive imagining. Fritjof Capra's warning, quoted in my epigram, reveals the whole scope of consideration that leads one to cherish Spinoza: we want our communities to live on, so we must examine and fulfill the conditions that potentiate our communities, which contemporary ecologists recognize as respecting the laws of sustainability that interconnect life. That is, we must clear the blinding soot of fancy from the lenses through which we conceive Nature and our place here. We must overcome imaginary relations with the world in order that adequate knowledge is inculcated that could sustain our species psychologically, socially, and ecologically. We just might come to flourish in our worldly lives with some level of blessedness.

Works Cited

Blake, William. A Memorable Fancy [A Printing House in Hell]. *The Marriage of Heaven and Hell.* Wu. 212-213.

——. "The Tyger." Wu. 197-198.

Brownlow, Timothy. "Only Connect". Essay. *Romantic Circles—Romanticism, Ecology, and Pedagogy.* Online publication. 30 Mar 2008 <http://www.rc.umd.edu>.

Capra, Fritjof. "Ecology and Community". Brochure. Center for Ecoliteracy. 5 Dec. 2005 <http://www.ecoliteracy.org/>.

Coleridge, Samuel Taylor. *Biographia Literaria; or Biographical Sketches of my Literary Life and Opinions.* Representative Poetry Online. 2005. University of Toronto. 25 Mar. 2008. <https://tspace.library.utoronto.ca/html/1807/4350/index-2.html>.

Richards, Robert J. *The Romantic Conception of Life: Science and Philosophy in the Age of Goethe.* Chicago: University of Chicago Press, 2002.

Scrivener, Michael. "Inside and Outside Romanticism". Criticism 46.1, Winter 2004: Review. *Project Muse.* 26 Jan. 2008. 151-165.

Shelley, Mary. *Frankenstein.* Ed. Candace Ward. Mineola, NY: Dover Thrift Editions, 1994.

Spinoza, Baruch. *Ethics, Treatise on the Emendation of the Intellect and Selected Letters*. Trans. Samuel Shirley. Indianapolis, Indiana: Hackett Publishing Company, 1992.

Wollstonecraft, Mary. "Introduction". *A Vindication of the Rights of Woman*. Wu. 279.

Wordsworth, Dorothy. *The Grasmere Journals*. Wu. 585-588.

Wordsworth, William. *Preface to Lyrical Ballads* [extracts]. Wu. 525-527.

Wu, Duncan ed. *Romanticism—An Anthology*. Oxford, UK: Blackwell Publishing, 2006.

389

Originally written for Philosophy 475
Topics in the History of Philosophy—Deep Ecology

As published in Athabasca University's journal, The Trumpeter, Vol 28, No 1 (2012)

Essay 8—Spinoza, Deep Ecology, and Human Diversity—Schizophrenics and Others Who Could Heal the Earth If Society Realized Eco-Literacy

Abstract: The author, who is a diagnosed schizophrenic and a student of Philosophy, explores the notion of the active love, of Spinoza and Arne Naess, in association with Fritjof Capra's concept of Eco-Literacy and with Gregory Bateson's ecological theory of schizophrenia. Via personal anecdotes and synthesis, the claim is made that enriching respect and understanding of our human diversity, and especially seeking the social integration of abnormal psychologies, should be a key goal of Deep Ecology-related thought and action.

Keywords: deep ecology; Spinoza; schizophrenia; eco-literacy; human diversity; social integration; mental illness; mental health; adaptation; feedback systems

Within its metaphysics of "Nature," and with its approach to emotional bondage and self-realization, Spinoza's *Ethics* can be read as a manual for psychological coherence, a state marked by the stable expression of innate freedoms and the flourishing of mental life beyond imaginative fancy. In the twentieth century, Spinoza's work provides a robust philosophical foundation for deep ecological thinking, because of its influence upon and comparison with contemporary systems theory, holistic and multidisciplinary approaches, integrative scientific reasoning, and methods toward reaching productive and beneficial realizations of the relation of self to nature. Spinoza spoke with the *Ethics* to his time and social context, but glimmers of contemporary contentions, arguments, and conceptual systems can be glimpsed today in his articulation of the human path to emotional and cognitive self-realization. He referred to an active love of "Nature or God", two words overtly interchangeable in the text, and in this respect compares to new age environmentalism, which sometimes ponders that all life and creation is part of a natural yet sacred unity. At the same time, uniquely, Spinoza and contemporary thinkers support the pursuit of active freedom in emotional expression and a disposition to intuitive, conscious interrelation of the self with other entities inside nature. Spinoza associated these virtues of sustained, positive relations with the development of "adequate ideas" or the reasonably and reliably ascertained knowledge of the constitution of the self and nature, and they are increasingly needed for humanity.

At this juncture of human development, in this world with its issues, the words of a preeminent ecological writer hold so much weight: "the transition to a sustainable future is no longer a technical nor a conceptual problem. It is a problem of values and political will."[1] In Spinozist language, it is a problem of "passive emotions": of endeavouring to fulfil desires that are based in inadequate imaginings and a lack of interconnected, well rooted, or conscious values.

In *The Hidden Connections*, Director for the Centre of ecoliteracy Fritjof Capra extends an emerging contemporary theory of life systems "to the social domain" by presenting "a conceptual framework that integrates life's biological, cognitive and social dimensions".[2] The framework constitutes a systems-oriented, interconnectionist, holistic, and ecological perspective of biological life, consciousness, and the feedback between these two. Capra's framework has several implications for "the social domain," and thus implications for the feedback between ecosystems of human ideas and the ecosystems of biological Earth.

One set of strong claims Capra makes is about "the profound impact of the machine metaphor on the theory and practice of management," indirectly speaking of general cultural organization.[3] In its more extreme forms, the machine metaphor regards all systems, including the living, as fundamentally mechanical, or dynamically contingent only on forces and conditions of an external and causally complete and causally isolated extended nature. The penultimate mechanical theory is the observer-independence or fundamental blindness of basic physical structure, which, as Capra argues, speaks also to automaton theories of cellular biology, theoretical presuppositions about organismal consciousness, and then further on to theories of social organization that give among other dubious conclusions "a view of [personnel and resource]

---

[1] Capra, Fritjof, The Hidden Connections—A Science for Sustainable Living, (New York: Anchor Books, 2002), 257.
[2] Capra, The Hidden Connections, xv.
[3] Capra, The Hidden Connections, 103.

management as engineering, based on precise technical design".[4]

When one takes "the view of organizations as living systems," however, including the conception of a healthy, life-filled planet as a complex arch-system of many subsystems of biological and psychological expression and interaction, one can "realize that [social organization] is capable of regenerating itself and that it will naturally change and evolve".[5] The tendency over time when inhabiting fortunate environments, of course, has been for living systems to grow ever more diverse and thus more dynamically expressive of bio-psychological powers. Capra endorses a view holding that social systems are part of the world's ecology and that human action enters into complex feedback mechanisms that in general will entail the successful adaptation and refinement of those social systems, or their failure and the way of the Dodo. One worrisome implication of Capra's theory about life and the machine metaphor is that certain cultural projects can stifle and homogenize otherwise adaptive, diverse systems. Many deem our age of consumerist modernity to result in economic and cultural monotony and lifestyle compulsion, like we're just part of some economic/ideological machine.[6]

Capra advises us to become " 'ecologically literate,' i.e., to understand the principles of organization, common to all living systems, that ecosystems have evolved to sustain

---

[4] Capra, The Hidden Connections, 103.
[5] Capra, The Hidden Connections, 104.
[6] If in need of examples, refer to any issue of Adbusters.org magazine, based in Vancouver, BC, Canada, for rich and dedicated perspectives on the issues of this essay).

the web of life".[6] Efforts to inspire eco-literacy, an adequate understanding of the general principles of life's organization, complement the related yet independent efforts of Deep Ecological thinkers to ground an ethical orientation to Nature in Spinoza's philosophy of the imaginative and of the active love. If we understand life adequately then we will aspire to love it, and a greater love of life will foster understanding. It even seems implicitly essential within the concepts of Deep Ecology that the relation within the preceding claim must have existence. In "Spinoza and the Deep Ecology Movement," a lecture delivered by Arne Naess at Katwijk in 1991, one ground for Deep Ecological thought emerges in Spinoza's figure of *amor intellectualis Dei*, or the intellectual love of God. Spinoza is very careful with what he takes to be the 'definitions' of concepts, because as a rationalist philosopher he builds upward from small, important beginnings to larger ideas and implications. God, to Spinoza according to Naess, is the immanent, eternal substance of all individual things, or simply Nature, but

> The *Ethics* furnishes no basis for assuming that the immanent God expresses its nature, essence, or power, in any other way than through each existent being. Therefore *amor intellectualis Dei* must *somehow* [by being a special kind] be a love of these existent particular beings of our everyday life—parts of the total richness and diversity of life forms on Earth.[8]

---

[7] Capra, The Hidden Connections, 230.
[8] Naess, Arne, Spinoza and the Deep Ecology Movement, (Delft: Eburon, 1992), 5, his emphasis

What Spinoza and Naess talked about could be expressed simply as mindfully loving Nature. More complexly, *amor intellectualis Dei is* the understanding and love, for all living entities, for their inherent capacity and potential to explore their birth right. By birth right I refer to the inherent features of life such as self-organization and homeostasis, to name a few, which life forms naturally express and in so doing evolve into beings of higher complexity.[9] Naess calls the intellectual love of God "more specifically a manifestation of love" or "a special kind of intuitive understanding of a particular thing which involves an internal love relation"[10] between oneself and every being in relationship with him or her. Spinoza aims to bring to his readers' lives active love over passive and imaginary love, which is ephemeral, fleeting, and fanciful rather than based in intuiting the deep relation of self to God/Nature and in participating in 'direct action' to express that relation. As Spinoza seems to have it, intuiting the relation of self to God invigorates the activity of the feelings and reasoning we have about life's personal and practical realities, by virtue of an ever-developing and loving connection between our human being, and the immanence of life—being an expression and pursuit of itself.

The active love of God/Nature that a human being should aspire to could be considered deeply as a brilliant expression of a human being's 'human nature,' such as

---

[9] I am reminded of the Aristotelian principle of an entity's inherent virtue being the entity's pursuit of its own naturalistically understood conditions of excellence. A conscious entity's natural condition of excellence might be most simply conceived as its emotional love of Nature and an active pursuit of expressing itself.

[10] Naess, Spinoza and the Deep Ecology Movement, 6.

intelligent understanding of ecosystems and the stewardship of them. We might be capable of it and it would be a pursuit of our ecological conditions of excellence. What Capra calls Nature's "principles of organization," Spinoza might think of as the "definite and determined expression of God's infinite power," to paraphrase the often used terminology in Part 1 of *Ethics*. I agree along the lines of Naess and Capra that Spinoza's "God" is no more and no less than the ecological totality of existing systems of beings, or what Spinoza called *Natura Naturans*, or Nature Naturing, and *Natura Naturata*, or Nature Natured. We should live in a deep, visceral, and intellectual communion with Nature. As the biological integrity of our world's history demonstrates, life systems can naturally flow toward the powerful expression of biological diversity and, we hope, into thriving, ecologically literate, and loving societies.

So? Connecting theory to practice has been a contentious issue in relation to Deep Ecological values and perspectives, such as the "Platform Principle" of Naess and George Sessions that the flourishing of non-human life is compatible with a significant decrease in the human population. Such an ethical concept makes sense to most reasonable debaters in terms of skyrocketing human population, dwindling biological resources, and a risk of intense climate and soil change; however, I have been routinely amazed in my experience of informal, somewhat heated arguments with people out there in the real world who are like me genuine agents of our social situation and its impact upon the ecosystem. The most common notions I encounter in certain sectors of the general public claim something along the following lines: 1) "They," my respondent says about everyone in general, "are going to do whatever they want no matter what they know." 2) "You," and my respondent really seems to mean me in particular, "cannot do anything about it." Just as Capra said, it is a matter of political value and will, and machine metaphors, and not at all a matter of adequate concepts or action plans. It is fundamentally a matter of psychological coherence whether people en masse can eventually make choices which defer what they want and reflect the reasoning and action they know is adequate and responsible. Spinoza would consider such a position the result of passive imagination that disregards the exerting and expression of a growing and diversifying social reality compared to the one we presently manifest.

As I see it, Deep Ecologists may need a more fertile ground than purely physical-environmental philosophical and ethical arguments, which my above example illustrates, for leading people to check their fanciful values and passive actions. Solidly, most people can immediately understand and accept the reasoning that ecosystems have creative powers and needs, and can accept that the health of the world's ecosystems actually provide the basis of our very survival. The passivity that treats Nature as an unwieldy machine of exploitative forces leads to the view that "no one can control or direct the necessary changes" as my passive interloper might have said. Since we understand perfectly the solution—unifying information, awareness, and involvement with the only reasonable actions that remain—the only way to lead people to correct their behaviour may be to stoke people to realize more about, and become more involved, with their inherent powers of emotion and intellect within Nature, rather than point to the world and to others, commonly considered distant, alien, and unimportant.

However, this understanding of self and God/Nature may have to be prodded forcefully, consistently, or at an early age in order to trip the switch in the brain that orients one with emotional love toward Nature and promote an interest in contributing to healthy ecosystems. I think of Gregory Bateson's warning that humans "are learning by bitter experience that the organism which destroys its environment destroys itself," in the essay "Pathologies of Epistemology," read at the Second Conference on Mental Health in Asia and the Pacific, 1969.[11] It is "epistemological lunacy" that provides the "massive aggregation of threats to man and his ecological systems".[12] Bateson is speaking to therapists at a conference on mental health and is addressing the need to overcome "errors in our habits of thought at deep and partly unconscious levels" which affect individuals, cultures, and ecosystems.[13] Most poignantly to where I am taking this essay, the final remark of Bateson's essay states that "there are patches of sanity still surviving in the world[;]…some of the inarticulate efforts of our own young people are more sane than the conventions of the establishment".[14]

I remember when I was freshly diagnosed by a psychiatrist as schizophrenic, and when I still didn't know it during my first hospitalization in the fall following high school, and my topmost priorities included picking up garbage and cigarette butts from the outside smoking area and discussing the ecological need of Earth for our growing responsible action and sentiment. I was also very concerned

---

[11] Gregory Bateson, ed. "Pathologies of Epistemology" from Steps to an Ecology of Mind, (New York: Ballantine, 1972), 483.
[12] Gregory Bateson, "Pathologies of Epistemology", 487.
[13] Gregory Bateson, "Pathologies of Epistemology", 487.
[14] Gregory Bateson, "Pathologies of Epistemology", 487.

about the suffering I conceived in the destination of every siren that left the hospital, and I also wanted to focus on interpersonal connections between myself and others around me. For hours on the grass I cried with my mom, while reflecting on ethically problematic interactions and relations between myself and figures of my past. My mom tells me the reaction of every nurse who dealt with me was to acclaim my shining spirit of compassion and my respect for nature and the well-being of others. I didn't really know where I was, or where I had been the previous weeks, and I certainly didn't have a sense at all of my extreme emotions and severe disconnect from certain relevant, socially shared realities.

Basically, I had betrayed several cultural expectations for an appropriately functioning human individual. I was disorganized and distraught, but really, I was closer to expressing my most innate desires than when I was in high school, deteriorating into alienated angst and preoccupation about what Bateson would call pathologies of my culture's epistemology. I didn't like that "garbage duty" existed as a punishment for students who would come to tell me "someone gets paid for that" when I would spend my lunch hours cleaning the school yard. One intense moment was when a few students laughed at the sound of the accent of an elderly Jewish woman who was describing in a video interview how her parents were murdered in front of her as a child. That happened the day I 'dropped out' of classes and left a note saying I'd rather be dead than experiencing my socially shared reality, which my principal interpreted as a suicide note. To me, it was quite the release to get away from 'those people' and climb to the top of that hill and scream before the surging Pacific and the wind-swept rainforest. In the light of Bateson's perspective, I had a rough patch of ecstatic, compulsive sanity.

By no means was I in a state of mental order, but I wasn't in any moral wrong. It was natural for me to have the perception and desire that I did to find an escape, release, or difference from my social surround, given my feelings and thoughts about my experience. I feel it was healthy to have that specific visceral aversion to such terrible laughter, as those boys in History 12 had produced, but I want to explore my outburst intellectually from a systems-oriented perspective. As James Lovelock expresses in *The Revenge of Gaia*, "the biosphere [is] an active, adaptive control system able to maintain the Earth in homeostasis".[15] It seems to me that my reaction to my teenage angst, particularly the outburst surrounding History class, was something like an "adaptive control" mechanism. My ideational structure dealt by erupting forcefully against the intense cognitive dissonance of keeping quiet in face of my perception of incredibly reprehensible apathy.

In his essay "Double Bind, 1969," Gregory Bateson explores potential reasons for the genesis of schizophrenia. To briefly explore Bateson's sophisticated theory of schizophrenia, he has a highly ecological perspective of it. During the exploration, think about the first severe symptom I remember in my case: I felt a lot of social angst growing in later high school, and to deal with it I laid the seeds for auditory hallucination by going into the woods and pacing while I would speak my mind and then imagine the responses. This symptom grew as my angst grew in feeling

---

[15] James Lovelock, "What is Gaia?" in The Revenge of Gaia, (New York: Perseus Books Group, 2007), 22.

and intellectual complexity, partially through hashing out my issues with imaginary friends, and the pace of my mind sped up and new, aberrant forms of thought developed across my late high school experience and afterwards.

First of all, Bateson claims that "[a]ll biological systems (organisms and social or ecological organizations of organisms) are capable of adaptive change [that] takes many forms, such as response, learning, ecological succession, biological evolution, cultural evolution, etc., according to the size and complexity of the system which we choose to consider". Further, "[w]hatever the system, adaptive change depends upon *feedback loops*, be it those provided by natural selection or those of individual reinforcement". In the interaction of feedback between physiology, environment, and ideational structure, "we" or biological systems in general "not only solve particular problems but also form *habits* which we apply to the solution of *classes* of problems".[16] For some schizophrenics, the healthy mind becoming ill has the experience of a shifting to aberrant habits of meaning, idea, and mental capacity. This shift to full-blown schizophrenia is characterized by disconnect from various classes of established social contexts, such as quiet on my lips with a talking storm in my head when the subjects were present.

To Bateson it is a shifting likely to occur not only in terms of some gene's random expression, but in terms of adaptations of the organism, within certain internal and external environmental feedback. In addition, the feedback occurs to and within the same system that we find

---

[16] Gregory Bateson, "Double Bind, 1969" in Steps to an Ecology of Mind, pp. 273-4, his emphasis.

aberrant meanings, ideas, and mental capacities. That is, the shifts in psychological function occur partly because of the impact and feedback of other psychological contexts. Specifically, Bateson writes that "experienced breaches in the weave of contextual structure are in fact 'double binds' and must necessarily (if they contribute to the... processes of learning and adaptation) promote what I am calling transcontextual syndromes".[17] In the essay "Minimal Requirements for a Theory of Schizophrenia", Bateson refers to the "schizophrenogenic" environment, an environment whose feedback loops have a potential to exert and maintain double binds.[18] For instance, the kids laughing in History 12 were merely laughing at the accent and not paying any attention at all, emotionally or intellectually, to other contexts of meaning. I, however, perceived that laughter as a breach of the appropriate context of a History class, especially in 2002 as the 'War on Terror' had just begun, as my grade 12 classes began, which being a world-scaled instance of war had basically set in flesh the context of my already developing social angst and intellectual anxieties, my talking storm and other growing numbers of symptoms. It simply hurt, in a deeply personally resonant manner, that just hours after those fateful planes hit those towers, already a few peers had complained "Stop talking about it, I've heard too much already." Such "experienced breaches in the weave of contextual structure" led me to all sorts of augmented behaviours and distorted ideas and feelings,

---

[17] Gregory Bateson, "Double Bind, 1969" in Steps to an Ecology of Mind, 276.
[18] Gregory Bateson, "Minimal Requirements for a Theory of Schizophrenia" in Steps to an Ecology of Mind.

which increased until I was a blubbering boy who could not care for anything except cleaning cigarette butts and negotiating diligent eco-literacy. I became utterly unable to sort out my thoughts and became a confusion of impulses, across a span of gradual deterioration and encounters with double binds.

Of course, Bateson's approach would probably find itself in much disrepute in our age of the pharmacopeia and so-called "medical model" of psychiatric illness. But even in the 60's Bateson knew enough about the inherently systemic nature of mind-body-environment that any proposed genomic or physiological/chemical disposition affirmed as the cause of schizophrenia still needed interconnection with and provocation by "internal" and "external" environments. Bateson's metaphysical assumptions are close to Spinoza's: anything which happens in the body is in some way identical with what happens in the mind. The mind and body are both aspects of a deeply and complexly organized life pattern. The medical model tends to represent schizophrenia as a brain disease, pure and simple, but I have to debate that. My own perspective and the testimony of countless 'survivors' of schizophrenia regard the obstacles and perseverance differently. Just as it makes sense to many schizophrenics to frame their symptoms in a context with meaning to the self, it is straightforward, given my particular interpretation and understanding of my experiences, to directly frame my illness in social and ecological terms.

Some of us tend to view our psychological symptoms as important parts of ourselves, even when we know there are forces, at odds within, which put us at a level of risk. Some of us tend to be proud of our perseverance, against those risks, and tend to relentlessly keep interpreting our symptoms, and engaging them. We might avoid developing the medical model's method of isolating proper functioning behaviours from dysfunctional behaviour, as though it were simple to do so, and viewing any deviance from normal and prescribed patterns as a potential reason to up the dose. Especially, it seems that the brain disease theories block out all potential for saying these psychological disturbances are in some cases an ecological adaptation within socially disturbed societies where abnormal psychological capabilities arise whose role to play and diversity in our species are inherently valuable.[19] The shape of the role of abnormal psychology is manifold, as successful as reactions to it can happen to integrate with the situation and resolve some contextual breach. Of course, there may be some cases when genes conspire and a child is simply born and will simply grow up autistic, but still the ecological perspective tells me to seek a way to include such a person and ennoble such a person, and see what such people can contribute, to self and to friend alike, through their innate being and their innate experiential capacity.[20]

---

[19] I know most ethnographic studies show that schizophrenia in some cultures is integrated in a different way so that the individual sensitive to double binds is healthier. There may be lower incidence of extreme forms.

[20] The autistic 'savants' who have learned to type essays and produce popular YouTube videos support such a claim that even when one perspective says the entity is closed and sick to the world, it is so open, and so profoundly brilliant in the world. In simplest terms, everyone's inborn way of being has an inherent value, and having diversity in our ways of psychological being is healthy for us. Healthy integration and constructive habits become key for both the individual with the deviance and those who may learn something and grow healthier.

Diversity is the positive expression of healthy ecosystems, be they ideational or metabolic in character. The present analysis not only defends the view of human minds and societies as inherently ecological systems, but also corroborates with the Deep Ecological perspective on the present ecological crisis. Opening their book *Hope's Edge* with a chapter titled "Maps of the Mind," Frances and Anna Lappé employ the example of realizing the need to expose their daughter to the hunger myth: "if we look at food, *really look*, our world can shift: We might just not only grasp for the first time the biggest ideas limiting our lives, but also discover for the first time whole new ways of seeing the world that release us from our march toward planetary destruction".[21] As 1 out of 2 people may be statistically likely to face a bout of clinical strength depression and 1 out of 4 another mental illness at some point in their life, which I convey by report of my friend who is in a psychology program,[22] I am tempted to consider that certain myths limit our views of and responses to psychological nature, in a similar way as certain myths limit our view of and responses to our biological predicament, especially in light of the need to develop adequate eco-literacy for solving social and environmental problems.

In my mind for a long time growing, there has been the impulse to conflate social predicaments of the human self and mind with ecological action and crisis. I mentioned, earlier, forces of cultural homogenization. In this capitalist

---

[21] Anna and Frances Lappé, "Maps of the Mind" from Hope's Edge, (Penguin, 2003), 14, their emphasis.
[22] I believe they are World Health Organization statistics from some study, actually.

civilization of explicit commercialization and making uniform of life style, economy, public discourse, and media content, it is a living hell for the psychologically deviant, especially when one reflects on the subtle-to-not-so-subtle paradigms of life achievement as the right career choices and of luxury and time off work as the appropriate fields of behaviour to reserve for our experience of meaningfulness. It is a hell for them because of the imaginative paradigms of intellect which socially dislocate them. As David Abram put it in "The Spell of the Sensuous," the "alphabetized intellect stakes its claim to the earth by *staking it down*, extends its dominion by drawing a grid of straight lines and right angles… according to a calculative logic utterly oblivious to the life of the land" or the curved minds which inhabit its oblong societies.[23]

If "there is no free lunch," do autistics waste their support group's time in preparing the food that the sun and living Earth have always freely and abundantly provided in their natural self-expression? I certainly think not, but instead of appreciating our differences and sharing the world's bounty, we ignore or "have forgotten the poise that comes from living in storied relation and reciprocity with the myriad things, the myriad *beings*, that perpetually surround us".[24] It seems to me the aspects of our civilization that render so many of us ecologically illiterate may also lead many of us to socio-psychological stigma and inadequate ideas about those of us who just aren't the same or the sane

---

[23] David Abrams, "The Spell of the Sensuous" from Time, Space, and the Eclipse of the Earth, (New York: Pantheon, 1996), 267, his emphasis.
[24] David Abrams, "The Spell of the Sensuous", 270, his emphasis.

or however it is that dominant paradigms conceive our useful and beautiful differences.²⁵

I think respect for psychological diversity constitutes a radically potent force to put toward respect for, and preservation of, Gaia's biological diversity. Deep Ecologists note the need for bridging the gap between Gaian needs and human activity, and global ecological flourishing could well begin with communal realization of the value of human psychological diversity, as well as with the integration of alternate forms of consciousness and understanding, and hence culture and economy. Our diversity is currently under diminution from forces of irrational stigma, antisocial paradigms, and imperial motivations. I am talking from a perspective of "deep social ecology," which sees how psychological, cultural, and thoughtful diversity addresses our ecological and social predicaments. Murray Bookchin in "Social Ecology versus Deep Ecology" makes an argument along the same lines as my argument from Bateson which conceives my experience of schizophrenia as a unified deep social experience. He advises Deep Ecologists "to fully anchor ecological dislocations in social dislocations… to give the human species and mind their due in natural evolution, rather than regard them as 'cancers' in the biosphere".²⁶ He doesn't like the tendency of some Deep Ecological thinkers to chastise humanity for its ecological impact; more importantly, it seems Bookchin is suggesting that human social systems are sick and out of touch with

---

²⁵ That "rehabilitate" instead of "integrate" is the most common language actually scares me sometimes.
²⁶ Murray Bookchin, "Social Ecology Versus Deep Ecology" in Environmental Ethics—Concepts, Policy, Theory. Ed. Joseph DesJardins, (Mountain View, California: Mayfield Publishing, 1999), 540.

their own "richness of potentialities", not just out of touch with Nature's.[27] He recommends in conclusion that "what we must 'enchant' is not only an abstract image of 'Nature' *that often reflects our own systems of power, hierarchy, and domination*—but rather human beings, the human mind, and the human spirit".[28]

Of course, human nature is manifold in its expression and possesses an indefinite array of cognitive, emotional, and intellectual powers. I have experiential and theoretical grounds for rationalizing the bio-psychological dislocations of my schizophrenia in my experience of ecological, social dislocation, but if we listen to Bookchin, the links only really go back and forth, continuously, between the world's principle patterns of life and the human patterns of idea and behaviour. To echo, extend, and integrate all the thinkers I have included in my analysis, I recommend that Deep Ecological thinkers ever-comprehensively explore the causal relationship between ecological and social dislocation, and that they explore the interconnecting effects on the cognitive, emotional, and intellectual well-being of individuals as well as the feedback effect unique individuals can have on those causes.

By promoting a deep and social eco-literacy, Deep Ecological thinkers have a hope of leading individuals to self-realization of their life in Nature and their life with Gaia. We must learn about how life actually operates, and slowly dissolve our fanciful imaginings into wild, well-ordered involvement and enchantment, with the myriad

---

[27] Murray Bookchin, "Social Ecology Versus Deep Ecology", 540.
[28] Murray Bookchin, "Social Ecology Versus Deep Ecology", 540, his emphasis.

beings that share and enrich our nature and our knowledge of our nature. I am reminded most poignantly of Spinoza's discussion in the *Ethics* concerning the genesis of our knowledge of emotions. If it is indeed true like Spinoza holds that any interaction with a thing which affects us tells us more about our own constitution and susceptibility to modifications then it does about what externally affects us, then it seems also true that to reach understanding about and respect for life external to us, it will be most doable if we first inspire an understanding about and respect for our own inherent human nature and potential.

The basic claim here is that the spirited understanding and active love toward life, which our ecological and social crises call for, inspires appreciation of life's diversity and the recognition that humanity is in need of, or the throes of, adaptive responses to shifting experiential contexts. Facilitating adaptation may represent a deep aim of direct action. If we understand life adequately then we will aspire to love it, and a greater love of life will foster understanding. Absolute stasis of Nature seems impossible, and as Spinoza held in the sole axiom of part IV of the *Ethics*, there is always a more powerful entity than any single and particular individual. Therefore, we must globally admit that our planet's biological complexity and our social systems are interrelated, and that we are deeply systemically threatened by self-destructive emotional and intellectual habits.

Whatsoever the outcome, there is only waiting for our civilization to pull up or crash on its own.[29] If all else

---

[29] I think of the metaphor of testing-the-airplane-by-running-it-off-a-cliff, a powerful image in Daniel Quinn's ecological fiction masterpieces Ishmael and The Story of B; the image brilliantly surmises the

fails—in that state of waiting—there is then committing relentlessly to the efforts implied by the issues of this paper. We might ensure that the feedback in this complex system, goes the way of reinforcing beneficial relations with ourselves and with nature, to get all of us collected, inspired, and focused on enriching the patterns of biological and cognitive diversity among the myriad beings surrounding us. In sum, Spinoza's *amor intellectualis Dei* is very close to Capra's idea of ecological literacy. Diverse forms of perception and consciousness have a unique capacity to sustain and provoke beneficially responsive feedback in our societies. We need to actively build on the urge in people to understand and love themselves and Nature, in order to realize our expressive potency.

Works Cited

Abram, David. "The Spell of the Sensuous." *Time, Space, and the Eclipse of the Earth.* Pantheon, 1996.
Bateson, Gregory, ed. *Steps to an Ecology of Mind.* New York: Ballantine Books, 1972.
Bateson, Gregory. "Double Bind, 1969." *Steps to an Ecology of Mind.* 271-278.

---

potential bristly outcome of human actions evolved out of reckless motives based in groundless imaginings about reality. When it comes to global deforestation and desertification, to the spilling, leaking, and dwindling of oil reserves, and to the seeping into arable land of heavy and radioactive compounds—for example—it is quite the plane-off-the-cliff test of the experimental craft called modern humanity. Will human biology endure?

Bateson, Gregory. "Minimal Requirements for a Theory of Schizophrenia." *Steps to an Ecology of Mind*. 244-270.

Bateson, Gregory. "Pathologies of Epistemology." *Steps to an Ecology of Mind*. 478-487.

Bookchin, Murray. "Social Ecology Versus Deep Ecology." *Environmental Ethics—Concepts, Policy, Theory*. Ed. Joseph DesJardins. Mountain View, California: Mayfield Publishing Company, 1999.

Capra, Fritjof. *The Hidden Connections—A Science for Sustainable Living*. New York: Anchor Books, 2002.

Lappé, Frances and Anna. "Maps of the Mind." *Hope's Edge*. Penguin, 2003.

Lovelock, James. "What is Gaia?" in *The Revenge of Gaia*. Perseus Books Group, 2007.

Naess, Arne. "Spinoza and the Deep Ecology Movement." Lecture. Delft: Eburon, 1992.

Spinoza, Baruch. *Ethics*. Translated by Samuel Shirley. Indianapolis: Hackett, 1992.

A personal essay, dated July 1st, 2010,
with no review or reality check by one of my excellent profs!

Essay 9
Uh Oh: Do You Have a Brain Disease You Didn't Know You Had?

As I revise and edit this short piece in the early morning of the formation of the Canadian Confederation (x143 short years), listening to Rose by A Perfect Circle, I am caught pondering the collapse of civil freedoms and incredibly uncompromising will demonstrated by the faulty powers that came to be out of that troubled, mixed origin that has been recently marked by the ludicrous farce of the G20 summit in Toronto.

Police and the military barely winked for a couple hours as they watched chaos ensue by the Black Bloc, whoever they were run and staffed by. The next day, tear gas, rubber bullets, and knees to guitars weren't enough to make most of the Kumbaya singing unmasked protesters close a fist in self-defense after they had walked calmly to the detention centre that are depriving protesters of the basic right of calling lawyers, contacting media, or having food and water. Now, in the mass confusion of the media fed ignorance wing of the cultural coercive apparatus, I can read comments on the YouTube video of the friendly, intelligent people singing and sitting on the ground being stomped, comments which describe how the police are justified to use force on terrorists and how Canadian protesters are gay for not *all* being violent.

Excuse me? Aren't I the schizophrenic? Aren't I the one people stigmatize as "schizo" like I might freak out ? (It is statistically quite less likely of schizophrenics to be violent compared to "normal individuals.") At the very least, I used to think myself to be weirder than most around me. My deepest delusions are finally exposing themselves. Oh, and don't forget all the people who will argue to the death that "no one can change the world or what people are going to do." They have kind of decided that they would rather be very bored and uninspired by thoughts of being life forms who put an effort to making the actual processes succeed of the ecological world they depend on and subsist in. And there is no point now or probably ever was of trying, if you trust the casual historians among these cynics.

I was diagnosed after an intense psychosis, after much self-admitted psychological deterioration and disordering, with schizophrenia in 2002, re-hospitalized in 2006 after another acute psychosis. And, previously through 2000-2001, I was developing more and more acute chronic pain, given the cute moniker—in its being technically vague *and* similarly precise—Pain Amplification Syndrome.

I deteriorated most significantly in my grade 12 year between September 11, 2001 when that day I heard peers claim "I've heard enough about this already, I don't care" and sometime in February, 2002 when I "dropped out" of school because the rest of the boys in my History 12 block chose to giggle incessantly as a Jewish woman in a video interview described her parent's violent death and their being thrown into a pit before her childhood eyes. I know well that undue apathy and lack of compassion can be two of the worst acts of violence conceivable. I'm glad I returned to final exams to graduate with the Governor General's

Bronze Medal for highest graded student in a given class and to earn the Clayoquat Biosphere Trust's 4 year $3000 scholarship that sent me to university to learn more about the purpose for which I'm writing these words.

I have always wondered about following the traditional "imbalance theory" of psychology that my chemicals are all topsy-tipsy-turvy. It is said I need pharmaceutical "psycho-decibel limiters and frequency dependent compressors" (my own word play) to control the highly activated Dopamine, Tryptamine, and Substance P (for Pain) molecules that are "imbalanced" in my brain system. Now, the brain system is really just a set of systems of genetic dispositions, adaptive synaptic clefts, and tangled axons and dendrites containing every variety of endogenous elixir crammed into dense vesicle berries. The idea is my chemicals are doing something funky.

Well, I will have to wholeheartedly agree with these theories that my mental illness entails that my brain and extended metabolic structure is a warped mass of inappropriate, painful, often effectively antisocial surges of magnetic activity and chaotic nerve communication. I *must* embody a brain disease, come to think of it. After all, I had a physics professor once who told me I had all my facts about quantum mechanics correct, but she interpreted the opposite of my interpretation and how it treated the philosophy of mind and revealed to me that she actually believed in the mind-brain identity theory.

What she said of her beliefs represented to me, in the words of philosopher David Armstrong, a feeling that science will eventually determine conscious life in all its multifaceted experiential essence to be "nothing but a physico-chemical mechanism" (p. 206 in Morton, Peter,

417

Ed. *A Historical Introduction to the Philosophy of Mind—Readings With Commentary*).

If we take mainstream quantum and classical physics as well as psychology and philosophy for that matter on face value, we could actually conclude that psychological elements like *effort* and *desire* have absolutely no part or role in the actual causal mechanisms of, say, devious and mutual play or even lovemaking. It's a matter of conditioned and instinctual responses and brain chemistry history: the fancies arising "due to" hormones and genes. We must after that, to be logically coherent, go one step farther in the way we construct the language of our interconnected claims, whether they are made in physics or psychology. We may therefore conclude that human consciousness itself is what's diseased, responsible for the calamities some would mistakenly conceive as the willingness of humanity to straddle ecological and social chaos. (Consider that many of the evils of civilization revolve around "normal" humans doing "normal" things to the world and other "normal" humans).

We may also safely conclude that schizophrenia and chronic pain are primarily nothing but more strange blindly random quantum physical mechanisms. Uh oh—do you have a brain disease you didn't know you had? I may occasionally have believed that an "evil daemon" possessed the world around me and was forcing it to die and kill itself as a lesson in the progress of my spiritual evolution. Like Robert Anton Wilson said, "of course *I'm* crazy, but that *doesn't mean I'm wrong.*" We often feel the right thing to do or right way to be before we totally understand the ethical item and its direct ramifications to action or before we creatively act indirectly in accordance with it.

Contemporary neuro-chemical psychological dynamics leaves the ultimate question of human meaning begged for in this dismal state of (admittedly loose, but nonetheless perhaps compelling) logical implication. This is especially the case when the mode and method of global civilization itself (within a plethora of revolutionary-psychedelic-memetic-altermodern-deep ecological theories) is "just completely bonkers." If normalcy is wilful ignorance or denial to act upon the fact that humanity is on a crash course of deep ecological, technological, and cognitive waste (think about the *lacking* interconnection between "Last Week's TV" and with the Earth and the human mind, for instance), then every normal human being on Earth has a normal yet severely dangerous neuro-chemical imbalance.

Of course, the standards of normalcy they use to gauge my "schizo/pain imbalance" compared to normal people who are chaotically governed by mad economic ideals and ignorant of the basic principles of social organization and ecology which are actually used by some, like myself, to label an arguably accurate diagnosis of absolute insanity on the whole human shebang. I not only read in studies and theoretical criticism all the time about the effects on our planet of neural-linguistic conditioning in the age of mechanized, oppressive info-toxins, but I also personally experience the occasional info-toxin spill in my own self.

What I am calling *cultural psychosis* would be an "imbalance" in terms of sustainable ecology and peace, and it *is* showing up in those affected as evidenced by their chaotic minds, diets, health, and social activities and involvement. Psychosis is a variable disconnect between psychological self and relevant, actually shared realities of relation with the surrounding environment, *including the ecological one*.

(DUH???) Now, The sheer scale of madness may be just an *acute social breakdown*, just a temporary psychosis, but in "civilized" peoples who have always gone to war and killed the "primitive" way of life and replaced its vibrant diversity and knowledge of practical biology with *ecomadness*, it is a full fledged, chronic, *ecological schizophrenia* with a historical breakdown and identifiable endogenous triggering in certain predisposed or retro-disposed-to-be-so individuals. Enough said: indeed I'm crazy, but doesn't mean you're not!

My own "brain disease theory" cynicism set aside, there really does seem to be something inadequate about the human genomic system in its collusion with such disabling propensities as the incredible conscious resistance to changes in our subconscious ecologically at risk culture's group-schizophrenia. And all this only a few geological moments beyond our species' origins of nearly complete impressionability and flexibility. Remember, we grew out of this planet's own psycho-physical environment. We stem from Earth's own potential to wonder and we did not make our brains. Yo got to check yourself, before yo wreck yo self...

I estimate it takes exactly part of one generation to be raised to intensely affect most of the healthy patterns of the past, and exactly part of one generation to be raised to indefinitely secure brand new healthy patterns for a human future. Keep busting them ads. You know, "we" are winning one by one, and "you" are recovering one by one. The genomic fluctuations that lead to radical transformations of flesh that some call the punctuated equilibrium model evolution will inevitably *keep overhauling* our psychological structures. I stew patiently.

We will keep dreaming and become like the breathing wind that a madman aims to shoot at but strong enough and conscious enough to slow his outbursts down from harm's velocity and dance between them...Whoa...What else is there to dream of left around here? I relish the future. Send me home!

Part Four

The Last Word

"The Gathered Part for the Book" by the author's mother, Michelle MacDonald

Reading Brenden's book was very emotional for me: his words and my thoughts and memories brought me to tears on more than one occasion. There is nothing more painful to a mother than to see her child in pain, confused or in an emotional upheaval. I think of Brenden as the brilliant light he is. His schizophrenia has made him a better person, lucky to have such special experiences that have opened his mind and heart. We are all better people for having him in our lives and I am proud beyond words to say I am his mother.

Brenden is my first born and he has always been unique. He was always very smart and has continually impressed me with the intelligent approach he took and takes to the world. I encouraged learning by always teaching.

At less than 12 months old...

He had figured out what it took to get himself separated from everything but his own thoughts and senses. We lived in a small trailer with a wood stove and not much room to 'baby proof'. He repeatedly touched what he was told not to and went to his crib happily. The crib just happened to be in the dining room with windows on three sides looking out at mostly forest and sky.

Brenden was different even then; he didn't seem to be clingy like other babies were. I was happy enough to let him play alone happily in his crib, and thinking back now, I have always been happy to let him alone with his thoughts if that was what he wanted.

Brenden's difference's starting showing up more and more when he was a bit older. He just wasn't the same as the other kids. I remember one day especially. We were in a park where other kids were playing too. Brenden had climbed to the top of the slide and was thoroughly enjoying the view before he slid down. He was oblivious to the angry (considered bully) child below next in line repeatedly telling him to go. Any other child would have gone as fast as possible to avoid the bully's wrath, not Brenden, he went only when he was ready and gained the respect of that bully for the rest of time they went to school together. I remember thinking about it at the time and wondering what it was that made Brenden the way he was. He was stubborn as can be and always argued if he knew he was right or in the case of his wishes and wants, he knew them, stuck to them and was oblivious to what was normal to others as their thoughts might influence their actions.

I look back to see that indeed he was just a bit different from the other kids. He did not conform, was very bright and seemed to be attracted to the 'misfits', and the handicapped kids. He was not into athletics, although he did play T-ball and enjoyed it. He could have been just as happy reading or watching a favorite T.V. show. He liked transformers momentarily because that was all it took him to figure them out. He liked exploring and learning,

Later on.......

He was very good at figuring out what the doctor and nurses were looking for, and thus behaved well, settled and gained his freedom on a minimum of medications. I being his mother was not always fooled; now reading his words, I realize just how far apart my and his worlds were. Maybe that can be my excuse to be guilt free from missing all the early warning signs...............

35 Early Warning Signs:

- Deterioration of personal hygiene
- Depression
- Bizarre behaviour
- Irrational statements
- Sleeping excessively or inability to sleep
- Social withdrawal, isolation, and reclusiveness
- Shift in basic personality
- Unexpected hostility
- Deterioration of social relationships
- Hyperactivity or inactivity or alternating between the two
- Inability to concentrate or to cope with minor problems
- Extreme preoccupation with religion or with the occult
- Excessive writing without meaning
- Indifference
- Dropping out of activities or out of life in general
- Decline in academic or athletic interests
- Forgetting things

- Losing possessions
- Extreme reactions to criticism
- Inability to express joy
- Inability to dry, or excessive crying
- Inappropriate laughter
- Unusual sensitivity to stimuli (noise, light, colours, textures)
- Attempts to escape by frequent moves or hitchhiking trips
- Drug or alcohol abuse
- Fainting
- Strange posturing
- Refusal to touch persons or objects: wearing gloves, etc.
- Shaving head or body hair
- Cutting oneself; threats of self mutilation
- Staring without blinking or blinking incessantly
- Flat, reptile-like gaze
- Rigid stubbornness
- Peculiar use of words or odd language structures
- Sensitivity and irritability when touched by others.

I excused away................

26 out of 35: many I excused just because he was a teenage boy, others because he was, even then, very concerned with the world and the greed of large corporations, others because it was Brenden and Brenden had always been unique..... He read endlessly, why would we think anything of the content. He journaled and wrote poetry and I never

snooped thus seeing the circle writing, preoccupations with religion or nonsensical ranting.

The decline in academics? He went from A+ to the odd B. Many early warning signs are so subtle, I didn't think of what I'd noticed or seen until later when reading them in one list. Such as: strange posturing, flat, reptile-like gaze, irrational statements, shift in basic personality, hyperactivity or inactivity or alternating between the two, inability to concentrate or to cope with minor problems, indifference, forgetting things, losing possessions, extreme reactions to criticism, and staring without blinking or blinking incessantly.

The social withdrawal, isolation and reclusiveness we thought was because his peer group was aggravating him, they laughed at him picking up garbage and caring about the world, affected by 9-11. Even now 10 years later Brenden still finds the 'social' side effects/disability the most difficult to overcome, I think. In the book he refers to himself in a couple different ways and almost jokes. It is easier at 28 years old being a nerd than at 16. I think this might be one of the hardest aspects for the general public and even families, the lack of 'normal social expectations' behaviours that come as easy as breathing to those who don't have schizophrenia.

His symptoms caused the family to stop turning on the T.V. when he was home. We thought he was just ranting about every single commercial and corporation, waste of time programming - when in reality or unreality he was actually hearing voices talk to him from the T.V.

Schizophrenia, when it became a full blown psychosis, affected the whole family, we almost lost Brenden in the

States, due to his condition and being taken advantage of by a pedophile. He was lost in the desert/ or somewhere unknown to us, for 10 days.

We heard from him 3 times, during and after the ten days. 1st. From in the hospital St. Marys in Reno, he said to me (read me a poem). He was underage and so had to be escorted back to the Burning Man site until he could be picked up by an adult to get taken to the airport. 2nd. In Gerlach, the little town outside the Burning man site, he said "I like it here, I am going to stay" 3rd. In South Oregon - sounding like he was 3 years old saying, "we saw the redwood forest!" We only then started to suspect a psychosis, and subsequently schizophrenia. Not until we heard from the hospital in Coos Bay, did we have any idea about the kind of man he was traveling with.

Then we heard from the hospital in Coos Bay Oregon —"We have your son, we are trying to bring him back. He has made sexual allegations about the gentleman he is travelling with, came in alone, where did he get the drugs?" Needless to say, we were surprised, concerned, frightened and immediately made arrangements to get his dad to the hospital were Brenden was.

In his book he has mixed up the timeline here and there, all irrelevant in the big picture and the point of his book, which was to inform and introduce himself, his life, and struggles, and figuring out how to live with schizophrenia. He was in three hospitals in the USA, and it was the third one that they put a needle in his heart to get it beating again. (*Interesting fact: BCAA Travel medical insurance does not cover mental illness*).

My INSANE:

- I = intense, insidious, insane, indelible, impossible, ideally, into, incredible, isolation, is, internal, identify, indeed, ignorance, illness;
- N = never, never at no time ever, nothing, nicely, needs, neatly, namely, nitwit, no, now, negative;
- S = sane, soothing, sadly, serenade, sever, social isolation, strenuous;
- A = absolute, arguably, artistic, asinine, assume, accomplishing, agile, arduous, alternately;
- N = nature, nicely, note, not fair, nurturing, nebulous, nada;
- E = eyeing, energy, evermore, eager, eyeful, endeavour, extent, experience, emotional instability and blunting, enthusiastic, earnest.

Before Brenden got sick, I had not considered schizophrenia. I thought maybe bi-polar disorder but its symptoms and Brenden's behaviour didn't match. I knew something was wrong but no idea what. When he was hospitalized and I was given information (every visit) to read, it became very clear. The early warning signs jumped out at me and I knew immediately that it was schizophrenia. Brenden himself knew years earlier and the doctors and nurses knew because of how well he responded to medication and with the help of a letter I wrote describing his behaviours in the past. They had seen it before.

His was a classic case, but only in the symptoms, because I would never refer to Brenden as classic, normal or predictable in his behaviour or personality or intelligence.

He proved much of the information to be incorrect in his case. It took me a couple years to get over being angry at the whole situation, the 'man', the school and teachers' ignorance and silence about his symptoms—anger at the disease, anger at myself. Now, ten years later I am over the anger, worry less, still feel the sadness occasionally, and am very proud of how well Brenden is doing, proud of this book, which I know will open many, many eyes, minds and answer questions of any young people experiencing the same symptoms that Brenden did.

The following letter is one I wrote to be passed on to his psychiatrist from his councillor after he was first hospitalized:

Hi Elaine,
Please pass these notes on to Dr. Loewen, I hope they can be of some help.
These are the early warning signs Brenden displayed, that I missed, dismissed or explained away. I think of them now after reading the material on Schizophrenia and feel sick with myself for not acting on my intuition.
They started slowly and gradually got worse over the past 10 months approx.

- *–sleep patterns changed*
    - *– regularly up until 2–3am but still getting up for school*
    - *– other days he was sleeping 12 or more hours*
- *–focus on pain*
    - *– headaches*
    - *– sleeping causes his pain*
    - *– convinced he could help me with mine*
- *–depression*

–withdrawal from most activities (this happened slowly, Feb./Mar. 02–June 02)
- school clubs
- volunteering
- theater group
- homework (actually quit school about 5 wks before the end of gr.12)
- socializing (80%)

–isolation
–moodiness
–indecisive
–several episodes when there was an over–reaction to disapproval
–personal hygiene
- against all commercial suggestions about body odor etc.
- stopped changing shirt, few showers
- room very disordered– floor six inches deep

–obsessions (don't know if this is the right word)
- words – placement on the page, use, context, meanings
- made up spelling and words in his poetry mainly but other writing as well
- writing in circles, up–side down, backwards
- very against commercialism, corporations "THEM"
- childhood nightmares
- helping me to improve myself and my life

–unpredictable moods
- anger
- depression
- excitement

–sensitive to noise
- T.V.. and computer hurt his head (to the point, the family shut off the T.V. when Brenden was around)

–eating less
- reading labels, going on and on and on about potassium/salt levels

–speech
- repeating the same thing many times
- speaking quickly
- jumping from topic to topic

–questioning his identity
–reading about mental illness

Post Risperdal:
Since Brenden has been in St. Joseph's he has been napping 2–3 times daily or going to bed very early when he hasn't napped. We have been home a week today.

–eating A LOT
–slightly depressed
- quiet, I've seen him a few times holding his head in his hands
- thoughtful
- not reading very much
- not always returning calls from friends

–watching T.V. again, had stopped completely over a year.
–spending a little time on–line
–avoiding reading about his possible mental illness (I suspect)
–started working Wed. 25, helping a friend with house repairs/remodeling

He was home two weeks only before he had gone off the meds and became very sick again, and was sent back to the hospital. I believe the letter helped in his diagnosis and he got on the correct medications, which helped him without having too many side effects. **The sooner the psychosis is addressed the more likely there will be a full recovery and the dosages can stay lower.**

The most important information I want to relay with this 'our story' is to parents and educators: what the early warning signs of psychosis and schizophrenia are. The importance of catching psychosis and schizophrenia early is huge in the treatment and outcome.

Every story is different and yet very much the same resulting in shock, fear, anger, anxiety, blame, devastation, depression and so many more.... I reread this and feel a need to add joy, relief, education, love and pride.

I didn't understand it at the time, but the nurses kept repeating to me that it wasn't my fault. I understood later when I was no longer in shock but reading and learning about the disease and also questioning my possible part in Brenden getting/having schizophrenia. What had I done when pregnant, was it anything to do with the food poisoning I had. Was my depression a possible reason? In the old days they blamed the mother, and I had a friend say to me that all she knew about it was that they killed their mothers. I was very alone in my feelings; not one of my friends had experienced what our family had. We could find no history of schizophrenia in our family's history.

I myself, spent many worried hours about my son Brenden the one and a half years before he had a psychotic break brought on by drugs while travelling in the USA. A psychotic break resulting in an attempt of suicide and in hospitalization. I continued to worry for years and years and probably always will to some degree.

Brenden's story began in grade eleven. His first very obvious (obvious now) warning sign was an obsession with words. Saying them, reading them, contextual meanings, inventing them, their usage and placement on the page. He began to correct my English every time I spoke. He also began writing with his own spelling—for some reason his teachers allowed it—I found later many examples of circle writing.

We all let him get away with it because he was a straight A student who also excelled in community service and peer helping. He was extremely difficult to reason with, and impossible to win an argument against. He repeated himself often and showed extreme frustration especially with me. I think I became his focus and he tried to improve my life by trying to get me to change all habits.

I don't remember the order of things and signs. It was an extremely difficult time for us both. I sensed something was wrong and couldn't/wouldn't ever think schizophrenia. Brenden apparently was reading all about it.

His obsessions broadened to commercialism, capitalism, religions, humanity and caring for the earth and its creatures. His personal hygiene dived, he started dropping out his usual activities, hated school, and he started picking up litter all the time.

We all just made an excuse for every single one of his early warning signs. In our case if would have made a big difference in our lives had we known Brenden was in a psychosis. Medical costs were huge, and worry and anxiety at home—off the charts.

Brenden began to complain constantly of electronic noise. We stopped turning the TV on when he was home. At least twice he reacted—over the top—when faced with criticism.

I have given it a lot of thought, and I think we could have benefited most, not from the stacks and stacks of statistics on schizophrenia, but from having an advocate, who understands the enormity of the diagnosis and steps in to help the rest of the family to make the transitions required. Some public understanding and much less stigma surrounding the disease would be a great help too.

I try not to think of schizophrenia and/or Brenden having to live with it for the rest of his life. I also think about it all the time, wondering how he is, always happy when he is in a relationship, keeping in touch on a regular basis. There is always that fear sniggering in my mind that he will have a psychotic break or slowly fall into a psychosis. I have faith in Brenden to do everything in his power to prevent that, and continue to look forward to his improving and growing and reaching his dreams: Promise of a long, healthy life of actively improving the world's condition. Always educating, creating, loving and being loved!

My advice to other parents, friends and the schizophrenic's families? Love and support your family member or friend, educate yourself, get counselling if you think it would help, find support groups, and know you are not alone.

For Brenden
Multi–dimensional thoughts
can confuse and enlighten
determine
rationally.........
the layers and edges
and fly
         through
the sky
           knowing

by Michelle MacDonald

Made in the USA
San Bernardino, CA
01 December 2019